Letters from
SKOKHOLM

R.M. Lockley

Illustrated by
C.F. Tunnicliffe

LITTLE TOLLER BOOKS
an imprint of THE DOVECOTE PRESS

This paperback edition published in 2010 by
Little Toller Books
Stanbridge, Wimborne Minster, Dorset BH21 4JD
First published in 1947 by J.M. Dent & Sons

ISBN 978-0-9562545-8-0

Typeset in Monotype Sabon by Little Toller Books
Printed in Spain by GraphyCems, Navarra

All papers used by Little Toller Books and the Dovecote Press
are natural, recyclable products made from
wood grown in sustainable, well-managed forests

A CIP catalogue record for this book is available
from the British Library

1 3 5 7 9 8 6 4 2

CONTENTS

PREFACE

Ann Lockley

MY PATERNAL GRANDMOTHER hailed from Milford Haven, daughter of David Mathias, Master Mariner. She met my grandfather while she was a nursemaid in London. According to my father, Grandpa Lockley was tall and handsome with a goatee beard like Edward VII. But I have no memories of him. He was the black sheep of our family: an incurable gambler, banished by the family before I was old enough to remember him.

Grandpa and Granny Lockley married in August 1895 and had six children: Enid, Kenneth, Kathleen, Aline, Ronald (my father) and Marjorie. Collectively, the Lockley aunts were a formidable bunch. My father, his mother and his four sisters were always deeply loyal to one another, which made life trying for those who married into the family and did not conform or unreservedly embrace the whole clan. When my father was eleven years old he was confined to bed for some weeks: he had the misfortune to be rolled on by a horse. Aged twelve, he suffered a very bad attack of appendicitis, and throughout his childhood he was troubled by having a weak chest. His four sisters cared for him, doted on him, and continued to do so for the rest of his life. Surrounded by Lockley aunts, Ronald was somewhat spoiled while growing up.

After Grandpa Lockley left home, Granny Lockley started a little primary school to make ends meet. In about 1922 she was able to help finance my father start a small poultry farm on the outskirts of St Mellons, then a small village near Cardiff. This is where he met my mother, Doris Shellard.

At the time, Grandpa and Granny Shellard had a smallholding in St Mellons, with a large old farmhouse, tennis court and outbuildings.

Grandpa Shellard was a highly respected and fashionable dentist, with a surgery on Cardiff High Street – the luxurious waiting room on the first floor was tastefully furnished with his latest acquisitions in the way of antiques, pictures and *objet d'art*. My mother – always referred to as Do as she hated her name Doris – ran the little farm, the garden, and bred black Labrador dogs.

As near-neighbours in St Mellons, the Lockleys took part in Grandpa Shellard's big tennis parties, and joined his organised walks, cycling trips and picnics in the nearby Black Mountains (on one picnic he was reputed to have run three miles across country to the nearest village to buy mustard when he discovered he had none in his ham sandwich). With a shared love of literature and nature, it was during these gatherings of St Mellons neighbours that my parents' romance began to bloom. It was also how my father first 'discovered' Skokholm.

Grandpa Shellard always liked to have the latest car, and in it he would take young Ronald Lockley on explorative jaunts, sleeping rough and observing nature. They journeyed through most of Pembrokeshire this way. And on the Whitsun of 1927, after driving westwards down to the village of Marloes, they employed a fisherman to take them across the choppy sea to Skokholm. When they arrived, both fell immediately in love with what they saw. From that moment my father could not get the island out of his mind. He wanted to make Skokholm his home.

My father told my mother about his discovery, and she too was wildly excited and longed to be taken to see this island. On August 6th my father, Enid, Granny Lockley, Do, Grandpa Shellard and her uncle all made their way to Marloes. The same fisherman took them over in his boat and they spent the night camping and exploring. Enid and Granny Lockley were absolutely horrified at the filth and ruinous condition of the house. But my mother and father felt differently: 'Do and I being more or less engaged,' my father wrote in his diary, 'propose to go and live on Skokholm Island.'

Back on the mainland, while he courted my mother, young Ronald Lockley found out that Skokholm was owned by Colonel Lloyd Phillips

Winching up 'Storm Petrel' on a stormy day.

of Dale Castle. He decided to approach him and discovered that although the Colonel was willing to sell the island, the asking price was more than he could afford. Instead, he and the Colonel began haggling over terms for a long lease, finally agreeing in late September that my father would have the island for 21 years, at £25.00 per annum, providing he compensate the present tenant and take possession immediately!

My mother and father fixed their wedding day for July 12th the following year. Skokholm was to be their home.

Most of the family were up in arms about leasing the island. The isolation, giving up the poultry farm, the forthcoming marriage, their age difference (he was 24 and she was 34), the house on the island was a ruin, how would they earn a living. . . But my father promised he could make the old farmhouse habitable before Do arrived, and said he could make money from breeding chinchilla rabbits, fishing, sheep farming and trapping wild rabbits. My mother threatened to elope. She did not, however, faithfully staying at home when all she really wanted was to take part in rebuilding the island house – and get away from her parents.

As soon as he had successfully negotiated the lease for Skokholm, my father quickly sold the poultry farm and moved to Pembrokeshire,

The Lockley's home on Skokholm 1927–1940.

staying with the Codd family who had a farm near Martin's Haven. He engaged a Marloes fisherman and boat owner, Jack Edwards, to help with the work and teach this 'greenhorn from up country' how to handle a boat, learn to read the tides, to fish, make lobster pots and cope with island life.

In the early days Jack had an ex-ship's lifeboat, the *Foxtrot*, clinker built and double ended, having no engine, she needed fair weather, being totally dependant on sail or oars. One of the first things my father had to purchase was a boat both light enough for hauling and with an outboard motor. With Jack as adviser he finally settled on a sturdy little 16 foot clinker built craft with a 3hp engine for £50.00, which he christened *Storm Petrel*. October 20th was an exciting day for my father: he had taken delivery of his boat and brought it round to Martin's Haven. There he and Jack loaded the *Foxtrot* and the new boat with furniture, new winch rope, rabbit traps, oil stove, fuel, cement and stores. Then, taking the *Foxtrot* in tow behind *Storm Petrel*, he and Jack made Skokholm within an hour in fine calm weather. Island life was about to begin.

In his diaries of those years, alongside records of his day-to-day activities, hardly a day passed when my father failed to record the natural world around him.

November 2nd. Weather too bad to cross . . . starting on the garden, clearing off the dead weeds and bracken, and digging deep into the rich, sandy, loamy soil, which is full of weed roots and a few rabbit holes. Noticed a woodcock, so followed him up at 4 p.m. to Spy Rock, where saw a buzzard soaring. The view from the rock was enchanting, the mist driving in from the sea over the red and green land of Skokholm like a cold breath of hell, and Satan himself roaring his foghorn at the gates of perdition!'

On Tuesday November 8th, his first birthday on Skokholm:

'. . . I am 24 today and I am realising my greatest ambition, which is to live happily forever on a bird-island, lonely, set in the sea, with the dearest girl in the world wishing and longing and going to be with me soon. How little I could have dared hope for a few months ago, and how often I have dreamed of this!'

Three months later, life on the island became even more exciting when a small schooner was wrecked at Skokholm. My father and his assistant-mentor, the faithful Jack, had been ashore to get a load of timber and corrugated iron. On their return to the island they had some difficulty tacking against a stiff south easterly wind:

. . . we downed sail and rowed easily close to the south stream, putting up sail off the stack and cruising in . . . Jack had laughingly said: 'look out for a schooner which was rumoured ashore here yesterday!' So we did not particularly look out for her, not believing that there could be a wreck anywhere in this weather. However, as we approached South Haven there the schooner was, with all sails set, fast on the rocks in a creek facing SE below Spy Rock. We hastily moored the *Foxtrot* and went to inspect the prize . . . the *Alice Williams* 1854 of Falmouth . . . her bowsprit and rudder carried away, she is fast bow and stern, broadside in the creek. I hurried to the lighthouse to get particulars . . . It seems that she had drifted ashore, having been abandoned in the night (flares and rockets had been lit aboard). The Trinity House ship had watched her go on the rocks, unable to help her as there was no one aboard the *Alice Williams* and a big sea was running, as well as a slight fog . . .

Sunday February 26th Wrecking all day, took the mainsail down . . . it is a brand new sail and evidently worth a sum of money. Below decks the cabin, hold and cargo are battered about and mixed up as her decks are awash at high water. An amazing experience this 'wrecking', though I had a few slight qualms as to the legality of it.

Restoring the figurehead of the 'Alice Williams'.

Early on the Monday morning my father had a chance to assuage his conscience and make things legal. He telephoned the Lloyds agent, who, on being informed of the position of the wreck, advised saving all they could and making a deal with him for what was worth having! My father made an offer of £5 for the wreck, which was accepted, giving him salvage rights for the 100 tons of coal and enough timber from the wreckage to help rebuild the island house and barn. For eight days, six men toiled with the help of two winches, lifting all the loose gear and several tons of coal safely above reach of high water, living on a diet of saltmeat saved from the wreck.

Wednesday March 14th. Cold and wet, wind blowing a gale force from the usual quarter SE This morning the *Alice Williams* still stood with her masts proudly erect, though the rigging was beginning to sag. At midday she had completely broken up and lay in fragments submerged in the roaring breakers! Thus the first high water with a strong wind destroyed her utterly. We worked hard after high water putting away planks and wreckage in the clefts of rocks above the high tide mark.

My father worked extremely hard to get the house habitable for my mother. I was to learn just how hard from the constant stream of letters my parents wrote to each other during the year of their engagement. In one of his letters to my mother, father describes feeling ill and stiff after carrying sand all day up a steep and stony path cut in the cliff – all the sand to mix concrete had to be carried by the sackful from the only sandy beach on the island, North Haven. In reply, my mother was always sending parcels of cakes and vegetables down to feed the inner man of her beloved. They compared themselves with Oisín and Niamh from the Irish legend *Oisín i dTír na nÓg*, one of the best known and best loved tales of the Fenian cycle: Oisín, poet and warrior of Fianna meets beautiful maiden Niamh Chinn Oir from Tír na nÓg, who asks him to come with her to her land of everlasting youth. After a while, when he wishes to return to Ireland, Niamh lets him go, warning him that if he goes he must not touch ground or he will become old and die.

My parents used a good deal of license in comparing this legend with their romance. My father always said later in life that the only reason my mother promised to marry him was so that she could share in his life on this island. My mother denied this, always. Whatever their truth, my father was one of the lucky ones. In his first book about our Skokholm life, *Dream Island*, he wrote: 'To dwell alone with birds and flowers in some remote place where they were plentiful and undisturbed was an ambition early cherished . . . '. He achieved his dream early in life. But he also found somebody to share it with, a partner as incurably romantic for their island life as he was.

Rare snowfall on Skokholm, c1931.

INTRODUCTION

Adam Nicolson

THE ISLANDS off the west coast of the British Isles are both hidden and rich. Most of them remain, except to a small band of islophiles, largely unknown and – at least outside the summer yachting months – unvisited. And most of them share a particular set of conditions. They are not oceanic specks, separated by hundreds of miles of sea from any other point of land but are within reach of the mainland, with all that the mainland implies of settlement and civilization. That is their east-facing, landward aspect: for many thousands of years these islands have been part of the human world.

But there is also the opposite. From the deck of a boat, Auden wrote in his 1940s poem 'The Sea and the Mirror', 'All we are not stares back at what we are.' That is the Atlantic, 6,000 miles of south-westerly fetch, a brutal and uncompromising world, a salt desert driven on to the hard western rocks of the British Isles. Wind and storm arrive unbroken at these islands. When they combine with the tides which are funnelled into races between the headlands and the off lying stacks, the result is some of the most difficult seas in the world, utterly exhilarating if you are at least half in control, murderous and devastating if you are not.

This is the potent amalgam of a western, British island: homely, but not; wild, but not; with the sensation, in island after island, that it is somehow a net spread across the currents of wind and sea, set there to catch any passing piece of fluff or flotsam. Nothing is inert here; the whole universe seems to be animated by the mobility of the elements in which the island finds itself. These conditions make for a world of dynamic polarities. It is a state of siege, but also one in which the besieging element is rich with food for man and bird. It also happens, by pure geological chance, that Britain's oldest and hardest rocks are set against this ocean. There is nothing here of the east coast slide into sludge and mud, all those estuarine ambivalences, the easing and oozing of land into sea. West coast islands might have been designed as stage sets for romantic drama. Failure is around every corner. Love seems highly poignant here. Turmoil is the setting for desire. Ambition is futile and the hugeness of the oceanic and atmospheric forces create, paradoxically, an appetite for the small and the delicate, for the domestic and the precious, for everything which seems more precious because the island makes one aware of the transience of things.

When in 1927 Ronald Lockley came across Skokholm, the small island within a few miles of the Pembrokeshire coast, it was the right place for the right man. He was 24, on the point of getting married and hungry for excitement. He had been brought up in the suburbs of Cardiff, where his mother ran a boarding school, and was working at the time on a poultry farm in the outskirts of that city. This was no setting for the life of a man who longed to live a life more intimately involved in the natural world than suburbia or chickens could ever provide.

Skokholm, to begin with, is nothing but a young adventure story. It was a late Romantic fantasy by a young man who could afford – just – not to plunge into the world of work but to indulge a larger vision of his life. Its foundations go back not to Robinson Crusoe, which is the story of a man deprived of civilization by an island condition he loathed and longed to leave, but Rousseau. It was the Genevan philosopher who in the 1760s invented island-love. On the run from aggressive and conservative forces in France and Switzerland, he escaped to the Île St Pierre in the Lake of Bienne. There he could feel secure, away from the forces of worldliness and reaction. There he could botanise with care and patience. 'They say a German once composed a book about a lemon-skin,' he wrote. 'I could have written one about every grass in the meadows, every moss in the woods, every lichen covering the rocks.' Île St Pierre was an Eden away from society:

I was able to spend scarcely two months on that island, but I would have spent two years, two centuries and the whole of eternity without becoming bored with it for a moment. Those two months were the happiest of my life, so happy that they would be enough for me, even if they had lasted the whole of my life.

Everything that the great nineteenth and twentieth century island lovers, the whole Gauguin and Robert Louis Stevenson story, the excessive island-love of figures such as Compton Mackenzie or Frank Fraser-Darling, all stem from the Rousseau moment, from the desire to escape the oppressive and mundane realities of a mainland existence.

Young Ronald Lockley sits centrally in this island stream. His coming to Skokholm with his wife Do and soon a little daughter Ann, with its ruins and its plague of rabbits, was an escape into another world, an experiment with his own life, a brave and undilutedly egotistical attempt to set himself off from the masses:

> Island life gives us not as some suppose a feeling of insecurity and isolation, but one of absolute security in our society and freedom from any encroachment by neighbours and the busybodies one unfailingly encounters in a mainland life.

It was exciting. His hair-raising adventures in a tiny boat among the tide rips and standing waves off the cliffed and fretted Pembrokeshire coast are as gripping a dramatization of small-boat sailing as I know. He told them again and again in a series of Skokholm books that came out in the first decade of his life there. *Dream Island Days: a record of the simple life* (1930) was followed in 1934 by *Island Days: a sequel to Dream Island*, by *Islands Round Britain* in 1935 and in 1938 by *I Know an Island*. All of them are characterized by Lockley's particular mixture of modesty and display, a sort of sweetness and bravado, both a childishness and a canniness in the telling.

> Nasty groundsea in South Haven . . . too rough to land Ann, so Do stayed in the boat with her and held on to the mooring ropes. Almost as soon as I

had jumped ashore and gone up to the house, Do lost both the oars when a huge swell shook the boat and carried them out of the rowlocks. What a predicament she was in: Ann very troubled and ready to cry sitting in the stern, Do holding on, not daring to let go, having no oars to manoeuvre the boat to face the breakers head on . . . What a life we lead, peril too near to be comfortable, yet starry sky, the still sea and warm sun on other days make the hazards worth while. The wash from the rocks brought the oars within reach, and she was retrieving them when I returned with the rabbits.

The virtue of Lockley's life and writing, though, is not in this half-boy, half-man style of adventuring. And if he had drowned on one of his big-sea, little-boat outings in the mid-30s, he would scarcely be remembered. What is interesting about him is the way in which this treating of life as a holiday deepened into something of more lasting and less self-indulgent value. This book, which was written in the first year of the war but not published until 1947, is the first testament to that more serious life.

Here, with these *Letters from Skokholm*, Lockley began to look less at himself than at the world around him. They are written to his great friend and brother-in-law, John Buxton, a distinguished naturalist on his own account, who had spent a great deal of time on Skokholm himself, had volunteered at the outbreak of war and had been sent as part of the British force confronting the Germans in Norway. It means that the situation of the letters is a little false: Lockley describes to his friend an island and its life which that friend already knows and probably understands at least as well as Lockley himself. In fact, the letters were years of notes, jottings, diary-extracts gathered 'together in essay form' and sent to Buxton as 'each was written'. So this, like much else in Lockley's writing career, is a bit of a performance.

But something else more powerful is in play. The world itself is darkening. The Germans are conquering Europe. The British military authorities are commandeering Skokholm and the Lockleys must leave for the duration.

I find it easier at this critical moment of history to summarize my observations on the natural history of the island in letters than to attempt a more ambitious form.

It is a kind of farewell, a treasuring of something precious as that thing is withdrawn. As the letters deepen and become filled with ever more descriptions, a catalogue of the detail of natural life on the edge of Europe and the Atlantic, the light thrown across them by the impending catastrophe becomes poignant and beautiful. Here, with 'a wide sky about us, and a clean atmosphere' he can contemplate a world which the rest of the world cannot. He can attend with 'great care and gentleness . . . in handling the captured bird', in a way that other prisoners in other places would not be. He can love and protect his 'remote little ornithological kingdom' in a way that other kingdoms would not be. He can surrender sovereignty willingly, while others would have it taken from them.

> When I see our ravens, I have a feeling, almost, that this island is not mine but theirs. They have been here since time immemorial.

That only means what it does because it is written in a time of death and invasion. Not that the way nature goes about her business is any less brutal than what the Nazis were then doing in Poland or would soon do in Belgium and northern France. As a naturalist he does not avoid that aspect of the natural world, but the dominant note is of a man suffused with amazement and affection, and with a kind of modesty in exactness, a desire to delineate in words what he sees before him, with no grand theatrical effect:

> The chough family toys in the still air over the bare cliffs like a group of great dark butterflies, or explores the soft cushions of the thrift with curved pickaxe beaks for insect life.

In a world on the brink of chaos, it is the miniature which starts to carry the heaviest freight of meaning:

> So that on these wild days when the gales roar over the island and the feeling of desolation and loneliness cannot be drowned by the magnificence of the storm waves beating in white foam on the red cliffs of Skokholm, there has always been joy for me in the company of meadow pipits.

This book would be valuable for moments like that alone, as vivid as any illumination in the margins of a manuscript, or a vignette in the corner of a stained glass window. But in the middle of this book – I will not ruin the surprise but I can tell you it is on Friday 14th June 1940 – there is a scene with a swallow that steps beyond both the pleasure in exactness or any sense of late-sunlit poignancy. For a moment, in which Lockley himself can provide no explanation, the natural and transcendent worlds seem to become one. For a few minutes, nature seems rich in omens, as much a system of signs as of biology or natural selection. 'You know I am not a superstitious person,' Lockley writes to Buxton, 'as a student of real nature cannot readily believe in the *super*natural. But it was impossible not to be moved and greatly comforted by the omen.' In the light of that sign, he finishes this letter, as so many, with a benediction from the island itself, sending its blessings to his friend in trouble in a foreign country:

One day all this agony and separation will be over and we shall meet you again on island soil. Meanwhile, from the calm June weather and quiet sea and the air full of the soft island summer, murmurous with nesting birds, I send you a message of hope, and my faith that soon we shall hear of your safe recovery.

That is Lockley's final testament, a life-long belief, carried out through many thousands of rigorous and groundbreaking measurements and observations, that nature was a cure and that the life of an island would outlast any horrors which men might imagine for it.

Adam Nicolson
Sissinghurst, 2010

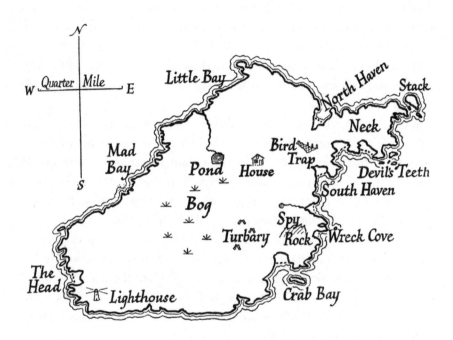

The Island

I. THE ISLAND

D EAR JOHN – You ask why I decided to live at Skokholm. The answer is fairly easy. Skokholm happened to be the nearest to my home of the many lonely, obscure, and uninhabited islands which lie off the western coasts of Britain.

Islands have always fascinated me, provided they were sufficiently isolated from the more crowded haunts of men, and provided they could support life in a simple way.

When I was very young I had a fervent wish, almost an obsession, to reduce life to its simplest terms. I wished to live as simply as possible in order to be free to enjoy life out of doors, unhampered by the thousand and one ties of the modern world. Such thoughts, mostly unpractical, were encouraged by the reading of those immortal books, *Robinson Crusoe*, *The Swiss Family Robinson*, and Thoreau's *Walden*.

When you consider the circumstances, Thoreau in his woods was far less isolated than many a cottager in a lonely country district today. We in our situation at Skokholm are more cut off from the world than was Thoreau, but yet not so cast away and forlorn as the fictitious Swiss family, or as was Alexander Selkirk, the real figure around which Defoe built his imaginary hero Crusoe.

Because Thoreau was a real man and wrote so delightfully of his life while living alone in the woods, he earned a popular reputation as hermit and philosopher which the very saints might envy.

Thoreau was my saint for the latter part of my school days. I practised, as far as I could, the doctrine of self-sufficiency and simplicity which his books preached. I lived much in the fields and woods, neglecting the class room, but seeking always to know and understand birds, flowers, trees, insects, stones, and the wind and the weather. My thoughts, even when I became farmer of a smallholding, ran to islands and remote places, lonely forests, moorlands, and desert. So that when at last I was old enough to have full liberty of action I began to put into operation these cherished ideas. And I found in Skokholm the only available site on which to carry out the experiment. I was lucky to obtain the island on a lease at a very reasonable rent.

So began my connection with this little patch of red sandstone in the open Atlantic (for the nearest land to the south-west is South America). According to the ordnance survey, Skokholm is 242 acres. It is rather less than one mile long at its longest from north-east to south-west and more than half a mile wide at its widest from north-west to south-east. At one point, where North Haven strives to meet Peter's Bay, it is less than 100 yards wide. It is in the form of a rough plateau sloping to the north-east where its height starts at 50 feet, rising to 150 feet at the lighthouse on the south-west point. The plateau is interspersed with outcrops of rocks, the highest of which is 170 feet above the sea. The rock of which the island is composed is almost entirely old red sandstone – but I shall hope to go more fully into the geology later, if we keep up our plan of exchanging letters from time to time.

Yours, R.M.L.

2. THE HISTORY OF THE ISLAND

15th September 1939

MY DEAR J.B. – It is interesting to try to picture man's earliest connections with this windswept, treeless island. From its wild and lonely situation and having no safe anchorage, there would seem to be little to attract the settler. True, it has good drinking water, some small streams and ponds, a turbary where the peaty turf was cut for fuel, and it can produce grass when not over-grazed by rabbits. These, however, are the only amenities; for the rest, the abundant sea pinks, heather, and bracken – but was bracken always present? – could scarcely have been an attraction to settlers. Nor was the inhospitable coast, with its soft red sandstone carved by the Atlantic into creeks and bays and caves – yet none of them safe for a ship to lie at anchor – inviting to the settler.

What, indeed, would attract any one to a place like that? An isolated, heathenish place where you found nature in the raw and the 'eat-or-be-eaten' rule as the guiding principle of its wild inhabitants?

Opposite the island, two or three miles across the sound and touching the mainland only at low tide, is a small islet of red sandstone, known as Gateholm, or, as the fishermen pronounce the word, 'Gattum'. It is elevated, about eleven acres in extent, and waterless. It is remarkable for the number of hut circles upon it. Excavations in recent years have proved, from some small articles found there, that these huts were contemporary with the Roman period. The island may have been a refuge camp for local inhabitants who, from the nature of the steep cliffs, could easily defend themselves against assault by sea or by land. The problem of a water supply during a siege must have been serious.

There is no trace of such hut circles or ancient primitive dwellings on Skokholm. But the surface of the island is so diversified and broken up by outcrops of sandstone that these natural walls may well have been used, with little or no excavations, to support the skin roofs of any primitive dweller on Skokholm.

The first mention of a house does not appear until the fourteenth century. But earlier than this the Danes, who in 878 invaded Dyfed, as Pembrokeshire was then called, had named most of the west coast islands. The word Skokholm is variously misspelt in old manuscripts and seems to be derived from *skokkr*, meaning a trunk or hulk, or *stokkr*, meaning a sound. If the latter, it seems that its real meaning would be the Island in the Sound.

Apart from the name of the island, there is no other evidence of Danish pirates. I have made a fairly extensive search of the more accessible material in the British Museum and the Public Records Office, and have seen a number of interesting documents from which I have made readable copies. The earliest of these (1219-31) shows that Skokholm was a feudal possession of the Norman barons who conquered Pembrokeshire.

From 1324 onwards for a period covering 150 years there is a series of accounts showing how, in conjunction with the neighbouring island of Scalmey (Skomer), the island was farmed for the rabbits. These were caught exclusively by means of ferrets and nets worked by ferreters who lived principally on barley-bread and rabbits. For instance, in the winter of 1387-8 John Wyllyam of Haverfordwest bought the skins of 3,120 and the carcases of 2,318 rabbits, 540 carcases having been consumed by the two ferreters and 262 carcases used as food for the ferrets. In the account for that winter is a charge of two shillings for the 'repair of a house on the island of Scokholm and of another house on the island of Scalmey, for the said ferreters, as well as for the storing of the rabbits.'

How long this house existed before this date I have not discovered, but it was then old enough to require repair. It may be that the very thick walls which surround the present central or main room of Skokholm house are the original walls of the ferreters' bothy. As the farm was developed the walls were heightened – and they show this today in the narrower width of the superimposed wall – to allow headroom for a sleeping-loft under the rafters. At the same time the new roof was extended to run down over four rooms which were built against the original structure, two rooms on the north side and two on the south. This completed the structure which is described by Fenton in his *Historical Tour through Pembrokeshire*, published in 1811, as 'a dwelling house built after a whimsical manner'.

The reconstructed house and the present farm offices were probably completed during the early part of the eighteenth century, in the period of agricultural prosperity. The island was farmed well with plough and livestock for a period of 150 years, during which time hedges of earth banked with stones laid herring-bone pattern were erected to fence in stock and crops.

Free trade, the manipulation of gold in the hands of the favoured few, and the rise in the standard of living are, I suppose, to blame for the decline in the prosperity of the island farm. At the beginning of the present century farming on the mainland became unprofitable enough; on the island, extra transport costs and the unwillingness of hired labour to live isolated from modern amenities, more than counterbalanced the extra profit from the high prices received from the sale of seed corn and fat stock for which the island was noted.

Tenants became dissatisfied. The house and buildings were allowed to deteriorate – which they quickly did on such an exposed site. At last no one would live there except casual rabbit-catchers and fishermen.

The rabbit-catchers tore open the hedge-banks to allow the article of their trade more housing room. In twenty years rabbits had overrun the island and converted its fertile pastures to bare dwarf turf. The burrow-nesting seabirds – puffins, shearwaters, petrels – extended their territory inland from the cliffs.

This was the condition of Skokholm when I took possession during the stormy October of 1927.

Yours.

3. GEOLOGY

Dear John – Thank you for your letter of encouragement. For my part I find it easier at this critical moment of history to summarize my observations on the natural history of the island in letters than to attempt a more ambitious form. Now as to geology, there is nothing very remarkable about Skokholm. The whole island is composed of a series of beds of old red sandstone of the same marly nature as that of the mainland of Pembrokeshire due east. The island coast shows this very clearly, and there are steeply pitched folds in the strata exposed on the cliff face.

This rock is usually red and soft, and, although porous and not very durable, it is easily worked for building purposes. As it outcrops everywhere on the island it is quite convenient for quarrying and splits well under the chisel. In one spot near the western headland of the island a bed of buff- and magenta-coloured sandstone is exposed to a depth of five feet. This is weathered and cleaved, and provides a pleasant coloured form of rock slates with which the farm buildings were once covered. At present only the barn carries these island tiles; I had to cut a few hundred of them from the quarry myself when repairing the barn soon after my settling here.

This greenish-grey marly outcrop has a fine grain and suitable-sized pieces make quite good hones or sharpening stones. Under the microscope this material has a beautifully speckled appearance, due to the mixture of quartz chips, chlorite and zircon crystals, and prisms of agatite.

So much for the bedrock. On the surface of the island lie scattered many large stones and boulders which have no connection with the sandstone. It is clear that the ice sheet once covered Skokholm, and when it melted it left behind boulder-clay and boulders. This material had travelled in some cases from as far afield as Scotland, in company with granitic boulders which came to rest on the mainland near by and on the sister island of Skomer.

There is one large stone which, when the lichen is scratched away, shows a beautiful bright green. It lies to the west of Crab Bay and it seems to have travelled from the western isles of Scotland. This is of augite-granophyre and resembles the granophyres of the Isle of Mull, Inner Hebrides.

Other boulders are of white-weathering rhyolite, felsite, and white quartzite. Some of them are too large to move. The less massive ones have been rolled into service as wall foundations and as guards to sheer off the wheels of farm carts from running against the ends of walls in entrances to field and yard. Flints and pebbles can also be found on the island, presumably carried there in the glacial drift.

The soil itself takes on a redness from the sandstone, is on the light side, and when it receives a sufficiency of humus and organic material from the decaying bracken and vegetation and the droppings of the seabirds yields good farm crops, especially as it suffers a dressing of salt each winter from the storms of the west wind blowing over the open Atlantic.

Yours.

4. ISLAND ECONOMY

26th September 1939

DEAR JOHN – Your letter must have crossed mine. I will, of course, gladly try to explain why I am content, as yet, to live at Skokholm.

A happy and reasonably comfortable existence here is dependent as much upon the fund of inward cheerfulness of the inhabitants as upon their ability to make use of the natural resources of this island situation. Our mental temper is on the whole very serene, since my wife and I, and our old helpmate the Baron*, are content with a quiet life, tending our sheep and garden; and our fishing and boating expeditions in the ever-changing current-swept seas provide a sufficient mild excitement to obviate the chances of monotony in our circumscribed position. Besides, we are all fond of the sea, and like to have a wide sky about us, and a clean atmosphere, and wild birds and flowers in abundance to study and live with. Ann, knowing no other world (except that of her school at Brighton), is yet young enough at nine years to want no other life but that of her island home.

There is a great deal of happiness to be found in living at home, and in our case home has a very significant and exclusive meaning. Our home is especially inviolable in the sense that it is a territorial entity, with its integrity assured by two or three miles of inshore waters on one side and the whole of the Atlantic Ocean on the other. Island life in fact gives us not, as some suppose, a feeling of insecurity and isolation, but one of absolute security in our own society and of freedom from any encroachment by neighbours and the busybodies one unfailingly encounters in a mainland life.

* Originally from Pembrokeshire, George Harries was a friend and handyman who was invited to live with the Lockleys on Skokholm in 1938.

This is not to boast that we are without those usual little fears and worries which at times cloud the domestic horizon; but I believe, from living so open a life, we may be nevertheless more free of them than most households. Our 'outside' problems are principally concentrated into the one day in the week or fortnight in which we make an expedition to the mainland shopping centre at Haverfordwest. Our simple wants have been listed on the island all the week and are then gathered in one furious round of the shops before we hasten to return to the boat. Even as we buy our groceries and goods and hear the shopkeepers' small talk we have one ear cocked for the sound of the wind in the eaves of the town buildings or the tree tops, and an eye for the speed and direction of the clouds overhead. We are more anxious about the return passage to Skokholm than the retail purchases over the counter; and I often find myself, tired of the shop assistant's delay in packing our stores, back in the street for a moment, gazing at the sky. As I do this, sometimes there gathers about me a crowd of idle people who stare up at nothing, and continue to do so long after I have returned indoors, I smiling, they asking each other what is in the sky, or is it an enemy plane?

This tyranny of our appointment with the mainland is a mild and salutary one, for it convinces us that, as long as we have good health and sound limbs and can move actively in our boat, our island is the best place for us. And that until the stiffening of our joints brings a warning of age and the inability to handle engine and oar we are justified in continuing to enjoy Skokholm.

Our mainland visits, then, act as punctuation marks in a life where time becomes almost illimitable, or at least is of less account than season and weather. We often forget which day of the week it is, or we may have to calculate the date by computation, or get it from the radio news, which, however, we are apt to forget to switch on. It is not that we take no interest in the news of the outside world, especially now that war has made news so stirring; it is simply that our normal island duties, whose proper execution is essential to our well-being, absorb our day almost completely.

Those duties are concerned with the economical use of the natural resources of the island, so as to make us, as far as possible, self-supporting. Our day vanishes in the occupations of shepherding, milking goats, catching rabbits and fish, collecting gulls' eggs and driftwood, cultivating two gardens, and digging, drying, carting, and storing peat.

We maintain at present one hundred breeding ewes of the Clun Forest breed. The rams are put to the ewes on 1st November, so that the first lambs are born early in April, which is soon enough in this exposed situation. We usually rear one and a quarter lambs per ewe, and so have for sale about a hundred and twenty-five sheep each autumn. The flock has the whole island for its range. At lambing time I walk the island thrice each day to examine the ewes, and if necessary assist them in parturition difficulties. This is a happy season for me, when my strolls reveal to me each new-arriving bird, each new flower, and all the rich and expanding business and beauty of nature in spring.

I am the shepherd of my own flock of sheep, and glad to be. I find shepherding has many idle moments and free days during which the shepherd can expand his mind by the study of his environment. I have delighted in this freedom to observe which is part of the work of a shepherd. But there are seasons when really hard work is called for, during the shearing time and at the dipping, and the ferrying of the wool and the lambs to market. But with the assistance of my wife and the Baron I am able to get through these periods comfortably.

Our goats are of a Swiss breed, crossed with the Welsh. Ann takes charge of the goats during her holidays. At other times the Baron and I do the milking. We usually have four in milk, each giving about half a gallon a day, which is quite a good yield entirely on pasture feeding. They are chained at night in an open-fronted milking-shelter which is moved to fresh ground each day, and always turned with its closed side to the wind. This simplifies cleaning, and the ground in the meadow is gradually enriched by the goat droppings as the shelter progresses over the grass. We keep one billy, running free and serving the nannies at the natural season of heat, which is August. The nannies dry off in

November in preparation for the next kidding; their collars and bells are removed, and they are free to wander and winter where they will on the island. The kids are born in January and the nannies are then brought in and their collars and bells restored. The kids we usually kill for meat, one female being reared each year to replace one old nanny. (As they grow older goats become less sure but never less bold on the cliffs; we usually lose one each winter in this way, when, looking for green blades in the steep cliffs, the eager animal loses a foothold, and falls to death on the rocks or in the sea.) As to names, these are left to Ann's fancy; at the moment our milch goats are called Sunshine-Snowy,

Longhorns, Pinknose, and Claribelle. Surplus milk from the goats we churn for butter, and we also make a sweet sort of cream cheese in the summer.

We keep a dozen Rhode Island hens and a cock, which provide us with fresh eggs and young chickens for the table. Gulls' eggs we are plentifully supplied with too. During May and June when the gulls are laying here, we endeavour to collect about two thousand to put down in barrels with preserving fluid. These will last us during the winter, and are useful for all culinary purposes. The surplus we feed, with meal and potatoes, which make a balanced diet for them, to the chickens; and in this way convert the pickled gulls' eggs into fresh hens' eggs. By the way, fresh gulls' eggs are not in the least fishy to taste (except in the imagination of some finicky persons), and are as delicious, and of much the same texture, as the egg of the domestic duck. I think you said you had enjoyed them. They are excellent to fry.

Wild rabbits, of course, are always available for the pot. For meat of the larger sort we kill a young sheep every few months, sharing part of its carcase with the lighthouse-keepers, and salting the rest. Of other meat we occasionally eat a woodcock or curlew caught in the bird-traps, and have tried other large birds, such as oystercatcher, puffin, shearwater, gannet, and gull, but only as a novel experiment, rarely repeated. For we are too fond of birds generally to want to kill them even for food, and besides we have a plentiful supply of protein foods in milk, butter, cheese, eggs, rabbits, and fish.

Our sea-lines catch pollack, mackerel, wrasse, whiting, and conger, and our withy pots – of which we generally keep half a dozen in and about the harbour – yield us lobsters, crabs, and, in the season from June to October, crayfish.

Add to this the considerable and varied items of our garden produce and you must agree we are not badly off. We can grow potatoes here very early in this mild climate; and we do not want for the usual garden vegetables: lettuce, beans, peas, parsnips, carrots, rhubarb, and so on. Of small fruit we are able to grow gooseberries and blackcurrants prolifically. Strawberries – both garden and Alpine varieties – do well. Since the first threat of war (Munich 1938) we have opened another garden some distance from the house in a sheltered pocket between Boar's Bay and South Haven; and here we have grown our main crop of potatoes and our cabbages, with a stock-proof fence to protect them.

Then we have an important daily duty in searching for driftwood in the several small creeks and bays of the island. According to the direction of the wind, to that side we go. There is always the hope, and sometimes the excitement, of finding a really good haul in the shape of a sound plank, a barrel of something (even an empty barrel is valuable to us), boxes, boxwood, corks, rubber goods, fruit, candles, and anything else that floats. It is hard work collecting and carrying this stuff up steep cliff paths, but it is very good fun and each of us willingly takes a turn. The wind that blows and converts flotsam to jetsam on our shores is often strong enough to assist you upwards over the cliffs with your bulging sack of driftwood acting as a sail.

If driftwood on our island shores is scarce we make an expedition to beaches on the mainland opposite which are only accessible by boat, and are therefore seldom visited by the mainland farmers. Hence we do not want for timber here, neither for planks for repair work, nor for matchwood, tree-roots and stumps, and firewood generally. Salt-impregnated wood burns with great heat, sending out blue-and-yellow flames and crackling and spitting merrily. Almost too spiritedly, for the little explosions send out into the room small fragments of red-hot charcoal which will quickly burn holes in carpets and chairs if not collected or put out promptly. But driftwood fires burn out swiftly, and we have learned to prolong our hearth fire by adding peat. This is an excellent combination, the peat being sullen and dull to counteract the bright and gay driftwood, the whole burning slowly with a central blue flame about the wood. And in the evening peat alone is heaped upon the grate, sufficiently to smoulder all night and be ready to blaze for us in the morning when a stick of dry wood is thrust into the ashes.

Our peat is not the true slow-burning bog-peat, it is little more than the ancient turf of the island: old grass and heather-root mingled. We cut it from a place near the south pond which is marked 'turbary' in old maps. It is also found plentifully on the south slopes of the rocky outcrops and in the wet parts of the central bog. After cutting it into small rectangular slices or bricks we set it up in the wind to dry, each three slices placed tripod fashion. Then it is carted to the yard and built into a conical stack resting on a platform of stones. From this stack a quantity is brought indoors as needed and stored in a dry ante-room ready for daily use.

I could write a good deal more on the economy of our island life, but think you will appreciate sufficiently from the above remarks that we are as self-contained as we can be with the available resources. I hope to mention in a future letter our bees (we get no honey from them!). Also the hay we cut and gather, since our rabbits were nearly exterminated; and that is an interesting story.

Finally I must mention our mountain ponies. Our stud consists of five: three young mares (named and trained by Ann), known as Petronella, Lollipop and Arabella, bred on the island, daughters of the old mare Judy and the stallion Sugarback. Sugarback is our draught horse, pulling the little luggage trap between landing and house, and also pulls the trams for the lighthouse-keepers.

To make full use of the island's resources, as we try to do, demands a full physical effort on our part, and it is joyfully given. Although my wife is naturally much employed about her house, cooking and catering for four months, she is gardener and boatman too, and cannot bear to idle. You would scarcely think from what I have written that we could find time to stand and stare at the pageant sea and sky, or absorb the beauty of bird and flower. Nevertheless in the letters to follow this I hope to prove to you, although a shepherd's life on a small island is a busy one, it has been possible to live in an increasingly understanding harmony with this wild environment about us. And that I have found time to explore intelligently a little of the life-histories of the fellow creatures of our island.

Yours ever.

5. BIRD RINGING

29th September 1939

M Y DEAR J – We all begin our study of nature in a casual way in childhood, noticing the pretty colours of the flowers and wild fruits we see on our first walks in the country, and the movements of the common birds in their flocks and by the roadside. If this curiosity is allowed to develop we become anxious to know the names which men have given to flowers and birds. There is a great satisfaction, at least for the moment, in being able to name a wild bird or flower at sight. But having learnt to recognize the common birds and flowers our curiosity is only the more whetted and we want to learn more about them. This we are able first to do by reading what other people have discovered about them, and secondly by making direct observations ourselves. Here the botanist has advantages over the ornithologist: his subjects are more or less stationary and he is able to note and study and protect the

individual plant accordingly. But birds are ever on the move and, except when tied by nesting cares – and not always then – it is impossible to be certain that the individual seen in one place yesterday is the same seen in the same place today. Yet how often we read the confident assertion that a certain blackbird or thrush or robin frequents a certain garden, day after day, year after year, when the writer gives no evidence that he knows the bird as an individual. The truth is that there are certain places where food and cover are attractive to certain birds who set up residence and establish a feeding and/or nesting territory which they defend against others of their species. But unless the bird bears some distinguishing mark the human observer cannot be certain from day to day that the individual bird has not been deposed by some natural chance. Thus we say that 'the same robin has been at the bottom of the garden ever since I was a boy'; when we should more correctly say 'there has been a succession of robins living at the bottom of the garden'. For birds in general live very short lives, and a robin is aged at five years.

Early in my occupation of Skokholm I was exercised in my mind as to marking of the individual bird for the purposes of identification. Fortunately my friend H.F. Witherby, the editor of *British Birds*, advised me to use the numbered aluminium leg-rings which were at that time supplied bearing the address of his firm, but which today have 'Inform Brit. Museum Nat. History, London' stamped on them. I began using these on the larger seabirds, especially the Manx shearwater. The results of this ringing I hope to communicate to you in subsequent letters.

When I put one of these rings on a bird's leg I note down in a little book against the number the date of ringing and the species of bird and any particulars of its sex, age, number of ring on its mate's leg, or if a young bird the numbers of the rings upon the legs of its nest mates, etc. These particulars are also entered on a card which is sent to the British Museum (Nat. Hist.) for filing. If and when the bird is recovered, elsewhere in Great Britain, or abroad, the finder sends (if he is a good citizen) the ring, or gives its number, to the British Museum, where the recovery is noted on the bird's record card.

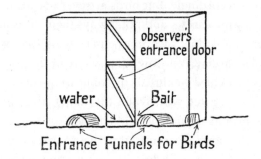

Entrance Funnels for Birds

The information is then sent on to the ringer. In this way we learn of the movements and migrations of the bird, and also gradually build up a picture of its longevity, attachment or otherwise to its nesting ground, etc.; while the advantage, indeed the necessity, of ringing as an aid to the intimate study of the individual bird at the nest, is obvious. Where birds are easily caught, as are some seabirds at the nest, and small birds which freely enter traps, numbered rings are sufficient; but where birds are shy and elusive and it is necessary to identify them in the field and not in the hand, a system of differently coloured rings may be used.

Such birds as gannets, guillemots, razorbills, puffins, shearwaters, and petrels are easily caught at the nest by hand or by means of long wire crooks gently hooked over their legs. But in order to catch active small birds some form of netting trap is necessary. At Skokholm – as you know – we built two or three such traps, of which the smaller kinds are either on the lobster-pot principle or on the drop-door plan.

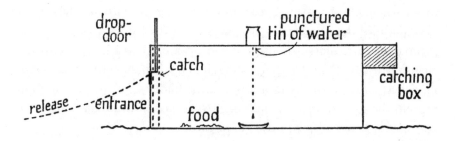

But our best trap is the Heligoland trap. This trap is so called because it is a replica of the funnel-shaped traps used by the ornithological station at Heligoland. If you have read Gatke's remarkable book *The Birds of Heligoland* (translated by Rudolph Rosenstock) you will remember his description of the *troossel-goard*, or thrush-garden of his day. This consisted of 'a few dry shrubs stuck in the earth. A space about twenty

feet long, and from six to eight feet broad, is surrounded by a fencing of bushes, ten feet high, and placed fairly close together, so that there is just room enough left between them to allow the thrushes to run comfortably through the bottom. . . . Over this a strong net is stretched, enclosing one side in a long semicircle.' The thrushes are driven in at the open end and caught in the meshes of the net the other side. That was fifty years ago. Today the strong netting of the thrush-garden at Heligoland is replaced by the concrete walls and wire-netting cages of the Vogelwarte Fanggarten, the bird observatory trapping garden, where shrubs and small trees, water and food attract the passing migrants.

By degrees, and with the help of visiting ornithologists, we have erected two such Heligoland traps at Skokholm. The first one is in the vegetable garden where it acts as shelter for various shrubs, currants, gooseberries, and elder bushes we have planted there and which now provide the green cover attractive to small birds. We can see it from our window and as a rule most small migrants that enter the garden make straight for its shelter. We have put down a small artificial drinking-pool for birds close to the wide entrance of this funnel trap.

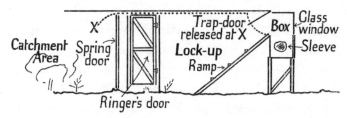

The second Heligoland trap is about twice as large and was put up, again with the aid of friends, during August 1935. We erected it over the rushes and wet growth of annual vegetation in the watery hollow below our drinking spring a hundred yards from the harbour. For cover we 'planted' tree and bush cuttings in the 'assembly area' and beneath the funnel or 'catchment' area, sticking these in the ground as they did with the *troossel-goard*. Owing to its position in the open meadow, with no wall or complete surround to protect it from wind and grazing animals (especially rabbits), we could not plant live bushes and trees with any hope of their surviving, so we have had to import tree and bush cuttings from the mainland from time to time to replace those too withered and rotten to be effective as cover any longer.

On Skokholm's bare tableland of sandstone in the midst of wild ocean these two man-made attempts to provide natural cover prove to be most attractive to the weary migrants. After days of haze and sudden shifts of winds – conditions which bemuse the travellers in the migration periods

– these oases are filled with warblers of many kinds and other small cover-loving birds.

It is fairly easy to drive these migrants through the bushes to the-narrow end of the trap, where a spring door, actuated by a distant release, shuts them into a netted compartment we call the lock-up. At the narrow end of this compartment is a window of clear glass about eighteen inches square. The birds fly to the glass, thinking to escape, only to flutter against it and drop down into a dark box which is then closed over them. They can now be collected, by way of a sleeve door, taken to the ringing office, identified, ringed (if not already ringed, in which case the number is noted down in the book of recoveries), examined for age, sex, parasites, etc., and released.

You might suppose this procedure has a bad effect on the birds, but how little some birds are frightened by this handling is suggested by the fact that many birds fly back to the cover of the trap immediately on release. And provided great care and gentleness is used in handling the captured bird I have found that there is seldom any ill effect resulting, even to a female bird with eggs.

Some individuals indeed become quite accustomed to handling, and wait to be lifted from the box almost with quiet composure. Such a bird is Pipette, an old friend, a meadow pipit of which I shall hope to write in a later letter.

From the above remarks you will understand that we are well placed as to the identification of some at least of almost all the species of birds which either nest upon or visit this remote little ornithological kingdom of Skokholm.

All best wishes.

6. RAVEN

1st October 1939

DEAR J.B. – Thanks for your notes about the ravens in the Tower of London. It was once suggested to me that ravens might be established, by way of tame birds at first, as breeders, wild and free, on the Houses of Parliament! And I was even asked to secure some young birds. But the war has stopped this experiment.

When I see our ravens I have a feeling, almost, that this island is not mine, but theirs. They have been here from time immemorial. They are, so to speak, indestructible, for they are believed to pair for life, and when one of the pair dies, a young bird immediately steps in to fill the gap. The ravens have been there through all the gaps in the occupation of the island by man, and will probably continue long after man has finished with Skokholm. Such continuity compels respect; you must admire the dogged persistence of the raven in clinging to its native crags, in lording it over all the other birds of the island, for it can mob and drive away every other bird, and will rarely suffer a mobbing itself. It is certainly one of the most intelligent – cunning is perhaps the more popular term – among birds.

The island is not large enough to contain more than one pair; and I have observed that, except in the autumn, no other raven is tolerated by the residents on Skokholm. Many a day in early spring, or on fine still days in December and January, I have heard them fill the blue sky with angry croakings. On these occasions I have watched our ravens attack other ravens, which, exploring or merely passing by, ventured over the island. These barking cries are very different from the softer, slower, deep, varied, rumbling notes which are used in conversation by the mated pair at the nest, when feeding, and when performing those curious and exciting aerial dances which are indulged in chiefly in early spring. These consist in rolling over sideways in flight, and gliding or flying very short distances upside-down; and often suddenly swooping downwards vertically with closed wings. On the ground the courting raven performs quite a series of bobbings and bowings and caresses to secure the response of his mate.

Our ravens favoured the steep cliffs of Mad Bay as a nesting site. From 1928 to 1939 they only nested twice on the south side of the island. For the rest of the time they had two sites, both close together, one on the north and one on the south face of the same projection in Mad Bay. They changed from one site to the other every other year. It may be that the old nest became rather verminous after two years occupation and needed a rest for the wind and the weather to spring-clean it. It was a solidly built affair with a foundation of sticks, especially heather twigs, lined with a first lining of mud, grass, and moss, and completed with the hair of our ponies and the wool of our sheep. A very compact and spacious cradle for the three to six blue-green eggs, spotted and blotched with brown, which were laid in February. When incubating, the hen seemed to sit deep in the nest, like a child in a bed too wide for it. But when after three weeks incubation the eggs were hatched, the nest was quickly filled by the rapidly growing youngsters, and in a very short time they overflowed on to the ledges of the cliff. As they got their glossy feathers they began to push each other out of the nest. There was no longer room for the mother to brood them and the parents had to sleep away from the nest when the chicks were three to four weeks old. A fortnight later, by the end of April, the young birds were on the wing.

The food of the island ravens consists of every sort of carrion and small fry, the eggs and helpless young of other birds, insects, frogs, and shellfish left by the tide.

We usually climbed down to our raven's nest by a rope, when the young ravens were about three weeks old, and ringed them. In 1936 we lifted two from the five young birds in the nest, and reared them by hand. These became amusing pets for Ann, then six years old, who dubbed them Tinker and Inky. They were as full of mischief as a pair of boys at six years, and as soon as they learned to walk freely and use

their wings they began to steal, play tricks, and tease in a delightful manner. The dog's tail and bare human legs were fatal attractions. The dog lost its temper very quickly and became sulky and retiring if the ravens appeared at a picnic. They had, indeed, a special fondness for picnic meals, but soon began carrying the joke too far: that is to say, from merely playing with food, silver spoons, forks, rings, eggs, and small articles, they took to flying off with these things, and losing or hiding them altogether.

It was time to shake them off and encourage them to go wild. When they first began flying up to the roofs of the buildings in which we had reared them they were quickly spotted by the adult ravens, who became very excited and flew over the house croaking wildly. This seemed to alarm Tinker and Inky and they would not venture into the air while their parents were in sight, but merely croaked back at them in a bewildered manner. Later when they could fly well, the parents often attacked them and compelled them to seek cover in the buildings. This was during the period when these adults were still feeding the other three fledgelings, now flying more strongly than Tinker and Inky. Later, in July and August, when ravens in this district become sociable and form quite large flocks of up to sixty individuals, the adults were less in evidence. Young ravens from other nests wandered to the island, and Tinker and Inky joined them. Our precious pair gradually drifted away from us. Once or twice they coaxed other young ravens towards the buildings, even into the bird traps. We caught and ringed two of these strange young ravens. Two years later one of these was picked up dead on the mainland opposite Skokholm. It had thus not travelled very far. Raven migration is probably very local; the young birds flock and roost together in the autumn, and probably remain vagrants until they have found a mate and a nesting site. The raven is now a numerous bird in Wales, where the sea-cliffs are its principal refuge, although many pairs nest on inland crags and on trees.

The very last we saw of Tinker and Inky was late in their first winter. For many weeks we had not had a visit from them. One day I saw a pair of ravens flying past at a height of about three hundred feet. I called my daughter's attention to them, and suggested that they might be her old pets. She ran over the grass and waved and shouted their names, whereupon they swerved from their course and stooped in unison, coming down to within a few feet of her head. One swift dip at her was all they made, then on they flew, leaving her delighted with this sign of recognition.

The raven is freely accused of attacking sheep and lambs. When going around my flock at lambing time I always kept a keen eye on the ravens. They were ever ready to worry a ewe that had isolated herself and was in any difficulty over the birth of her lamb or lambs. They attacked and killed sickly lambs. If a ewe heavy in lamb was 'cast', that is, had fallen over on her back and was unable to get up without assistance, the ravens watched her carefully, hopping around her in a sinister manner. I have observed this behaviour at a distance through glasses, as the raven normally will not permit a close approach. The ewe is aware of her danger, and makes great efforts to roll on to her side and so on to her feet. Her panic grows until she is exhausted and can no longer shake her

head to keep the ravens from her eyes. They become bolder and bolder, and soon attack her soft parts such as the eyes, mouth, and ventral openings, eventually disembowelling her. But it is not long before the great black-backed gulls are attracted to the horrible meal; and the ravens, having fed enough, depart, leaving the carcase to the gulls, who are often surprised there by the shepherd who may wrongly suppose they had killed the animal. The shepherd on the cliffs and mountains has a special care to watch for cast and lambing ewes and the weak lambs of his flock.

Yours.

7. CHOUGH, CROW, ROOK, AND JACKDAW

2nd October 1939

DEAR JOHN – While on the subject of the corvine tribe, I may as well deal briefly with the other members which frequent the island. That smaller but not the less intelligent and tenacious sort of raven, the carrion-crow, is one of the regular residents here. Not less than seven, and sometimes as many as twelve pairs nest in the cliffs and craggy outcrops of the island. This is a large population – one pair to about twenty-five acres – a much greater concentration than is usually found on the mainland, but as its name implies the bird is a scavenger and there is much on Skokholm to be scavenged: from rabbit and bird carcases to shellfish and the small life of the shore. In fact it is a decidedly useful bird and forms an almost indispensable part of the ecological economy of the island. It is not powerful enough to be a nuisance to the wild or domesticated creatures of the island, and it engages my sympathy to some extent for it is unable to live the normal freebooting style of life of inland-dwelling crows, because in the securing of food it has a good deal of powerful competition to face from the gulls.

In using the term 'not less intelligent' than the raven, I had sound evidence in mind. The carrion-crow is able to secure food from under the beak of the great black-backed gull, as I have several times observed. When this gull has killed a rabbit, puffin, or shearwater it is powerful enough to make all other gulls and even the ravens keep at bay, but the brainy crow, working with its mate, plays a trick on the gull. The pair of crows hop around at a safe distance and wait until the gull has begun to disembowel its victim. When the tempting mass of entrails is drawn forth by the wicked-looking bill of the gull, one crow makes a rush towards the gull while its mate stands, apparently an innocent spectator, at a distance on the opposite side. The gull leaves its victim and advances angrily to intercept the audacious crow. This is the signal for the spectator crow to dart in and take a dig at the food, and gulp down as much as it can before the gull returns. The infuriated gull rushes across the body of its victim and tries to reach and punish the thief.

The first crow immediately turns round and follows on the gull's tail and takes a turn at the food, gulping eagerly until, with a desperate squawk, the gull comes back and drives it away – only to find that the second crow is back serving itself to a second helping of meat and entrails. This seesawing goes on until the crows have had a good meal or until the weight of the victim is reduced enough for the gull to lift it in its beak and fly off to sea, where it will devour it on the water, safe from the more terrestrial crow.

A great enmity exists between gull and crow – the enmity of rival thieves. Gulls mob crows which approach their nesting ground and this means that the crows are constantly harried in early summer. But a crow can escape aerial attack by quick manoeuvring with its short black wings; the gull with its very long powerful wings, built for long-distance flying and gliding, is unable to follow closely.

Usually the crow manages to drive away gulls and even ravens that venture too near its nest containing young. The gulls have the advantage, however, when the young crows leave the nest and are half hopping, half flying about the cliff edge. The adult crows, with the supreme courage that causes most creatures to defend their young, endeavour to drive away the gulls, but more than once when I have passed close to these fledgelings and so caused the crows temporarily to abandon their watch on the youngsters, a gull has swept down before me and knocked the young crow's life out with one or two sharp blows on the head.

In twenty-three crows' nests which I have examined on the island the number of eggs has been ninety-one, an average of barely four. The young reared from these nests is usually about two, sometimes three, seldom four, and often one per nest. What happens to the other eggs I do not know, but I believe these percentages are low compared with figures for mainland-nesting crows.

The island crow is not a great wanderer. Only one ringed crow has been recorded off the island, and that was picked up on the mainland at Angle, in sight of the island, nine months after ringing.

The rook is only a migrant here. It never comes over to feed with us for the day or part of the day, although there is a very large rookery only four miles away on the mainland at Dale, due east of Skokholm. Early in March the first rooks appear, usually flying against an easterly wind. Their cawing voices are pleasant to hear on this treeless island. Some of them wear the 'bare' face of maturity, but the majority have the fully feathered all-black face of the yearling rook. This migration of year-old rooks continues until the first day or so in May. The extreme dates I have are 5th March and 4th May.

In autumn the rook is a comparatively rare straggler. We have no arable land to attract it.

The jackdaw is even more casual and less numerous than the rook, with which it appears on migration. Considering how plentiful the daw is in every bay and cliff on the mainland a few miles away its almost rigorous avoidance of Skokholm is surprising.

As for the chough, I am glad to say this beautiful bird is a resident here, though it has only once bred – in 1928. It breeds at Skomer and along the mainland coast, regularly crossing over to feed with us. In

July the young choughs accompany their parents about the island. Their bright red bills and legs, their rich black plumage with its royal purple gloss, their powerful, sustained soaring flight with widely splayed wing-tips ever thrill me and cause me to run to gain the closest view of them. Their progress is a series of graceful wingbeats with gliding intervals: at times the chough flock hurries purposefully, but they are at their best in the aerial manoeuvres in the up-draught above the perimeter of the cliffs. Here they shoot upwards and dive downwards playfully, now almost closing the wings completely, now opening them so that every primary feather is widely spread. The ringing double note 'kee-arr' has a far more musical sound than the shorter similar squawk of the jackdaw. The chough family toys in the still air over the bare cliffs like a group of great dark butterflies, or explores the soft cushions of the thrift with curved pickaxe beaks for insect life. Every call from the ground is accompanied by a curtsying dip of the head and a flip of the wings. Suddenly the whole flock takes to the air, and flies restlessly on to some fresh feeding site.

Although we do not get the large flocks of up to seventy choughs in the air at one time, as I have seen them in the west of Ireland, we often see up to ten here in a flock and I have once counted sixteen together.

Yours.

8. MEADOW PIPIT

D EAR JOHN – Is it not wonderful that such a small, slender, and insignificant bird as the meadow pipit can fly as far away as the south of Spain on its winter migration? Am I not right in believing that you share with me a special affection for this little speckled bird of the waste land? It has cheered me with its plaintive call as I have climbed over desolate mountain tops, walked through arid sand dunes, and wandered by lonely shores. 'Seep-seep-seep' cries the meadow pipit rising apparently from the earth, for at rest its drab brown and grey-green plumage hides it so well against the grass and the heather. Then, unless it has a nest and is anxious about your presence near it, when it will follow you with a querulous note, away it flies into the blue distance – or vanishes with equal success into the ground it sprang from. It is the small voice of the spirit of the wilderness.

So that on these wild days when the gales roar over the island and the feeling of desolation and loneliness cannot be drowned by the magnificence of the storm waves beating in white foam on the red cliffs of Skokholm, there has always been joy for me in the company of the meadow pipits.

Some thirty to forty pairs nest annually on the island, but not many remain over the bleakest period of the year. That meadow pipits migrate is, of course, obvious on the island. In August and September the young pipits gather together, roving the limits of the island restlessly. I would sometimes see them take off from the island, flying south or more often south-east towards the mainland. Or I might meet a small flock going south to the island when we were crossing the sea in our small boat.

In October these movements continue, but in November and December they subside, and the smaller parties of meadow pipits are then fewer, and roaming seems to be confined to the boundaries of the island. In

February and March there is a big return of meadow pipits and great numbers pass northwards through the island. But how far they migrate north and south was until recently unknown. Until we began ringing them in numbers, I had supposed that all our breeding birds moved south in the autumn, possibly to Cornwall and the Isles of Scilly, and that meadow pipits from the north, the Hebrides, the Highlands, even from the Welsh mountains, moved into Skokholm in winter, returning northwards to their breeding grounds in the spring.

Ringing, however, has told us a more surprising tale, and revealed to us the delicate truth of their migration. Briefly, that while some of our meadow pipits in winter reach the south of France, Portugal, and Spain, others stay at home with us over the cold months.

From Skokholm three meadow pipits have reached this continental wintering ground. H 9088, ringed on 21st August 1933, was reported from Portugal on 15th January 1938. The circumstances of its recovery are not so clear as one could wish. Although the number was stated quite definitely by the writer who sent the information to the British Museum, no exact locality was given, and the description given was a 'red bird', which the meadow pipit certainly is not, unless accidentally tinged by a sunset. This bird had lived long – for a meadow pipit. LL 765, ringed as a bird in the nest on 25th August 1935, was reported from Jerez de la Frontera, near Cadiz, southern Spain, on 1st January 1936. HE 851, ringed in the nest on 19th August 1937, was recovered at Capbreton, Landes, France, on 25th October 1937. So that if we accept the record of H 9088 (of which I myself feel some little doubt) it may be learnt that the old as well as the young meadow pipits are capable of this migration; in other migratory species (as, for instance, the gannet) it is the young birds that go farthest south, the old birds, being the first to feel the call of the breeding season, remaining nearer home. It is always pleasant to have news from abroad of individual birds that one has held in the hand, examined and ringed, either nestlings or adults. But generally the price paid for such news is heavy: almost every recovery abroad means that the bird was killed, captured, or found dead, and so will never return to Skokholm. Until ringing stations for migratory birds, similar to the one we have set up here, have been established all along European and African coasts, we must inevitably expect the recoveries abroad to be both meagre and fatal.

Nevertheless, as I have said, it is pleasant to hear of such recoveries, which are the reward of our strenuous ringing work on the island. But there is a greater joy for me in recovering, after one, two, three, even five years, a bird ringed on the island as a youngster. Such an individual is my cherished LL 770 – I think you met her several times – which first came to my hand as a juvenile not long out of the nest on 29th August 1935. Nine days later I caught her again and noted that her tender pink-edged gape was hardening and she was now strong on the wing. Possibly she flew off to Spain that winter; at any rate, I did not catch her again until 4th April 1936, when she settled down near the garden with an un-ringed mate. I then learned that she was female, by the constant singing of her mate. He, in the ecstasy of the fine spring mornings, would leap from the ground and flutter upwards to perhaps fifty feet or so. As he rose in the sunshine he gave out his faint, tinkling rapture, a thin string of notes coming faster and faster until the top of his flight was reached. Descending, he changed his tune to a prettier trill, a run of notes which sounded at the last almost pleading. On 27th April I saw her in the garden-trap, picking up loose shrivelled blades of last year's grass, in a most busy manner. The nest, placed in a little hollow on the hill behind the house, was soon built, and by 2nd May there were four dark-brown marbled eggs in it. In less than a month the four healthy nestlings had flown.

Perhaps my constant eager looking into the nest resulted in the second nest being placed higher up the hill and farther from the house. Maybe our chickens scratched it out, or more likely a gull found it, devoured the eggs, and threw the nest cup of dried grass and horsehair aside. At any rate, one day early in July the nest was rolling in the wind over the short turf. Next year, however, she showed both confidence and common sense and placed her first nest right on the stone and earth bank of the garden wall; and her second nest was inside the garden, against a well-used path.

This apparent seeking of our protection, whether real or accidental, gave us much pleasure, and indeed LL 770 became so tame that she would do no more than flutter out of our way as we passed close to her when she was busy hunting insects and worms between the cabbages and carrots and under the currant bushes. We knew her by this tameness, and we forbore to catch her when, as constantly happened, she was foraging inside the wire-netting frame of the trap. Besides, she had learnt the trick of flying out past us when she found herself being cornered in the funnel of the trap.

Winter and summer LL 770 remained on the island, frequently visiting the garden in company with other pipits, when we were able to catch her.* We came to know her affectionately as Pipette. She is, of course, not the only meadow pipit with whom we are on familiar terms. Her present husband, HE 925, was first ringed as a juvenile on 29th August 1937. In 1938 he mated with LL 770 and is with her today. Apart from this distinguished couple, there are some thirty-one recoveries in subsequent years of meadow pipits ringed on the island. Of this number eighteen have been recovered after one year, ten have been recovered after two years (most of these also in their first year), and three have lived to return to the island for three years running.

These figures are taken from the card index of recovered birds, which you helped to build up and which has become so indispensable in a study of this sort. This index now has another hundred and twenty-four cards representing meadow pipits which have been recovered in the same year as ringed, records which show in varying degree the nature of their residence here. Most of these recoveries are of young birds ringed after leaving the nest. At this tender age they form small parties and rove about the island in July and August. They are augmented by arrivals from northwards.

These inexperienced birds are fairly easy to drive into traps. An

* As I write she is still with us, and in fact, I can add that she successfully reared a family in June 1940. She is now more than five years old, which can be considered 'aged' for a small bird.

analysis of the records show that the majority of young birds leave during September, probably flying south on their journey to the Iberian peninsula.

Yours.

NOTE (added on 30th November 1939). According to the records here, you yourself ringed DL 17,18,19, and 20, four of Pipette's children in the nest, on 16th June 1939. Of DL 19 nothing further has been heard, but DL 17 was subsequently retrapped on 11th August, DL 20 on 25th July, 11th August, and 1st September, while DL 18 had also been re caught on 26th July and 11th August, before going abroad to be reported from San Sebastian on 11th November.

9. ROCK PIPIT

7th October 1939

Dear John – A still and sunny day, the surf from yesterday's storm beating on the rocks. A great migration of house martins, more than I have ever seen here before, about two hundred flying around our flagstaff, with many swallows and sand martins. One of those fresh mornings worth living many storms for. Pipits were also numerous.

As I have written on the meadow pipit I may as well give you next such information as I possess on the rock pipit. This is a larger, stouter, stronger, greyer, and altogether more robust bird. Its breast is dull and less obviously striated. Its outer tail-feathers, such a clear white in the meadow pipit, are much duller, almost a sooty white. Rock pipits nest in the side of the cliffs and in rocks above the tideline of Skokholm. They are almost as numerous in these situations as the meadow pipit is on the grassland plateau above.

The rock pipit has its special charm as it moves between the edge of the sea and the tops of the cliffs. Apart from the wild-piping oystercatchers and the gulls, which seem as remote and as inhuman as the waves themselves, the rock pipits are usually the first homely little birds to greet us when our boat enters the haven at Skokholm. Their very short and almost plaintive whistle, 'pheest!' became a familiar welcome as the boat turned around the harbour rock to the landing-steps; or a snatch of song would greet us from a bird walking on the rock itself. At the end of March it begins its song flights, the pleasant song a stronger version of that of its cousin, the meadow pipit. Probably because it is often uttered below the level of the cliff-top it has a resonance and penetration lacking in the song of the meadow pipit. Each pair selects a section of the coast for territory and jealously holds to it. For instance, these landing-steps are held by a pair of ringed rock pipits whose numbers are usually known to us. Thus for a while the female (as we believed) was a bird first ringed in 1934 as MR 444 and was for three years with a mate whose number we never quite determined. In 1937 he took as mate ZA 549, a bird first ringed in juvenile plumage in 1936. As far as we know this combination may still reign supreme over the harbour steps today. But if so, MR 444 must be seven years old. Her place, however, may well have been taken by a younger ringed bird.

It was possible occasionally to drive this pair from the harbour into the mouth of the Heligoland trap, following the course of the water which runs through the little valley. Or sometimes the pair ventured so far on their own. Thus the pair in possession of the harbour was under our most frequent observation.

But of the other thirty or so pairs none could be observed more casually. For lack of time we could not develop and put into use a technique for catching and ringing them in their respective territories. They were very shy of traps and did not readily enter the portable cages as did, for instance, the robins which, as I shall relate in some future letter, I trapped in these very territories of the rock pipits during the winter.

One of the loveliest natural sights on the island is that of the nest of the rock pipit beneath a clump of sea pinks or other maritime flowers. Many times, in an exploration of some part of the island rocks, or when ringing razorbills and puffins, or more often perhaps when in search of driftwood, we have come upon the rock pipit's nest in this pleasant setting. Sometimes the nest is in a crack beneath the long leaves of hart's-tongue fern or of the sea-beet, or half hidden under the white aiglets of the sea-campion, or the yellow fingers of the kidney vetch. Even when in a recess in the bare cliff the nest looks well, with its neat cup of dead grass, lined with finer grasses and hair and occasionally a fringe of grey lichen gathered from the upper rocks. The contrast with the deep red of the rocks is always pleasing. In this nest the three to five rich brown eggs are laid.

The rock pipit settles down to the cares of the nesting season with great energy, rearing two broods, and taking exactly one month of thirty to thirty-one days over each, from the laying of the first egg to the fledging of the last nestling. The parents gather all sorts of small animal and insect life between the sea and the tops of the cliffs to feed their young, and I have seen them gleaning marine organisms by the edge of the sea and searching under jetsam for sand-fleas and hoppers, of which they seem especially fond: while they also catch flies and insects on the wing. They are careful not to betray the nest while you are watching, and will sit with a beak full of food, piping plaintively, until you have either remained immovable for an hour or have gone away in despair.

The young birds, like the young meadow pipits, soon after leaving the nest band together and rove over the island, readily leaving their normal territory of the rocks. Early in July the first youngsters come into the garden-trap. At this warm time of year they are much irritated by the parasitic fly, *Ornithomyia lagopodis*, a glossy, flattened creature which readily slides under the plumage, and, like the wren hidden in the eagle's feathers in the fable, must often be transported wherever the bird migrates. And, as young wheatears, meadow- and rock pipits are often together in these warm, summer days, the parasite is communicated to all three.

It is interesting that the two kinds of pipits, which are really so very distinct in the hand that one cannot easily picture them interbreeding, should intermingle in the early autumn, for later on they sort themselves out and go their respective ways. Without much doubt food is the deciding factor. Food is more abundant on the surface of the island than in the rocks, as by July the rocks would be overcrowded with young pipits if the ten to a dozen youngsters reared by each pair (making with the adults some four hundred rock pipits) were to remain close to the tideline.

As autumn moves to winter the young meadow pipits, and many of the old, too, dwindle and disappear on their southerly migration. Ringing tells us that a fair proportion of the young rock pipits remain on the island, still haunting the surface rather than the sides; so that in winter the number of pipits on the island, though much reduced, is in the ratio of something like three rock pipits to one meadow pipit.

In the wildest storms of December and January the rock pipits (which, from the fact that they are almost all ringed, are probably old birds) haunting the shore are driven up to the plateau and may often seek protection in our garden and in the lee of the island buildings. Here, out of their true environment, they are never quite as tame as the meadow pipits.

What has happened at this season to the rest of the rock pipits, mostly young birds? Probably they are along the mainland shore, feeding in the sheltered bays, estuaries, and mud flats where in winter, but not in summer, it is usual to find them.

The number of rock pipits on the island in winter seems to vary somewhat. At times they appear scarce, and a walk around the island one day to obtain a count might show only twenty. On other days they are twice or three times as numerous, even in the depth of December and January. It seems, therefore, that there is some local movement between the island and the mainland in winter; and, in fact, it is not uncommon to observe pipits flying over the sea then.

As soon as March is in the rock pipits begin to retreat to the edge of the island, and by the end of the month they are all paired off and in possession of their territories, the males singing blithely.

Among the many hundreds of meadow pipits which migrate northwards over the island in the spring, there are no rock pipits. The return to the nesting ground is after all a local movement and can be accomplished quietly.

In the wild Hebridean islands of St Kilda and North Rona the rock pipit practically takes the place of the meadow pipit. This is understandable, for the inland areas of these islands are as savage, as rocky, and often as barren as the shore. Both bird and habitat are thus removed inland. So, too, on the wild west end of Skokholm, where rocks and maritime vegetation extend inland, one or sometimes two pairs of rock pipits will be found nesting a hundred yards from the sea.

Ever yours.

10. WILD FLOWERS

8th October 1939

MY DEAR JOHN – Your own considerable knowledge of wild flowers will, I hope, make this letter of particular interest to you. Although without special talent as a botanist, I have always included wild flowers in the phenological record or diary which I have now kept fairly consistently since I was seventeen years of age.

There is a simple pleasure in recording the appearance of the first flowers of spring. The year is young, the days are lengthening, and there is promise of summer in the increasing warmth of the sun. But how few of us find the time to keep up our diary of wild nature when in May and June the rush of blossom and bird-song demands a daily searching and identification!

It is an easier task on a small exposed island, where the flora is limited. On the two hundred and forty acres of Skokholm it is possible, after one or two seasons, to become familiar with all the wild flowers. The list is not large – I have recorded one hundred and eighty-five species to date. But its compiling has given me some pleasure, that same pleasure which can be got out of exploring and naming and learning the flowers and birds of a garden, a field, or some enclosed land of which one has obtained possession. As a man gets to know and love the flowers of his garden, so have I come to know and love the wild flowers of my island.

The wild storms of winter blowing over the unsheltered plateau of Skokholm do not encourage a luxuriant plant growth. There are no genuine trees. But in spring there is a beautiful display of certain flowers. The flora of a district is conditioned as much by the fauna as by the wind and weather. The rabbits and sheep of Skokholm ensure that what the weather does not harvest they will crop. But certain plants are never eaten by these mammals; for instance, wild arum and bracken. Bracken, being reasonably hardy, thrives and is constantly spreading wherever its requirements are met in a deep soil and a not excessive exposure to salt gales. But wild arum cannot survive severe winds: it needs shelter, a moist soil, and shade later on. So it only grows in such situations on the east side of the island, and where bracken later provides the shade for its ripening fruit.

Some plants are disliked by rabbits, but are regularly grazed by sheep; these include bluebell, violet, sea-campion, ground-ivy, scurvy grass, and sorrel. Sheep in fact are more omnivorous, yet not so destructive to grass: their droppings enrich the land, whereas the pellets of rabbits seem to have no great manurial value, and the countryman considers that the urine of rabbits has a scorching effect upon good herbage, and is good only to promote rank weeds. Perhaps the truth is that rabbits graze too closely, eating the heart and strength out of the long grasses and clovers, so that only dwarf grasses, moss, and the smaller edible plants can survive in the native turf of Skokholm. Three succulent plants much loved by rabbits and sheep are the dandelion, kidney vetch, and wild carrot, but these are confined to walls and cliffs out of reach of Skokholm's grazing animals.

What remains of the original farm pasture, chiefly in the meadows around the house, seems to consist largely of the common and rough-stalked meadow grasses (*Poa pratensis and trivialis*), with a little cock's-foot and crested dog's-tail grasses. In damp places there is plenty of Yorkshire fog and in dry spots the sheep's-fescue is abundant. All sorts of weeds struggle for existence, gaining roothold wherever the ground is too dry or too wet for the grasses. In January this rabbit-grazed mat is still brown-green with salt, and the stalks of last year's bracken are beaten down almost to the level of the earth. The heather leaves are russet-coloured, the empty cups of last year's bloom faded to palest brown. Only in the creeks facing east, out of the prevailing wind, does the ground respond to the new strength of the morning sun.

Here the tightly rolled spears of the wild arum (*Arum maculatum*) or lords-and-ladies shoot forth and slowly uncurl during a mild January. In this month the tips of the leaves of the lovely vernal squill pierce the wet ground. This is the *Scilla verna*; its light-blue upward-facing bells appear in April, rather earlier than the hanging bells of its relative the wild hyacinth or bluebell, *Scilla nonscripta*. But the rich dark-green leaves of the bluebell do not appear above ground before February.

These are the few simple signals of the awakening flora of the island spring. Not until March is in does the first flower open. In the first week a few lesser celandines appear. In the second week primroses begin. In the third week *Cochlearia* or scurvy grass, of which we have three kinds, the common, the English, and the Danish, shows a few early white clusters, while its leaves are still insignificant. In the fourth week ground Ivy, predominant in territory occupied by bracken, flowers. Early in April dandelions, growing on walls out of reach of animals, open. The scentless dog-violet, *Viola riviniana*, appears in the fields and between the clumps of heather. The brown winter pasture is slowly changing – in the damper patches the field woodrush shows the black flowers which have earned it the title of 'chimney-sweeps'; and here too are the first wild forget-me-nots, *Myosotis collina*, to be followed by *arvensis* and *versicolor*, and still later by the lovely *scorpioides*, the water forget-me-not, as well as the first member of the stitchwort family, the mouse-ear duckweed. *Poa pratensis* and *Poa annua* and *Poa trivialis* are the three principal meadow grasses and these show green at the end of the month.

April is the month when the sea pinks open and the sea campion begins hanging out its multitude of veined white bells. But not until May do these flowers burgeon and form a richly coloured carpet over acres of the exposed cliff edges and the narrow peninsula known as the Neck.

This display lasts for the month of May and gives the surface of the island a warm glowing appearance as seen from the mainland, a warmth matching the bright pink sandstone cliffs. And early in the month, while the bluebell beds are spread like a purple sheet in the hollows on the east side of the island, Skokholm is, I think, at its freshest and loveliest moment of the year.

Primroses flower from March until August, but the few cowslips we have are opened and soon faded in the middle of April. At the end of April the lady's smock or cuckoo-flower appears in damp places. Beside it grows its insignificant cousin, the hairy bittercress. Bracken is thrusting upwards, to uncurl its fronded head at the end of April, and to grow rapidly until it has hidden the bluebells and ground-ivy and sorrel which, their time of flowering over, enjoy its cool shade. Its fern-like leaves do not overlap and darken the ground until the end of May; I have seen much bracken blackened by sudden fierce gales in May and June.

During May the island pasture becomes starred with the small flowers of tormentil, milkwort, the germander, ivy-leaved, and field speedwells, the rich red common vetch, with scarlet pimpernel, eyebright, and the pink English stonecrop, with lady's bedstraw, with the heartsease pansy – the perennial variety *Viola curtisii* – and the pink-tipped yellow cushions of the *Lotus corniculatus* or birds'-foot trefoil.

All these small blossoms are there in June, too, but the pasture is enriched further by the appearance of wild thyme, trailing St John's wort, hop trefoil (lesser clover) and white clover, lesser stitchwort, silverweed, creeping buttercup, centaury, self-heal, yarrow, and wood-sage. The pastoral year moves on to the flowering of the heather in July, the bell-heather preceding the ling. These are the only two kinds of heather on the island. A small percentage of the ling is white. On the stone and earth walls there are a few flowers which do not stray to the pasture, needing some small shelter or at least protection from the wind and from the feet of man and beast. Wall pennywort is abundant. Figwort is much less plentiful.

Foxgloves rear their red-purple spikes high above the tops of the walls early in June, and late in the month the sheep's bit scabious shows its untidy blue heads, generally out of reach of rabbits – it is most numerous on the natural rock walls of Spy Rock. Samphire grows on rocks close to the sea, and so does the shore-weed.

The main pageant of the island's flowers is over with the coming of August, bringing with it as it does ragwort and golden rod and greater knapweed, as well as the blackberry, which is late to flower in the cool island air, and only fruits in warm summers. In September the autumn hawkbit appears in the grass, and is about the latest flower to open. The ponds and damp places have their special flora. Watercress and its associate brookweed grow plentifully by the drinking water spring. Here, as in the marshy places generally, are the three rushes – the common rush, the toad rush, the heath rush, and two sedges, the vernal and the tufted.

Water blinks, *Montia fontana*, covers every small open pool as soon as the sun is strong in the spring. Not long after occupying the island we had to cover and darken the drinking water well to keep out this green growth of *Montia*, and also the long tresses of the starwort, *Callitriche aquatica*.

Bog stitchwort and marsh St John's wort, marsh bedstraw, marsh pennywort, water mint, waterpepper, fill the fringe of the wet ground. The lovely bog pimpernel spreads its pale pink cups profusely in the open damp places, enjoying the midsummer sunlight.

Floating in the largest pond, the lesser crowfoot or water buttercup stars the water of the north pond in May. *Amphibious persicaria* erects its red turban over much of the pond too, and until the leaves hide the flowers these red brushes give the pond the appearance of a company of toy marines, awaiting to embark on the edge of a fairy sea. Between the leaves of this dominant plant can be found the long wide leaves of the floating pondweed, as well as water purslane, and the tiny forms of the lesser duckweed and the cudweed, *Apium inundatum*.

Hemlock, water-dropwort, cow parsnip, and meadow-sweet provide a rank growth in sheltered marshy places by the end of June, and still later the graceful marsh plume thistle rears its tall stem highest of all. In one spot on the island, in the hollow where the spring runs out from our drinking-well, these plants provide, with some nettles and bracken, almost a jungle of annual vegetation, and here sing and nest the sedge warbler, the whitethroat, and the water-rail. It was here that we found it convenient to erect a trap for the catching and ringing of migratory birds.

This letter runs on, and I am not yet at the end of the island flowers. In general, rank-growing plant life is confined to the sheltered situations, but the magnificent Scotch or spear-thistle and the creeping thistle grow tall in the open pasture. The sow- or milk-thistle likes the protection of bracken or nettles, above which it lifts its head. Burdock grows near buildings and the pathways used by man, together with the evil-smelling poisonous hemlock.

Strictly we have no trees, apart from what we have ourselves planted in the shelter of our garden. The bare plateau of the island is too windswept to encourage a woody growth, although there are some quite tough old, if small, living branches of the creeping willow, *Salix repens*, surviving in and around the east pond. These are semi-prostrate, as is the habit of this species. But other deciduous trees are represented only in stunted specimens of privet and blackthorn growing in North and South Havens. Here too grow the evergreen ivy and the remains of one ancient and now dead furze bush.

Furze was formerly plentiful, being cultivated for fodder purposes, according to the Welsh farming custom in the eighteenth and nineteenth centuries. Chopped fine and mixed with chaffed hay and straw it was a valuable feed for horses and cattle.

In the shelter of the North and South Haven cliffs grow plants found nowhere else on the island. In spring there is the early purple orchis, honeysuckle is luxuriant, and the royal-looking blossoms of the tree mallow mingle with the shaggy heads of hemp agrimony. The yellow cat's ear and the white ox-eye daisy thrive. Here too the bitter-sweet lives in company with such ferns as the sea spleenwort, the hart's-tongue, and the male fern.

The exposed cliffs have a very different flora. Where the wind and spray strike incessantly on the west-facing rocks there is no vegetation for at least seventy feet above sea-level, save yellow and grey lichens clinging to the red rock. At that point you will find the tough leaves of the wild beet flourishing. When the winter's storms have died away a brief annual growth appears consisting principally of chickweed (*Cerastium viscosum* and *Cerastium tetrandrum*), sea mayweed, shoreweed, and the glabrous orache.

Higher still, where the deposit of rubble and earth begins, the sea pink and the sea-campion share the territory between them. But between the rocks and the sea pinks there is often a stretch of shallow soil hardened by much travel by rabbits and seabirds. Exposure to wind and sun dries this area excessively between the periods when it receives moisture through sea mist, spray, and rain. This terrain is usually covered with a closely grazed mat of buck's-horn plantain and sea stork's-bill whose tight rosettes, like those of the daisy, are firmly spread around them, to defy too close a competition from rival plants. With these plants can be found the minute flowers and foliage of allseed and of the sea pearlwort.

I have not been able to cover all the flora of the island in this letter. Nor have I mentioned the weeds which have appeared in the garden during the years we have cultivated it, some of which, such as charlock and borage, have escaped to spread outside its walls. Even such common weeds as shepherd's-purse, petty spurge, spurrey, corn marigold, the dead-nettles, Good King Henry, do not however care to wander from the cultivated land, and are not found outside the gardens. One weed seems particularly at home on the island, and is found in abundance in the gardens at the lighthouse too: this is the lesser swine-cress, whose finely divided leaves seem to be especially fond of associating with the fine leaves of young carrots! Which reminds me that one of our rarest plants is the sea carrot (*Daucus gummifer*), found only in the cliffs of Wreck Cove. This has been identified by Mr H.A. Hyde of the National Museum of Wales, who has kindly edited the list (see Appendix II) of our flora.

Very best wishes.

11. RABBITS

14th October 1939

DEAR J.B. – In an earlier letter I mention the interesting series of documents dating back as far as 1324 which proved that rabbits were a valuable source of revenue for those who held the island – at that time it was in the possession of the Earl of Pembroke and his heirs.

There is no document to tell us when rabbits were introduced to Skokholm. But the Pipe Rolls and Ministerial Accounts reveal the methods by which they were caught. Thus the Pipe Roll of Edward III records:

> Carcases and skins of rabbits caught in the islands of Schalmey, Schokolm, and Middleholm, Michaelmas 1325 to January 30, 1326, £15 12s. Expenses: Stipend of 3 ferreters, 12s. 3d., salt for the rabbit carcases, thread for rabbit nets, boards, nail, and cord used for the boat in the said islands, 3s. 2d.

Ministerial Account 1207, No. 11, for the winter of 1387-8 records: '3120 carcases from the islands of Scokholm, Scalmey, and Myddleholm, besides tithes, sold, 2318. Food of 2 ferreters, 540 carcases, and food of 2 ferrets 262 carcases.' The 3,120 skins in this winter were sold for £8 to 'John Wyllyam of Haverford, in gross.' (I mentioned this transaction in an earlier letter.) The following expenses are noted:

'2½ qrs. of barley for 2 ferreters in the said island for 21 weeks, price 6d. per bushel, 10s. 2 bushels of salt for salting rabbits, 2s.; 1 shovel bought for digging out rabbits, hire of cooking utensils for the ferreters, 6d., repair of a house on the island of Scalmey, and of another house on the island of Scokholm for the said ferreters as well as for the storing of the rabbits, 2s.; thread for the making of rabbit nets, 4d.; repair of the boat and the purchase of 3 new oars, 6s. 10d.'

It can be gathered that the ferreters worked the whole winter for three or four shillings 'stipend' plus their food, which averaged out at about five pounds of barley and a pair of rabbits per man per day.

I should estimate by knowledge of the rabbits inhabiting these islands today that the 3,120 rabbits were caught in the following proportions on the islands: Skokholm, 240 acres, 1,000 rabbits; Skomer (or Scalmey as it was then called), 700 acres, 2,000 rabbits; and Middleholm, 30 acres, 120 rabbits. The figure of 3,120 rabbit skins occurs regularly (from 1387 to 1453); probably the ferreters reached this maximum figure each winter and then stopped in order to leave a sufficiency of conies for breeding. The cony returns varied between £12 and £14, a very large sum in those days, and showing a profit above expenses of some £10 yearly. So that strict preservation of these profitable animals was probably enforced.

These figures might be compared with the returns of rabbits caught in these islands 540 years later.

Year	Skokholm	Skomer	Middleholm
1388	1,000	2,000	120
1928	2,415	4,500	120

The difference is explained by the fact that there was less breeding cover for rabbits in the old days, since presumably none of the present stone and earth banks and hedges had then been built. (Middleholm was always uninhabited by man and therefore its rabbits did not vary.) Also there was a good deal of summer pasturing of cattle on the islands, the 'agistment' thereof fetching various sums, from £2 15s. in 1324 to 15s. in 1358, and from 5s. 8d. in 1387 to 60s. 4d. in 1545. In 1472 the 'hunting of conies' in the islands was released to the tenants by William Earl of Pembroke for 40s. per annum.

The rabbits did not come into their own until early in the present century when the farms which had gradually been built up during the previous one hundred and fifty years began to decline, and were finally abandoned about 1900. After that Skokholm and Skomer were left to the rabbit-catchers, who tore holes in the stone-faced banks which bounded the fields where once corn and hay and potatoes flourished, in order to give the conies dry breeding and sleeping dens. In forty years the islands have become rabbit warrens as well as the delightful seabird sanctuaries which we know today.

Many attempts were made in the past to improve the strain of rabbits on Skokholm, by the introduction of tame varieties, and also, according to men who have had the grazing and cony-hunting rights in more recent years, by the transportation of wild rabbits caught on the mainland of Pembrokeshire.

The Skokholm rabbit is somewhat smaller, and weighs about two pounds, that is, an average about four or five ounces less than the mainland rabbit. It is slightly darker on the upper parts, due to the greater proportion of the long black hairs there. Albinos are rare – I have only seen two here in twelve years – but black specimens are common and may be as numerous as five per cent. Other mutations suggest descent from tame rabbits, particularly a variety with very long fine wool-like hair of a rich grey-brown tint, perhaps descended from introductions of Angora rabbits; and a variety with a white nose stripe and neck and foreparts – the so-called blaze and saddle of the 'Dutch' variety of the tame rabbit. Occasionally these 'Dutch' markings are incorporated with the long Angora wool in one aberrant individual.

An expert rabbit-catcher told me his dog could not keep up with mainland rabbits, but it easily caught those of Skokholm. This seems to me proof that the Skokholm race has lost speed through speed having no survival value for it.

When I first settled here I had an idea that I could cut a quick way to fortune by breeding the Chinchilla variety of tame rabbit, whose pelt at that time (in 1928) was worth from 10s. to £1. I had therefore only to breed a few thousand of these each year to make a very comfortable living. As you may guess I did not know the island so well then as I do now.

My plans were to exterminate the wild rabbits on the island and replace them with the Chinchilla variety, which incidentally weighs about four pounds and is twice as large as the native island rabbit. When after one year I found it impossible to exterminate the wild rabbits, which could not be dislodged in their cliff and boulder fastnesses, I laid out a number of wire-netting enclosures in which I turned down the young Chinchillas from the original breeding stock of twenty does and a buck kept in hutches in the island buildings.

These enclosed warrens of Chinchillas did quite well as long as a natural flush of grass was maintained during late spring and summer, but in dry weather and in the winter they were unable to maintain their condition without generous artificial feeding. Moreover they were growing wild and difficult to handle, and this was a disadvantage, since at killing time it is necessary to watch each pelt carefully and, if maximum prices are to be secured, the rabbit must be killed at the precise moment when its winter coat is free from all signs of moult. But the chief reason for my abandoning the scheme altogether was the severe slump in the price of skins during 1929 and 1930. The market for them was practically closed, and you could not secure more than one shilling for the very best pelts. As I was importing grain, hay, and roots with which to feed my large rabbitry I was now losing money rapidly. I therefore sold the does and turned loose the remainder, some forty young bucks.

These Chinchilla rabbits were seen about for the next two years, but ultimately disappeared. They were too big to go down small rabbit holes, so they lived in the larger, older rabbit thoroughfares in the hedge banks. For a few more years we were to catch from time to time one or two large wild rabbits weighing three to four pounds each, but the beautiful grey Chinchilla colour was not to appear in the offspring of these released males.

During the succeeding years I continued to hunt for a means of exterminating the island rabbits. The use of gin-traps, with all the cruelty they involved in the broken legs of the screaming tortured wild birds as well as of the rabbits, grew abhorrent. Yet neither traps, nor snares, nor long nets, nor ferrets and dogs, could reduce the rabbit population to less than a significant breeding nucleus. But let me give you some figures and bring the story of the Skokholm rabbits and my search for a means of controlling them up to date.

During 1927-8, 144 steel-toothed traps in daily use caught 2,415 rabbits – approximately two-thirds of the estimated population. In 1928-9, 288 traps and 120 wire-noose snares caught 2,908 rabbits, again leaving about one-third on the ground. It was found that traps were too slow to catch sufficient numbers in a limited time, and in both winters considerable numbers of wild birds were trapped and so killed. Traps were given up as being inefficient and inhumane. Snares could only work successfully in the few flat and wide areas where rabbits could run fast enough to draw them. Snares fitted with various humane devices were proved too clumsy and conspicuous to be successful. Nets and fence-netting traps were successful only in the flat, open meadows, but were useless in the major portion, which consists of a honeycomb of bird-burrows in rough ground.

Ferrets were unsatisfactory, possibly because for centuries rabbits on Skokholm have known no underground enemies such as the stoat and weasel, and they would not bolt in sufficient numbers.

During the years 1931-6, rabbits were not worth more than 2*d*. or 2½*d*. per pound, and could not have been economically marketed even if they had been caught. They were therefore allowed to increase almost unhindered and soon reached a climax state of about 10,000, the natural increase of summer or its equivalent dying out each winter from natural causes, it is believed chiefly from diseases associated with overcrowding and malnutrition, the common fate of rabbits on many small islands where no human control is attempted.

In the summer of 1936, Sir Charles Martin suggested that the introduction of the virus disease *Myxomatosis cuniculi* might be effective in controlling the population of rabbits. He had found that this malady was 100 per cent fatal to wild rabbits, and in two experiments the disease had exterminated colonies living under natural conditions in an enclosed area of 500 square yards in a paddock at Cambridge. The virus of myxomatosis had been tested upon a variety of domestic animals and wild fauna in the United States, England, and Australia and, so far, found to be entirely specific for the European rabbit. The disease produced by it has an incubation period of five to ten days, at the end of which time the animal becomes feverish and ill, and the eyelids and the nasal mucous membranes become swollen and inflamed. Afterwards a purulent fluid is exuded from the conjunctivae and nose. Sometimes the mucous membranes at the anal and generative orifices are similarly affected. The exudation from all these situations contains the virus, and the infection passes to other animals by contact.

During the last two weeks of September, eighty-three rabbits were marked, inoculated, and released at points scattered over the whole island; twelve of them were afterwards discovered dead in the open. Unfortunately, it was not possible to make this first attempt earlier in the year, so that rabbits infected from those inoculated would not be likely to be found dead before 4th October, when the island was abandoned for the winter. It is, therefore, not possible to say to what extent spread of the disease occurred; but when the island was visited in the following spring, there was no trace of the disease in a population which seemed as numerous as ever.

A second attempt was made during the summer of 1937, when fifty-five rabbits were inoculated with the virus and distributed as widely over the island as before. It was hoped that closer contacts in the breeding season would result in the wider spread of the disease. Both marked and unmarked individuals were found dead of the disease, proving it had spread somewhat; but it appeared to have died out by September, and with no obvious effect on the numbers of the rabbits. A final inoculation of seven rabbits in one warren in the spring of 1938 had the same result – the disease spread but soon died out without exterminating all the members of the warren. Sir Charles Martin had shown that with the strain of virus used intimate contact of healthy and sick animals was required to ensure transmission of the disease, and it may be that the instinctive behaviour of the sick animal in isolating itself and squatting about in the open at the most contagious period was responsible for the failure of the virus as a means of control under natural conditions.

Smoke pumped into burrows from a cartridge containing sulphur was found expensive and difficult to handle, and produced a painful death. In 1938 the Universities Federation for Animal Welfare (then the University of London Animal Welfare Society), through Captain C. W. Hume, arranged to make the Skokholm rabbit population the subject of a demonstration of humane rabbit control, using calcium cyanide in the dust form known as cyanogas. The dust is blown through the passages of warrens by means of hand-pumps, and on contact with the air gives off the fatal hydrocyanic acid gas. As the dust emerges from exits in a warren, these are blocked so as to ensure concentration of the gas within.

Work was begun in the winter of 1938-9, when tests made on rabbits in rock crevices and shallow holes proved that death occurred within a few seconds, the animals stretching out without excessive movement and without screaming. All the accessible holes were then closed, as so many were bird-holes only. The reopened holes were treated a fortnight later with the dust, and it was possible to fumigate all holes except those in the steepest parts of the cliffs and among cliff-falls and boulders. When this first treatment was completed, it was estimated that about 90 per cent of the rabbits had been killed. Rabbits from the cliffs seemed to be responsible for many holes afterwards found reopened inland, and it is probable that had the island been connected with the sea without cliff or boulder 100 per cent extermination would have been achieved.

As it is, after the holes had been gone over for a third time, it was calculated that only about 400 of the original 10,000 (in round maximum figures) rabbits were left, and all of these appeared to be rock-dwellers coming to the top of the island to feed only at night. On this showing, cyanogas was therefore 96 per cent successful for the island as a whole; excluding the economically unbeatable cliff-land, it was still nearer complete success.

Proof of this success was forthcoming in the summer of 1939. White clover appeared where it was always rare and stunted before, grass grew long and luxuriantly, and the absence of rabbit-pellets was remarked. As much as four tons of hay were cut from an acre of the best land; and hay had not been cut since the land was farmed in the last century. The grass continued to grow; our hundred breeding ewes were found quite inadequate to graze it down and it was eventually beaten down by winter storms.

The residue of rabbits in the cliffs began to breed with rapidity. Normally, under climax conditions, the island rabbits only breed from March until July inclusive, and their litters are normally small, from two to four young per litter. At present they are breeding all the year round as a result of the abundant feed, and gravid does are carrying up to eight young. During the summer of 1939 they spread somewhat inland, helped by the seabirds, which opened all the blocked holes in that spring. We are now going to try reducing this remnant by means of cyanogas, and at the moment of writing two men are here for this purpose.

From this experiment it is clear that fumigation with calcium cyanide dust is a successful means of extermination, and but for the inaccessibility of the cliff areas at Skokholm, would have achieved 100 per cent destruction of the island rabbits. We may judge therefore that it would be completely successful under most conditions existing on farm lands on the mainland. Until the cost of the dust is reduced, however, it is not likely to be universally applied. But it might be used as the first step in a campaign organized by the Ministry of Agriculture, and largely at the ministry's expense – since, by not taking measures in better time, perhaps the ministry is a good deal responsible for the present rabbit nuisance in west Wales, Cornwall, Devon, and Somerset. The gin-trap is very cruel and therefore immoral; but, apart from ethical considerations, it is quite ineffective, and, by killing off the natural enemies of the rabbits – fox, stoat, and weasel – it has actually encouraged the multiplication of both rats and rabbits, to the great detriment of our agriculture. So that today our western counties are swarming with rabbits and there is a huge and well-established rabbit-trapping industry – even accepted by the farmers and the local agricultural committees as part of profitable land husbandry!

Such an official campaign by the ministry would have to be accompanied by an Act of Parliament forbidding the use of the gin-trap; and power would be given to local authorities to secure the entry of competent persons into farms and infested premises for the purpose of killing rats and rabbits without fees being payable to the farmer or owner thereof. Rabbits treated as vermin in this way would soon dwindle to their former insignificant numbers of fifty to a hundred years ago, and be confined principally to the rough woodlands and warrens where they belong. Stoats and weasels would increase again, and rats would become correspondingly scarce. The slaughter and torture of many thousands of wild birds each winter, to say nothing of domestic animals – dogs, cats, poultry – which are caught in the traps, would cease.

From your home near Aylesbury you may most likely regard our rabbit problem in the west as a local one, but it appears of some magnitude to us here on the spot. And we consider you are fortunate in your better balance of nature: poachers, ferrets, dogs and gun, and stoats and weasels combine to keep your rabbits and rats properly controlled. With you the rabbit is almost a special and rare dish for the table along with the hare; and from being able to live in spacious conditions in your woods and spinneys is a much larger and finer creature. Here in the west the traps have exterminated all hares, and our rabbits, from being overcrowded and lacking natural enemies, are small, comparatively inactive, and much diseased.

Yours ever.

12. ATLANTIC SEAL

16th October 1939

D EAR J – There was great excitement fourteen days ago, for Ann had come running to the house to report that the old cow seal which for days had been haunting the North Haven, was ashore high up on the red boulders with a new-born calf in its wrinkled yellow-white coat. She reported that the cow seal had growled a little at her as she looked down from the cliff edge eighty feet above.

We all went down to peep at the wonder, while a fresh north-east wind sent little white-lined ripples to spill on the red slabs above the golden sand of North Haven. Mother and child lay about eight feet above high-water mark.

The young seal left the beach today at fourteen days old.

In most autumns a young seal is dropped in North Haven, but usually our inquisitiveness, and the necessity of collecting driftwood from the beach there, has led us to disturb cow and calf, and the cow has then abandoned the calf during the day, returning to suckle it only at night. And this has usually led to the calf taking to the water earlier than is natural.

This autumn we determined to avoid the beach and try to study the cow and calf, through glasses, and make notes of her natural behaviour when completely undisturbed. We therefore got the lighthouse-keepers to keep clear of North Haven also.

Frances Pitt in the *Romance of Nature* states that the mother Atlantic or grey seal tucks her baby away 'in some sheltered cove well above high-water mark. She must go and fish, and the young one as yet is unable to swim so far.' Fraser Darling, however, finds that where the breeding grounds are quite undisturbed by man, as at North Rona, the cows come as much as three hundred yards inland in order to calve, and they do not leave the land until two or three weeks later, and during this period they normally do not feed at all.

Our observations here also suggest that the cow goes to sea during the calf's suckling days only when disturbed by man, or when (for lack of suitable low uninhabited skerries) the calf has to be dropped so close to the sea that it is easy for the cow to slip into the water. It is certainly not true that the mother *must* go and fish; and it is more likely that she uses the sea principally as a refuge from man. I have never seen a mother seal feeding during the time she was suckling, but this I admit is no proof that she does not feed then. It is well known that cow seals (of several species) can be ashore and feed their calf for weeks without taking any food themselves. The calf thrives on the rich milk manufactured from the reserves of fat and blubber of its dam, who loses weight in consequence. The fur seal and the elephant seal, according to L. Harrison Matthews, haul out on Antarctic beaches and remain some two months ashore, each bull gathering a harem of several cows, and both sexes remain fasting ashore for several weeks until the calves are weaned and mating has been completed.

On North Rona Darling found the same thing happening. In September the mature bulls haul out of the ocean, where they have wandered for nine months, and climb up on to the grass. The cows follow as each nears calving, and gather about these bulls which have assumed definite territories. These they defend from other bulls, although cows are free to wander from one bull's territory to another's, quite promiscuously. Mating takes place eleven to fourteen days after calving, so that the gestation period of the Atlantic seal is fully fifty weeks. Maiden cows mate with young bulls that are waiting on the rocks, close to the sea. These young bulls are waiting for an opportunity to climb up and take over the territory of a bull which, ashore for perhaps three weeks without food, and satisfied sexually, is weak and willing to yield it up. The cows suckle their calves for periods varying between two and four weeks, and then abandon them. The first calf is born in mid-September.

Here in west Wales it is harder to observe the breeding habits of seals which are driven by the persecution of man to breed in deep caverns and upon beaches on lonely islands. The behaviour of the cow seal, whom we named Clementina, and of her calf, whom we called Anne and who left the North Haven today, was, I think, typical of seals on this coast.

Clementina was a rich golden brown with blotches of black-brown on her upper surface. She was about eight feet long and two feet in girth. From our look-out on the cliff above we could, by keeping very still, watch her without being recognized as enemies. (I have often crept up to a seal dozing on the shore: each time the animal stirred and opened its eyes I have remained motionless, and in this way have stood within eight feet of the animal without its realizing that I, in my brown corduroys, was more than a part of the neutrally tinted background. Its sense of smell on these occasions seems not to have been of use as a warning of the nearness of an enemy.)

For four days Clementina did not stir from beside her child, which she fed at least three times a day, probably oftener. To watch the calf suck the retractable breasts, and see Clementina paw and fondle her very lovingly, very humanly, was a happy sight. During this time a fine bull seal patrolled the sea in the region of North Haven. On the fifth day there was a heavy surf splashing up over the rocks and Clementina was obviously uneasy and watchful. She had disappeared by dusk. She was back again next day, another rough one, and on the next day. For the three following days we ourselves were absent from Skokholm, but on our return on 12th October we found Clementina still with her baby. She herself looked much thinner and leaner, with her 'hips' showing, which had hitherto been disguised by her very bulging 'waistline'.

Anne lost her white coat early in her first week, her iron-grey juvenile pelt breaking through and pushing out the white hairs so that they lay spread around her in a downy circle. She scarcely moved from within this rampart, while Clementina with her heavy body had flattened a distinct groove in the red marl close by.

On the 13th and 14th Clementina was observed swimming at high tide in the shallow water of North Haven while Anne watched her with her large sombre eyes.

On the morning of the 15th Anne was quite alone, but was looking very fat and thriving.

We had two visitors today (the 16th), and it was agreed to go down into North Haven and show them the baby seal, and we ourselves also wanted to have a closer look at Anne, so much observed at a distance. Clementina was not in sight. Anne, who by the way proved to be male, wept tears of what seemed to be fear and anger as we came close. He snarled in a businesslike way, and vigorously bit the segment of laminaria which was used as a wand to stroke him with. He measured about three feet in length. And although we withdrew discreetly when our curiosity was satisfied, Anne decided that he would not stand any more of this, and shuffled away over the wet red rocks to the sea.

For a moment he hesitated when the wave licked over him, but after rolling about uncertainly in the flotsam, he swam bravely away, making one brief dive, and then, with his head well up, swam out of sight, closely following the line of the shore.

Whether he was now weaned and fit for the sea I do not know, but as Atlantic grey seals can swim at birth (though they normally prefer not to), it is likely that Anne found his mother and she looked after him for as long as her milk lasted. Just about this time (fourteen days after calving) Clementina would be seeking a male and this may have accounted for her absence on 16th October.

There is no regular meeting and mating ground here as there is for instance, in north Scottish waters. Perhaps this has caused the time of calving of the Atlantic seal in Pembrokeshire waters to become spread over a long period. We find calves are dropped here any time between late July and late December – a period of five months; whereas at the large sealeries on Treshnish and North Rona Darling found the carvings took place from September to November only. Bulls in Pembrokeshire waters have a hard task in patrolling their individual cave and beach territories, for they do not lie out on the beaches with cows except when completely undisturbed by man, or when the bull has momentarily been called by a cow which is ready to mate. Mating takes place on the edge

of the sea, as the pair lie sideways to each other, tails uphill, and flippers interlocked like arms entwined, and it also takes place in the sea. As the cow seal is promiscuous she is willing to be taken by the first bull available, perhaps by several bulls if these are numerous. From what I have seen, however, it seems that certain stretches of the coastline, with or without caves and beaches, are patrolled by individual bulls, the best breeding areas being secured by the most powerful and experienced bulls, and the most unsuitable stretches by the weaker, less mature males.

Research into these and other problems of the life-history of these seals would be possible if some convenient method of marking the calves were devised. A number branded on the forehead (with caustic?) seems the obvious way for easy distant recognition of the swimming seal. Ordinary metal clip rings and tags such as we use for cattle would soon wear away in the salt water. For instance, we know almost nothing of the small local daily or large seasonal movements of seals or of longevity and attachment to locality, or even of the age when breeding begins. There seems to be a good opportunity for original research here, especially as these fine animals are fortunately increasing, and will increase still further during the war. For when men are at war, the wild creatures are usually left in peace.

Atlantic seals are noticed about Skokholm in all months of the year, but are most scarce in January, February, March, and April. They increase from June to October as they gather along the littoral for breeding.

On warm days in the summer parties of these seals lie out to bask on the reefs exposed by the falling tide around all the islands. There they doze, yawn, scratch, quarrel a little, and moan in a pleasant key until the rising water washes them off. Seals can rest and sleep (or at least doze) as they float perpendicularly at right angles to the surface; they can also sleep underwater for five or six minutes at a time, rising at intervals to blow but without opening their eyes or appearing to be other than fast asleep.

As you know their fur is useless as an article of trade, and probably this fact has saved them from extinction in the past. The colour of the adult pelt varies very much: a velvet black is not uncommon, and a rich cream is frequent; the majority are of some shade of grey-brown or brown-grey with large spots and blotches of a darker hue.

As for the other British seal – the so-called common (I prefer to call it the harbour) seal, as we have no considerable sandbanks in west Wales, this lover of flat and shallow shores is never seen here.

All good wishes.

13. FINCHES AND BUNTINGS

22nd October 1939

DEAR JOHN – It is a fine Sunday, very pleasant and full of birds. Calm warm days are helping to lengthen St Martin's summer here. There is more cloud today. We have caught quite a lot of finches this morning.

In general, finches and hard-billed birds have little to attract them here; for we grow no corn crops. Therefore my heart is a little heavy when I see the great autumnal flights of finches rushing past the island almost non-stop! On calm days such as these, however, when flying is something of an effort, they seem glad to settle for a while, but the majority, finding no food, fly on to the mainland.

On 18th October we caught thirty-six birds in the traps, of which twenty-four were greenfinches, eight chaffinches, two song thrushes, with one starling, and a meadow pipit.

Today we caught thirty-five birds, of which twenty-one were greenfinches, twelve chaffinches, with one goldfinch, and a blackbird. One of the chaffinches had been ringed on the 18th, and had returned to the trap on the 19th and 21st also. This is unusual, and although a ringed female chaffinch remained here once for sixteen days, it is more usual for them to pass swiftly over, or at most to stay for one or two days. Thus of one hundred and five chaffinches caught and ringed in the traps, approximately one-third were re-caught subsequently, some individuals twice or more times. But, of course, this is only *a third of the birds caught*; many hundreds more were not caught.

Greenfinches are the same, visiting us on their autumn migrations in October and November, and again in March and April. At other times of the year – excepting June to August when none is seen – they are very casual visitors. Only one has remained for so long as a fortnight, during May, and this was a tired individual which was unwilling to leave the island and cross the sea. We caught him each day in the garden-trap where he fed on groundsel and dandelion seeds. In fact he became so tame that we called him Buddy, and he would wait to be caught in the trap without fluttering or fussing much, and he would fly back into the garden as soon as released. But on the fifteenth day Buddy flew away to the mainland and we missed his cheerful chirrup. He never sang his full merry whistle, but at times he would give his trilling call more loudly as if he was anxious for a reply from one of his own breed. But out of the blue sky and the still bluer sea surrounding the island reply there came none. All his kind were by then breeding in more sheltered mainland fields and gardens.

Goldfinches also visit us but do not appear usually to associate with the main movement of chaffinches and greenfinches. They come singly or in twos and threes. Their sweet tinkling notes are most welcome to me, as they speak of the orchards and waste margins of the country lanes of my Monmouthshire days.

None of these finches and none of the buntings are likely to breed on this windswept island in its present condition: coverless and with no arable land.

The only finch that has bred here is the linnet. In 1929 a pair built a nest in the only furze bush on the island, a very old plant that has since perished of exposure and age. The nest was constructed in May of twigs and moss, plentifully lined with hair and wool. And while the hen sat on her four red-spotted blue-white eggs the cock half opened his wings and spread his tail to her and sang his lovely inconsequential twittering melodies from the honeysuckle and blackberry stems close by. So long as the wind lay in the south and west they were sheltered in their niche in the cliff. And all went tolerably well. The eggs hatched early in June, and two weeks later the family of four came to feed daily in the garden. But after 21st June they had vanished and I did not see a linnet again that year on the island until 9th October. As a migrant the linnet is erratic, but I have seen it here in every month, although it most often visits us in the winter months when there is, nevertheless, almost nothing for a hard-billed bird to feed on. No doubt it would breed more often if I had been able to plant some furze and blackthorn.

Bramblings pass overhead on the autumn migration with their common cousins the chaffinches, and more rarely in the spring. The northern races of the redpoll have been recorded in the winter by the lighthouse-keepers, and I have seen redpolls in their gardens on the cliff edge, but have not been able to determine which race of *Carduelis flammea* these might have been.

The corn, the yellow, and the reed buntings, all fairly common on the mainland, are surprisingly rare visitors. At times a corn bunting, and more often a yellow bunting, will turn up in the spring, uttering a brief chipping call note. Only once, on a bright quiet golden morning late in May, has a yellow bunting cheered us with his 'bread and no cheese' song, uttered from the chimney of the island house.

For birds which are migrating and are thus out of their normal feeding and breeding environment very seldom sing. The males have here no territories to defend by song, nor have they the environment in which they are accustomed to sing when advertising their presence to the female. A different urge is upon them, the urge to beat their wings on migration, an urge which is as seasonal and almost as automatic as the natural functions of the living body.

We therefore rarely or never hear the migrating bird sing.

It will utter the sharp call note, the keep-in-touch sound of its species, but will not normally utter the generally more prolonged and often seductive call note used at the breeding ground. These are the rules of voice on migration. But once winter quarters are reached – I am thinking particularly of those species which winter at Skokholm – song is indulged in. Thus robins, wrens, song thrushes, blackbirds, and dunnocks sing during winter and early spring on this island. And again, stray migrants, passing late through the island after the main migration has gone by, sometimes sing, though not often: certainly the turtledove croons, and sometimes a willow-wren or a whitethroat will sing for us.

Yours.

NOTE. It may be worth adding that one of the chaffinches ringed here on 27th October 1939, was recovered on 6th October 1945 at Hoboken, near Antwerp. This bird was over six years old, which I believe is considered aged for a small passerine. I wonder why it was so far from its (October 1939) autumn halting-place? Perhaps it was on its way west from some mid-European breeding ground, for it is known that the general autumn route of these continental chaffinches is in a west and south-west direction, and many reach Ireland, including chaffinches ringed at Heligoland and in the Low Countries.

25th October 1939

DEAR JOHN – The wheatears have gone. I saw what is probably the last one on 22nd October, having seen none since the 19th. The year is gathering to the end, and we are left with only the red rocks, the brown seaweed, and the dead bracken The fierce north-westerly wind is beating down the russet stems and driving the small birds to the crannies of the cliffs where they find shelter from this cool autumnal blast. A few flies dance when the sun comes into these windless nooks. A stray chaffinch or a rock pipit rises to snatch at them hungrily. Already the rocks are polished by the autumn rains and the whitewash of the nesting seabirds has vanished from the cliff ledges.

But we are grateful that the wheatears stay so long as seven and a half months with us. These brisk and neat and pretty birds are a great adornment to our landscape. They are comparatively tame, or perhaps I should say bold. They run or flutter before you with almost a challenging behaviour, restlessly bobbing their heads and flirting their bright wings and white-banded black-tipped tail in a conspicuous manner. The cock in his new spring plumage, I always think, is very handsome with his rich blue-grey mantle, black-brown wings, tail-tip, and facial stripe with white line above the eye. Nor are the rich buff breast and brown back of the female much less pleasing by their pleasant contrast with her mate's finery.

About a dozen pairs of wheatears inhabit Skokholm during the nesting period, and many hundreds pass through on their migrations. Birds ringed as nestlings in one year have returned to breed with us the next year. Two wheatears ringed as breeding adults have returned to breed in the following year and the year after; that is to say, they have bred three years in succession, and would then be getting old (for a small bird).

Wheatears like exploring holes in the ground. At Skokholm they roost in holes before nesting begins. They used to be caught in numbers by the shepherds on the South Downs who took advantage of this habit by setting hair-noose snares in shallow tunnels in the turf. The captured wheatears were sent to town to be prepared as 'larks on toast' for the benefit of gourmets. Here we capture wheatears in tunnel-traps and in house-traps, ring them, and set them free. Not many adults enter these traps in the spring. They seem too busy about their nesting affairs then to have time to go exploring as the young ones do in July and August.

These newly fledged young birds will play for hours about the structure of the traps, chasing each other in and about the poles and netting, especially on calm sunny days. They freely enter the wire-netting tunnels of the house-trap, although there may be no bait inside. And once one wheatear is inside and fluttering about there the other wheatears outside get excited and hunt for the way in. Rock-and meadow pipits share this curiosity and all three species mingle at such a moment. They are like children playing in the sunlight and seem fully as happy and absorbed.

This 'play' period lasts about two months while the young wheatears are moulting their juvenile body-feathers. Early in September many of them are ready to migrate. They are powerful fliers. They seem to reach their wintering grounds rapidly. Three of our wheatears have been recovered abroad, all three early in September; one on the 3rd in Gironde, France; a second on the 6th at Rabat, Morocco; and the third on 12th September at Arcachon, France.

The migration of the wheatear is one of the easiest to observe, for it frequents the most open ground, where its numbers are quickly assessed. In general they arrive with us in bulk during the third week of March, and the bulk pass southwards again during August and September.

The large Greenland race of wheatear usually appears late in April and May and is often in considerable numbers. For instance on 28th April 1938 we estimated 1,500 were present – a very grand sight, for they seemed to cover the foreground like a carpet – and 500 on 8th May of that year. In some autumns the return passage is almost as heavy, and many Greenland wheatears are present during October. With a little experience you can identify the more typical specimens of this race, especially the males, by the greater size and the very much richer buff breast and belly, and the browner back. (They are also addicted to perching on twigs and vegetation.) But size and colour can be deceptive in certain lights in the field, and it is only by catching them and carefully measuring the wings of these wheatears that we can be sure of the sub-species. Any male wheatear with wing measurement of a hundred millimetres and above can be regarded as of the Greenland race; and any female with wing measurement above ninety-six millimetres we can safely put down as of this larger race. Once again the value of ringing is proved.

Wheatears nest in unfinished rabbit scrapes, or holes in the stone hedge-walls. They lay five or six eggs of a delicate pale blue colour and usually rear two broods, at Skokholm. The second nest is built a few days after the first young are on the wing. The song of the male is one of the first to be heard long before the sun rises on summer mornings: 'Pu-ee, pu-ee, ee- wheet-tio!' – you will hear this musical jangle mingling with the song of the lark, the blackbird, the lapwing, and the strident piping of the oystercatchers.

Yours ever.

15. STORM PETREL

8th November 1939

DEAR JOHN – This morning the last young storm petrel had left the hole in the wall of the meadow. I had been watching it carefully all this month, as each morning I fetched water from the well. What a delicate-seeming, dainty, and altogether charming bird this is! In the hand it is as fragile and light as it looks on the wing, a fragility enhanced by its wayward flight when released; for then – on land – it appears to be blown hither and thither by the slightest breeze, or as if it were following the ups and downs of a confusion of imaginary storm-waves. I have a great fondness for this little bird which is no bigger than a sparrow and yet can ride out the endless hurricanes of the Atlantic winter.

For all its weak appearance it must be a powerful flier, and although from its habit of skimming low over the troubled waters of great oceans it has come to adopt this erratic flight which suggests frailty (in comparison, for instance, with the powerful-looking direct flight of gannet or gull), it travels at a great pace for a small bird. I have admired the ease with which it follows a fast-moving ship as it hunts for the small fry and planktonic organisms churned up by the propeller. In its side-to-side movements then, and its circling about the ship's stern, it covers about four times the distance travelled by the ship. So that if ten to twelve miles per hour is the average speed of a modern ship the petrel can easily fly at forty to fifty miles per hour.

Skokholm for its size, I think, contains one of the largest storm petrel colonies in the British Isles. Making a rough count of the nest sites in the farm walls, and allowing for the numbers of nests in the cliff areas, and amid the shearwater burrows, there are at the moment some six hundred pairs nesting here.

The storm petrel is very rarely identified within close range of the shore at any time during daylight. It is strictly nocturnal in its arrival and departure on the island. The breeding adults first come to land during the last week in April. The following table may interest you:

Year	First Arrived	First egg found	Last young bird seen on land
1927	–	–	30th October
1928	29th April	1st June	7th November
1929	26th April	5th June	25th October
1930	26th April	31st May	2nd November
1931	30th April	28th May	21st October
1932	28th April	–	1st November
1933	28th April	28th May	3rd November
1934	26th April	29th May	–
1939	1st May	1st June	7th November

I usually heard them first by their purring, almost crooning note coming from the hedges near the house on some quiet evening in late April. 'Purr-r-r-r-r-chikka', the new arrival crooned, a warm, a thrilling note to me it became, signifying the full moment of spring by this swallow of the sea abandoning the storms and waves to come to nest.

The nesting sites selected are many; in fact you can safely say they include almost every variety of sufficiently dark crevice and cranny, natural but also often artificial (as under a pile of wood), afforded on the island from just above high-water mark to the talus and debris of the weathered sandstone on the highest point of the island. Naturally the old herring-bone pattern stone-banked hedge-walls are in favour because the earth behind them is soft and easily burrowed, once the petrel has squeezed a way between the stones. And it is in these dry banks that I found it most convenient to study them. Here I could find a site not too far back in the wall, to which my hand obtained access by pulling out one of the 'vertebral' stones of the patterned wall.

Unfortunately a series of nests which I had marked for observation in 1930 were deserted owing to the excessive shyness of this bird. Having learnt of this readiness of the bird to desert I took much greater care when

I made a second attempt to study the storm petrel by the ringing method. And in 1931 I marked ten suitable nests, of which six were successful.

The shearwater, cousin of the storm petrel (they both belong to the *Procellariiformes* or tube-nosed birds) has a grand assembly place between the two islands of Skomer and Skokholm. Here, an hour or so before sunset, gather many thousands of shearwaters; they rest on the surface, preening and bathing or merely quiet if it is calm, but skimming to and fro in long flocks over the water if the sea is rough. They await the night before they dare venture to land. It is a great experience to sail through their ranks at sunset and study their beautiful gliding and easy manoeuvring.

No such rendezvous is adopted by the storm petrel. Very rarely a solitary bird may be seen zigzagging between the shearwaters as the sun leaves the edge of the Atlantic in the west. Yet as soon as it is dark the storm petrels begin to arrive from the sea. They circle around the nesting-wall or rocks for quite a long time, often singly, but sometimes a second bird joins the first and a pretty kind of aerial chase goes on. More rarely a third will join the circle, and, as far as one can make out in the dusky light, a very rapid display flight is then indulged in. Possibly on these occasions two males are pursuing a female – the excitement is high, there is a whirring of wings and sometimes a curiously soft but vibrating call is uttered. It sounds like 'Quick-er, quick-er,' as if indeed the birds were, appropriately enough, actually urging each other to a greater speed and excitement in their wild circling dance.

Suddenly, round about midnight, the dance is done, and down the birds drop. You hear a fluttering as one of them scrambles for a second or two at the narrow entrance to the nesting crevice. The wings rustle as they are folded, and the bird has disappeared. Perhaps the courtship will be carried on at the nest. I often heard a variety of monosyllabic squeaks and grunts which I interpreted as being part of the courtship, mating, and connubial exchanges. And usually one or both would begin the crooning note again.

In the open it runs nimbly about with the tips of the webbed feet touching the ground, while the weight of the body is really sustained by the rapidly beating wings, and by this curious half run, half flight it gets in and out and over every kind of surface, even up a perpendicular rock or cliff face. But at rest it sinks down with the tarsi flat on the ground, and like the shearwater it cannot maintain that upright stance often seen in the stuffed bird or in pictures.

Indeed this petrel has many shearwater-like habits. For instance, it does not visit the nest regularly, either before or after the egg is laid, but each of the pair seems in turn to spend several days at sea. I should say that just before the egg is laid the petrel spends approximately only one day in three at the nest over the hours of daylight. It is these birds which have stayed at home that begin crooning so early – just after sunset – long before the others return from the sea.

The single large oval white egg is usually zoned about the big end with very fine reddish-brown spots, but is frequently pure white. There is no attempt at a material nest beyond a slight scrape in the earth. When I first began recording a series of nests I found the new-laid egg was frequently abandoned by day, and I put this down to my ringing and handling of the adult.

But I have since discovered this is not entirely due to the birds' shyness. Other petrels and shearwaters, I find, also frequently leave the new-laid egg unincubated in the first few days. Fortunately the embryo in the egg is not developed enough to suffer seriously, but this habit does make the length of time between the laying and the hatching of the egg a variable one, even if the number of hours spent in incubation is constant.

In handling this bird in 1930 I found – before the pair deserted as a result of this inquisitiveness of mine – that incubation was undertaken by both sexes. In this instance what I took to be the female (because I found it on an egg laid that day), which I had previously ringed, sat on the egg for the first two days. On the third day a different bird (the male) was brooding and he sat for three days. The female then sat for one day, but left the egg on my handling her (to ascertain her ring number). The egg lay cold and deserted for two days, during which we can presume the male was away at sea on his three days 'rest cure'. He was back then for one day, but on my handling him he deserted altogether. Nor did the female ever return to this egg.

This experience was disheartening. In 1931 I took greater care not to disturb a series of nests which I marked. As soon as the date of laying had been ascertained I left each nest unvisited until after four weeks it became desirable to watch out for the chick's appearance. Here are the results from six successful nests:

Nest	Egg Laid	Hatched	Incubation Period	Young bird left	Fledgling Period
A	2nd June	12th July	40 days	6th Sept.	56
B	17th June	27th July	40 days	26thSept.	61
C	17th June	27th July	40 days	28thSept.	63
D	4th June	14th July	40 days	16thSept.	64
E	1st July	8th Aug.	38 days	1st Oct.	54
F	6th July	14th Aug.	39 days	21st Oct.	68

The average incubation period, therefore, was 39.5 days; that of fledging 61 days. Probably under normal conditions of noninterference by human inquirers, the incubation period is not more than 38 days. (I have a note that in the case of both nests A and C the egg was left cold for one day after laying occurred.) I do not understand the wide variation in the fledging periods, and why one nestling should fly two weeks before another, but perhaps in nest F one parent had given up feeding the chick (owing to natural death or to my inquisitiveness again?) and it had not been fed so well or grown so rapidly as a result?

The newly-hatched chick is a feeble little thing covered with a sooty-grey down, darker on the back and the head, in the centre of the crown of which there is at first a curious bald spot. This first down, as in the shearwater, is pushed out by the second growth of down still darker and of a firmer texture, to which it remains attached. Finally at five weeks old the feathers shoot from the same follicles in a continuous growth, so that the nestling looks like a soft ball with the double down still clinging to the tips of the juvenile plumage. At seven weeks the down begins to fall out.

The new-born petrel needs and gets a good deal of care at first. It is very small, weighing less than five grammes, and its head wobbles about – the chick cannot hold its head up for more than a moment. Like all petrels it is fed by regurgitation and slowly gains in weight. The parents brood it by day for the first two weeks, after which it is left alone by day (apart from rare occasions when I have found one adult with a half-grown chick).

Feeding of the baby petrel takes place when the parents come in about midnight, their stomachs loaded with a thick oily, fishy, white or yellow substance which they throw up if handled on these occasions. This is swallowed by the chick, who seems to thrive well on this one good helping each midnight.

But as each chick assumed the adult plumage, and as the double-down dropped away, the parents seemed gradually to lose interest in their adolescent child. Even as early as the third week they might have omitted a visit by night occasionally, but now as the chick matured their visits became more irregular. There is not space here to give you a detailed table of the visited and unvisited nights, but I found that in the sixth and seventh weeks the nestling might not be visited for two or even three nights, especially if the moon was shining in a cloud-free sky. To some extent the storm petrel does shun the land on moonlit midnights, but it is not so particular about this as the shearwater.

To record accurately this visiting or non-visiting was quite easy. I simply placed match-sticks or wedged light twigs of dead bracken in the entrance to the nesting hole or crevice; these the parents easily brushed aside when entering or leaving.

Take the case of the young bird in nest F. I found it was visited at night only on 5th, 7th, 10th, 11th, 12th, and 15th September. On the 13th one parent stayed all day in the nest! During the twenty-one days of October this chick in nest F was visited on not more than seven occasions, and not at all in the last six nights. It had vanished, therefore, on 21st October, after six days complete fast.

Probably the adults were now beginning their annual moult, which takes place from September to December, and like the shearwater, they had gradually lost all interest in their child as this annual phenomenon made a new demand on their physical resources. So they deserted the nestling before it was able to fly with them.

Fortunately, after its week's fast, the young petrel has lost its dumpy fatness and its long wings are well developed. In its tiny burrow there is not much, if any, room for the wing-flapping exercises which the young shearwater indulges in outside its burrow. The young storm petrel must crawl out – often from some complicated labyrinth of stones and boulders – and, as I have never seen it sitting about, it evidently flies straight away. I think this is certain, because I have myself taken young petrels from the nest at this stage and allowed them to fly off, which they do with ease and grace, though they have never tried their wings before.

When I have taken fledgeling storm petrels to the sea, and released them within a few inches of the water I have been greatly interested to find that each time they have shown eagerness not to touch the sea. They flew away without doing so, and as long as I could keep them in sight they continued to fly out to sea, with the characteristic swift wing beats of their dancing side-to-side progress, low over the waves.

Yours.

16. DUNNOCK

9th November 1939

DEAR J – This morning I caught for the third time DL 81, a dunnock (or hedge sparrow) which you ringed in the nest when you were here last summer – the index card shows that DL 81 was ringed on 26th July and retrapped 11th August and 17th October. Although small and of a tame and apparently confiding nature the dunnock is wild and intractable when caught, and like the wren, will dash itself against the glass or netting of the trap furiously, often rubbing the feathers from its forehead and wounding itself in this way. Its plumage is very soft and pulls out easily – it will lose its tail-feathers if these are held awkwardly. Occasionally it will die in the hand, as if from sheer nervousness. The meadow pipit, although haunting wilder scenes in nature, is far more friendly and docile when handled and will fly off apparently unconcerned afterwards.

Nevertheless, if they are not altogether a species which one can become intimate with, it is very pleasant to have dunnocks about our home. To hear the rather high sibilant warbling song on nearly every fine day throughout the year is a continuing comfort in our island wilderness, reminding me of the dunnocks I watched in more sheltered wooded scenes before I lived on Skokholm. And the lovely deep-blue eggs, set in a neat cup nest in a bramble bush or other light vegetation, are a delight. They rear two broods here as a rule.

The dunnock seems to have cycles of good and bad years. In 1928 five pairs nested here. This increased to seven pairs by 1934. It has since decreased and this year I was sorry to find we had only one pair breeding. Probably the reduction of cover such as bracken and weeds, due to farming and to our bird-ringing activities, has assisted the decline in the number of breeding pairs; but from 1936 onwards (when seven pairs bred) we have not had the usual influx of young migrants by which the number of breeding birds is strengthened annually. Many disasters due to rough weather and birds of prey must overtake the timid and defenceless dunnock on Skokholm; so that a high population built up in good breeding years by immigrants from the mainland can easily dwindle to vanishing point in bad years. Only two of our ringed dunnocks have lived as long as three years on the island; two have lived two years, and seven one year.

Yours.

17. BUZZARD

20th November 1939

MY DEAR JOHN – I well remember my excitement on seeing a buzzard, that eagle-like hawk, for the first time – when on an expedition in north Pembrokeshire with two other boys, about twenty years ago. And little thought then that I should ever have the fortune to dwell on Skokholm, which could be seen, from the site of our camp in Caerbwdy, by looking southwards across the wide bay of St Bride's, and through Jack Sound. Yet that same thrill comes back to me as I watch a buzzard soaring over the island today. And there is an added pleasure in the knowledge that the buzzard is steadily increasing in Britain today – certainly it has become very numerous in Wales.

A few months after my arrival at Skokholm the rabbit trapper caught one of the pair of resident buzzards here and stupidly killed it. Rabbit trappers hate predatory birds because they are always eating rabbits caught in traps and snares. For several weeks afterwards the mate of the dead bird spent much of each day in circling and mewing about the island as if searching for its companion. The long plaintive 'pee-ee-oo' echoed from the desolate rocks and we felt sorrow for this bird, which was a large, very pale specimen, probably from its size a female; far more sorrow perhaps than the bird felt itself. For this mewing of the buzzard is never a happy sound to the human ear, even when buzzards are calling in the ecstasy of the spring mating time.

Two months later on 12th March 1928 there were two buzzards flying about the island again, the white female and a small dark mate. The ravens now had eggs on the point of hatching in their nest in Mad Bay, and they would not tolerate the presence of the buzzards. The buzzards themselves were seeking a nest site, but the ravens did all they could to prevent their settling. If the buzzards soared high enough in the air to be seen from Mad Bay, the ravens rushed croaking to the attack. All day long this persecution went on. The buzzards could only avoid it by diving to the shelter of the eastern side far from Mad Bay – to the bays of North Haven, Peter's Bay, or Crab Bay.

The buzzard loves to soar at mating time, when for long periods the pair circle, heads facing each other, in the sunlight, mewing and playing together in a kind of slow aerial dance.

The young ravens began to leave the nest on 7th April, and now the adult ravens became less watchful. The buzzards settled on the cliffs in North Haven. They built a large nest of heather and bracken stalks, lining it with green roots, grass, wool, and bits of seaweed; and from time to time they laid fresh leaves and sprays of ivy and cow-parsnip about the nest with a strikingly decorative effect. Early in May three white eggs were laid.

The adult ravens were now moulting and in poor condition. If they passed close to North Haven the male buzzard swept at them fiercely and drove them away, but never pursued them far. He would quickly return to his perch on the cliff-top about fifty yards from the niche where his wife sat on the eggs. Two of the eggs hatched. For a while the cock fed the hen at the nest with rabbit and shearwater meat and she then fed the young. But soon it needed the hunting of both to secure enough food.

The buzzards would hunt for shearwaters which had failed to take cover – in that stupid way of shearwaters generally – before dawn. They also took mice, beetles, and young nestling birds. Once I saw the hen catch a crow not long out of the nest. The principal food was young rabbits, often the black ones which are numerous on Skokholm.

The young buzzards were on the wing by the end of July, and mewed for attention and food as they flew with their parents. Another group of buzzards joined ours, and in August and September we frequently saw eight buzzards in the air together. There was good hunting now – plenty of innocent young rabbits and plenty of still more untutored young shearwaters exposing themselves every morning after their first night's adventure in the open.

A truce had at last been signed between the predatory birds, now that the fierce emotions aroused by the breeding season had died down. You might see eight buzzards, ten or twelve ravens, many crows and great black-backed gulls, even perhaps a kestrel, in the air together on calm September days – while the feast of the young shearwaters made the plateau of the island seem like a table laden with delectable food.

The buzzards did not breed successfully in 1929 though they frequented the old nest site and brought many green fronds and sprays to decorate it during May and June. I could only surmise that the female, who had grown even more hoary and was now nearly as white as a herring gull, was beyond egg laying. She hung mewing about North Haven, for the most part a solitary bird after early June. On 14th July two young buzzards arrived from the mainland direction, and for the rest of the year she had plenty of her kind for company.

Old White One (as we called her) must have died in the following spring. I did not see her after 20th April 1930. On 1st May my diary records three buzzards soaring over the island. After that no buzzards were seen until 1st September.

In 1931 a pair of buzzards nested in Crab Bay. Their eggs were taken by crows. In 1932 they nested in North Haven; one pair has done so every year since (with two years – 1934 and 1939 – back at Crab Bay), usually but not always selecting a fresh site within the shelter of that haven.

Very best wishes.

18. SLOW WORM, NEWT, AND FROG

25th November 1939

Dear J.B. – We have no snakes here, but we have slow worms, newts, and frogs. Lizards and toads have been casually introduced, but are not established as breeders.

The slow worms here vary greatly in colour and are sometimes a very pretty salmon or coral, and sometimes pale and silvery. They inhabit chiefly the region between the house, Crab Bay, and South Haven, being partial to the more sheltered climate on our east side. We can always find two or three on a fine day lying in the dry warmth beneath an old sheet of corrugated iron in the corners of the home meadow. There is nothing very exciting about these little creatures, but my daughter was fond of keeping them as pets and never tired of watching them – and I dare say helping them – tie their long bodies and tails into knots and figures. Then she would put them on the table and see them glide out of the tangle very gracefully and interestingly. They would take small worms, insects, and flies from her hand, and seemed to recognize her as a friend, being rather slow but certainly not blind or deaf. They seem to have the habit of contracting themselves when frightened and are then more brittle and apt to lose their tail, which is so long that if it breaks, the animal has lost half its total length. They are then a considerable time in growing another and this never seems to be as fine and as long as the original tail. So Ann learned to be as gentle with her slow worms as they were with her. They were fond of water, which they licked with their curious forked tongue, while holding themselves with the neck lifted gracefully, and the bright eye giving an intelligent appearance. Ann was most anxious that they should nest in her glass vivarium, but we were never able to study this side of their lives, and it is still a mystery to me how such a slow and quiet creature maintains itself in the confines of an island full of the danger of rough weather and predacious birds.

It was, I think, in the slow worm that the curious parietal or vestigial third eye was first found.

The newt of Skokholm is *Molge palmata*, the palmated newt, so called on account of the distinct webs to the feet which it acquires during the breeding season. The male develops a crest and a whip-like tail filament during the spring, and has a handsome orange-yellow belly. None of the Skokholm males is large, and some appear to be breeding in an almost immature state. The minute eggs are hard to find, fastened snugly to pond weeds underwater, but our home aquarium revealed glimpses of the life history. Tadpoles of the frog develop hind legs first, those of the newt the front. Cannibalism was rife in our glass pond and none of the newts survived quite to the stage when they forsake the water and crawl over the island. They are found numerously wherever there is the least moisture, especially under stones that have fallen from walls and hedges, and are then without the fins or crests which they display in the aquatic period of their year. They feed on insect larvae, amphipod Crustacea, mites, spiders, worms, and bugs – these items have been recovered from their stomachs.

Almost the first sign of spring on this wild Atlantic plateau of ours is the appearance in January of frog spawn in our two larger pieces of water, the south and the north ponds. But because of our comparatively cool temperature they are slow to hatch and the young tadpoles do not grow rapidly until the shallow pools are heated by May and June suns. They then appear to mature quickly, drop their tails, and go on the land to escape nesting seabirds in the shelter of ditches where persicaria and rushes and the lush vegetation make a damp but secure cover. There they live for three years until mature and ready to breed. The number that survive to this stage is few, and as the island gradually wears away in future centuries the supply of Skokholm frogs will doubtless dwindle to extinction. We only find these large frogs when cutting down vegetation in the summer: they are usually a rich brown-red in keeping with the peaty colours of their habitat.

Yours.

19. MICE

30th November 1939

DEAR JOHN – On the neighbouring island of Skomer there is the common long-tailed field-mouse and also a rather pretty variety of the short-tailed bank-mouse or vole, which, in isolation, has become larger than the related mainland vote – it is richer brown and has rather different dentition. This vole is believed by some to be the descendant of the early type of British vole which inhabited Skomer before it became an island. Skokholm from its position is an older island, and may have been separated from the mainland before the vole had immigrated to these western districts. Whatever the cause we have no indigenous mice or other indigenous rodent. Rabbits were imported and so were house mice.

The story goes that the common house mouse, now far too abundant on Skokholm, was accidentally brought to the island in a boat which had been filled with straw on the mainland beach of Martin's Haven in readiness for loading a young horse required for use on the island farm.

At least one pair of the house mouse was in the straw or got in during the night. When the boat was unloaded in South Haven the straw was thrown on to the landing-place and the mice escaped on to the island. This story was told me by a fisherman whose brother once farmed Skokholm; he said the importation occurred about 1903. A few years later they were abundant and caused (the fisherman said) an influx of owls in the winter.

The house mouse has covered the island since. It is only house mouse in name, for it lives principally out of doors, surviving entirely without the aid of man. There have been long gaps in the human occupation of the island farm and house, during which this mouse would have perished had it depended on the larder and crumbs and harvest of the island farmer. The lighthouse at Skokholm was rendered proof against the entry of mice; while it was being built in 1913 a plague of these mice caused special precautions to be taken.

These mice do invade our house in great numbers as soon as the weather grows cold in October and November. As I write this one can set a dozen traps in our kitchen of an evening and have them all sprung within half an hour of leaving the room. The cats which we imported used to get weary of killing them and preferred rabbit- and bird-hunting in the end. This invasion eases off with the coldest weather in January and February, and presumably many of the mice then die off.

Some fears were expressed that, when the inhabitants of remote St Kilda evacuated that island in 1930, the house mouse there, given sub-specific rank by Barrett-Hamilton on some slight differences evolved in isolation, would perish. But if it is as tough as the Skokholm house mouse, it is certain to survive, although on St Kilda it has to face competition out of doors from the St Kilda long-tailed field-mouse.

I suppose Skokholm is too small an island to support a very stable population of mice, which are notably subject to high and low population cycles. Our house mouse is more abundant in some winters than others. It may be that both the bank-vole and the field-mouse once inhabited Skokholm, while it was a larger island than it is now. The size of the island slowly diminished and the population of these species at last fell too low in a bad year ever to recover.

But at present our one mouse thrives, the great majority living on a grass and vegetable diet almost exclusively. It has numerous enemies in the form of birds; gulls eagerly devour them, as do ravens, crows, jackdaws, buzzards, kestrels, and owls.

One is obliged to admire the power of adaptation displayed by this thrusting immigrant which, we are told, only arrived in Britain within historic times.

Yours ever.

5th December 1939

DEAR J – A remarkable accident took place this morning. I happened to step outside the door at the moment when a peregrine falcon stooped at a starling. The starling dived earthwards, screaming in terror, and skimmed low over the ground with the peregrine rapidly closing upon it. The starling flew straight for one of the walls – about seven feet high – of the farm fold, and managed to rise in time to clear it. But the peregrine failed to check itself, crashed head first into the wall, and fell dead, with scarcely a quiver afterwards.

This bird was quite small and from its colouring proved to be a male with not quite the full adult plumage and therefore about eighteen months old. I am forwarding it to the National Museum of Wales.

As far as Skokholm is concerned this falcon is truly the peregrinating kind, for it comes and goes in a most unsettled manner. It does not breed regularly. In 1930 it reared a brood of three and in 1932 two eyases were safely brought off. The site in both years was an old raven's nest on the south cliffs, just above the Sugarloaf Rock. The male or tiercel would play an aerial game with his lady, the falcon, on fine days in March, pursuing her above the Sugarloaf with gentle stooping flights; only to sway clear and soar up again when she turned to meet him. Now and then they would meet in mid-air, as if 'kissing' bills, and a curious double note could be heard, though they were generally silent during courtship. And if raven or crow or buzzard came near they both drove it away, but with less vehemence than they were to exhibit when nesting cares had actually begun.

In 1930 the first egg was laid on 1st April. The falcon seemed to do most of the incubation, with the tiercel sometimes on guard, but more often, when I went my shepherd's rounds and passed softly over the carpets of thrift on Peregrine Cliff, he was away hunting. She would sit very tight when she saw me across the little gully in the lichened rocks, and only slip out if I came near enough to look down, some twenty yards into the nest. She would rise screaming into the air, and if the tiercel was anywhere near, he would rush to join her. But they only rarely made a stoop at me; their annoyance on these occasions was usually vented on some nearby gull or oystercatcher.

It was pretty to see the tiercel bring food to the cliff. He would call the falcon out and she would fly under him eagerly. Then he would drop the prey – generally a puffin – for her to catch in mid air. She would carry it to the larder or plucking platform in the cliffs. This went on until the young were well grown in the nest. During June my friend, H.F. Witherby, twice witnessed with me this 'pass' of food between tiercel and falcon. The plucking ledges were thirty feet east of the nest and were full of puffin heads and wings, with some pigeon remains, including the legs (with rings) of racing pigeons, and a few starling and pipit feathers.

I cannot understand why the peregrine is not a regular breeder here, since it has every encouragement of food supply and sanctuary to rear its chicks unmolested. But it does not do so, though it wanders here to feed at all times, and is frequently seen crossing to and from Skomer or the mainland.

Homing pigeons, which frequently lose their way in races, and come to live on our charity, are usually killed, sooner or later, by peregrines here. In any case these pigeons, a racing expert tells me, are useless to their owners – any pigeon is that fails to get home promptly, for a bad homer remains a bad homer all its life, and will never make a valuable breeding bird.

Sometimes this falcon seems to play wantonly with its victim. I once saw a peregrine fly down into a flock of puffins, grasp one for a moment, carry it a few yards, and then release it apparently unhurt. On another occasion a peregrine dropped upon a party of starlings flying over the sea, and rose again with one bird in its talons. A herring gull immediately pursued it. After a chase of about three hundred yards the falcon dropped the starling (now dead) into the sea and turned upon the gull, which at once retreated with all the motions of desperate fear. But the peregrine only made one stoop at the gull, and failing to touch it rose high into the air and flew quietly away.

Such is the force of the blow struck by the keeled talons of the stooping peregrine that the prey is sometimes quite dismembered. We were sitting down to a picnic in South Haven one day when we heard a wild shriek above our heads. Looking up we were in time to see a peregrine strike a curlew at about one hundred feet above us. The curlew's head was struck off close to the base of the skull, and fell beside us. The body fell into the sea, from which the peregrine made no attempt to retrieve it, but on seeing us flew away.

At other times, however, though more rarely, the peregrine takes its prey in a less spectacular manner. I have surprised it with a young rabbit on the ground, and also in the act of plucking an adult shearwater which it had seized at the entrance to the shearwater's hole, half under a rocky ledge where the normal stoop would have been a physical impossibility.

Yours.

21. BLACKBIRD

16th January 1940

D EAR JOHN – Do small birds live long? Observations, chiefly by way of ringing, prove that most small birds are, on the average, short-lived. Thus a sparrow would be considered old at three years, and aged at four.

Today I had in my hand a blackbird whose acquaintance I first made in 1934, six years ago. For me there was a great pleasure in handling this bird and finding it alive and well after so long an interval. You know I hold the not universally accepted belief that the song of the blackbird is superior to that of the nightingale. I cling to that belief still, although I have not heard many nightingales singing, and perhaps have never had the luck to attend a really brilliant performance by Philomel. We do not hear the nightingale in west Wales, and certainly it has never wandered so far as Skokholm in its migrations. Although nightingales are reported almost every year from Pembrokeshire, investigation usually reveals the night-singer to be a sedge warbler or a blackbird singing in the dusk.

One of the many incidents that pleased me when I first set foot on Skokholm in the early summer of 1928 was the hearing of the songs of blackbirds on this bare storm-swept island. I found two pairs nesting in that year: one pair had a nest on a shelf in the roofless part of the island house, and a second pair had a nest in the creeping willow by the east pond.

The male of the house-nesting pair used to sing from the peak of the house, and this site has always been a popular one with the blackbirds nesting on the island. I could lie in bed in the early May mornings and hear the rich fluting song within a few feet of my ear, with only the barrier of the roof slates between us. And I could imagine myself for a moment back in the green valleys of Monmouthshire, once more a young boy listening enraptured to the songs of the woodland birds. So that in listening to the blackbird I could feel that for a moment I had captured the best of the two lives I had lived – it brought back sweet memories of the sheltered woods in the midst of this vivid open life of the island.

There was one little disappointment in the song of the blackbird heard at such close range. After the mellow, languid delivery of round flute-like notes, the singer would end with a little creaking, grating squeak, as if the wind had somehow failed to fill the bellows at the finish. This is a queer characteristic which spoils the full enjoyment of the blackbird's song at close quarters. But at a distance you hear only the loud, easy, and continuous rich fluting which distinguishes the song of the blackbird from the sharp, short, and clearly defined notes of the other thrushes.

When we first visited Skokholm there were two pairs of blackbirds nesting. But perhaps because we disturbed them when we repaired the house and building, only one pair nested in our second year there. In later years, from 1936 onwards, the blackbird did not nest on the island again. This was not really surprising. We had reduced the cover so much by mowing bracken and grazing sheep that, together with the disturbance caused by our movements on the island, the blackbirds must have found conditions for breeding unsuitable.

We first began marking blackbirds with leg-rings in 1933, the year when we put up the garden-trap. The resident pair were very shy of the trap and the female had a trick of darting out of the entrance as soon as you approached it, and in fact she was only caught once. The male was equally shy of the trap and was only caught twice.

In 1934 this pair reared a brood of five; these juveniles all came to the garden and were caught once or twice there during July. They were ringed, and in that autumn they migrated, and all but one were never heard of again.

This bird, F 9717, a female, unexpectedly turned up on the island on 30th November 1938, four years after ringing. While just as I write this, on 16th January 1940, she has again appeared, looking very fit and well, in spite of the bitter cold winds and snow showers. The thermometer registers nine degrees of frost to-night, which is exceptional for this mild climate. The condition of F 9717 was the more surprising because several days of frost and east winds had brought many birds to the island in a weak condition, especially golden plover, woodcock, snipe, and lapwing.

It is interesting that F 9717 during her long life of six years returned for two winters to the island. Born in June 1934, ringed in July 1934, recovered where ringed in November 1938 and January 1940. That is the glimpse we are permitted of the life of this island-born blackbird. Can we fill in the gaps? We can try. Ringing on the mainland of Britain has so far proved that British blackbirds are largely sedentary, except in cold, exposed northern districts. Movements are largely local and dependent on weather and shelter. We can imagine then that in the summer F 9717 might be breeding on the mainland opposite or near the island, but that for part of the winter she returned to Skokholm.

There are days in winter when the blackbird population of the island is very large. Today there were, I estimated, over sixty present, and in continued cold weather as many as three to four hundred may be counted, far more than the island could possibly support. But F 9717 did not necessarily retreat to Skokholm in cold weather. On the date of her first winter recapture, 30th November 1938, the weather was cyclonic, mild, and wet. Skokholm was part of her 'winter programme'.

The island is probably the winter home of many Welsh-breeding blackbirds – but ringing alone can establish individual records. At present my daily observations prove that the first migrants appear on the island in mid September, and that it is one of the commonest birds in midwinter and up to the end of March.

Although it is rare for British-bred blackbirds to reach the Continent, many continental-bred blackbirds reach this island in hard winters. I spent the night of 29th-30th October 1937 at the lantern of the lighthouse on North Ronaldsay, the most northerly point of the Orkney Islands. It was a dark night with a south-west wind and a drizzling mist, conditions which bewilder the migrating bird and hold up its journey.

From 10 p.m. to 3 a.m. the tower of this lighthouse resounded to the thuds of birds hurling themselves at the glazing. A crash, a flutter of feathers in the wind, and a small body dropping to leeward, with a final heartrending smack to earth or pavement or roof. The migrants came in twos and threes, half-dozens, dozens, and scores, wheeling up like large pale moths in the revolving beams, trying to avoid the lantern at the last moment, but often instead too blinded by the flash to steer clear. These birds were wind-drifted with deathly force against the lantern glass. Using a hand-net from the gallery rail my wife and I were able to save many of the migrants before they hit the glazing. We also picked up those which fluttered more gently to the glass and remained dazed and exhausted on the sill. Our total captures, all of which we ringed and released at dawn, comprised eighty-three redwings, forty-four starlings, thirty-three blackbirds, six fieldfares, and one each of brambling, ring ouzel, golden plover, and turnstone.

All these birds were probably from the Continent, migrating south from Scandinavia. Of the thirty-three blackbirds ringed one was recovered six weeks later in southern Ireland at Inchigeela, Co. Cork. A second bird was recovered at its breeding ground at Hardanger in Norway in July 1939. These two recoveries clearly indicate the usefulness of ringing to define the approximate limits of the blackbird's migration, which passed through North Ronaldsay on that occasion. Ringing informs us that the Norwegian blackbird is, as might be expected from the cooler climate of Scandinavia, more migratory than the blackbirds of Wales.

Yours.

ps. I have just received your letter about your being posted to a unit at Aldershot, for special training in the Intelligence branch, ready for the expedition to northern Europe.

9th March 1940

DEAR JOHN – This morning opened with a brilliant pearly look in the sky, such as you see during uncertain weather when the air is very moist and fog is about. There is more than a feeling of spring in the air. To my great joy I caught the first migrant today – a chiffchaff – and I knew then that spring had fairly begun. I ringed and released this olive-greenish harbinger, and almost immediately it gave out two or three distinctive call notes, even had I been in doubt – as I was not – of its identity. (But, of course, the wing formulae, size, and dark legs of the bird in the hand are conclusive enough without the song; and the thrill of sure identification was thereby added to the joy of meeting the bird again.)

We also caught a pair of black redstarts today, and two robins, a male and a female which appear to be full residents.

The male robin has been singing for many days, and I am hopeful that this pair will breed this year as they did – or the first time in my occupation of Skokholm – last year.

Thanks to our catching them in traps and marking them with numbered leg-rings we have quite a picture of this pair. They were first ringed in the late winter of 1938-9, one on 15th January and the other on 17th February 1939. They kept strictly to the landing-place and the vicinity of the Heligoland trap and here they eventually nested, in a mossy bank beside the stream. The first brood was a failure, but a second was successfully fledged on 12th July.

So I am hoping they will nest again this year. Their sweet if rather melancholy song and their tame ways have a special appeal for us in our rather forlorn and treeless home.

Before this incidence of nesting the robin came to us as a winter resident and passage migrant only. You would find the new arrivals in August, singing in defensive occupation of certain well-defined 'territories' on the island. These were usually seven; the homestead, North Haven, South Haven, Boar's Bay, Crab Bay, Windmill Gully, and the lighthouse buildings. In the wildest storms of midwinter the three last named, being more exposed than the others, were abandoned, and the resident robins were then reduced to four birds.

Robin HH 128 was first ringed on 22nd September 1937 and took up residence in Boar's Bay, where I caught him by means of a portable trap. He flew to the mainland in the summer of 1938, but was back on 3rd September 1938 and was re-caught on a number of occasions up to 16th February 1939. He then flew away for the summer as before, only to return to his favourite territory in Boar's Bay on 3rd October 1939. He was last trapped there on 17th October 1939.

The robin which frequented the homestead was LL 801, first ringed on 30th August 1935. It returned to sing in our garden on 18th September 1936. In this month another robin disputed possession of the precincts. This was JA 225, who was to spend three winters with us thereafter, from the date of his first ringing, 4th September 1936, to his last appearance on 4th February 1939. Usually robins are very wild at Skokholm, but during this time he became more tame and occasionally entered the house. But had we not had the evidence of ringing we might have supposed LL 801 was the same bird as JA 225!

I have drifted into the use of the masculine gender because all these robins sang a good deal at Skokholm, but students of robins confidently assert that the female is more migratory than the male, and as the female can also sing, though not so well, I am, of course, only using the term for convenience and to avoid the difficult 'it'. We do know, however, that some males winter with us, as the male of the pair that bred in 1939. From records of robins ringed elsewhere we can suppose that on the whole the adult robins are not great migrants and travel only short distances, very few going abroad. Our autumn robins very likely come from nesting-places on the mainland quite near the island. They are principally young birds in search of winter quarters. The majority have disappeared before winter, leaving only one in each of the 'territories'.

On the spring passage robins are comparatively rare at Skokholm.

Robin and wren are bracketed together in the mind of the average person, if only through the sentimental rhymes and songs. On Skokholm they have such a similar status that I may as well give you a sketch of the wren now.

You might with every good reason expect the common wren to nest with us, as it is found breeding on many smaller and more remote islands, but in fact it does not. On the neighbouring island of Skomer wrens breed freely, but chiefly in the high cliffs on the north side where there is a lush growth of maritime varieties of such plants as red campion, sea-campion, plantains, orpine, grasses, ivy, and some bramble bushes. Similar conditions obtain only in one part of Skokholm – North Haven. I can only presume that this lack of cliff vegetation, plus the small size of the island, is responsible for the absence of the wren from May until August. In autumn and winter it is resident and common. It sings with increasing frequency up to the time it leaves. It leaves us so late in the spring that I am always in hopes a pair of these delightful birds will stop to breed. But no. Wrens are elusive to catch in ringing-traps. Of the few we have marked one has returned, like the robins, to spend further winters with us. This was JA 385, first ringed 1st October 1936, and recovered on 12th April 1937 and 10th April 1938. Others are recorded as spending one full winter with us.

As the average expectation of life among small birds such as robin and wren must be very low, probably less than a year from fledging time, these individual robins and the wren, quoted above, can be considered quite old at two years. Genuine records of small birds living to ten years or more are few.

Ever yours.

23. OYSTERCATCHER

M Y DEAR J – It was pleasant to get back to the island after being detained a whole day on the mainland by a severe north gale. The sun was very warm and birds began singing again immediately. Each pipit soared up from his little territory into the light until his dark fanned wings and tail turned golden in the sun.

Life is at last pushing up through the gale-scorched grass, which this year is unusually long owing to the almost complete absence of rabbits. Primroses are struggling out, their virginal buds half open to the warmth, only awaiting the first April showers to burgeon fully. The leaf spikes of the bluebell already star the earth. The first honey-bees are searching the blue, violet, and dull white corollas of the ground ivy, the saviour of our island hive-bees in early spring. But humble-bee queens are also abroad and active, and today we met several of them at sea, sailing like Gavran over the glassy water in search of new empires to found. Travelling at thirty to forty miles an hour these buzzing balls blunder across the sea probably for hundreds of miles before weariness invites death by drowning if no land be raised in time.

The amorous herring gulls, long paired, sit like true lovers, touching each other, from time to time wailing melodiously, beaks wide in a slow duet. When a third interrupts or man appears there is a gruff 'wow-wow' of disapproval and warning.

Rock mates of the gulls, the oystercatchers alternately doze on one red leg, carmine bill on shoulder, or go for little flights about their selected area, as if beating the bounds and watchful for trespassers. They seem to be happily mated already, two months before the eggs will be laid in a saucer of fine pebbles.

The post today brought the reprint of your valuable paper on the oystercatcher and I reread it with pleasure. I see you 98 record thirty-five nests of this bird at Skokholm in 1939, which is close to the average of forty which is maintained at Skokholm over the twelve years 1928-39. What a grand and vivid bird this is, and well worthy of the time you devoted to it!

The oystercatcher is here throughout the winter, but is reduced in numbers to about half its summer strength. During the short winter day, and in fact from September to the end of the year, it keeps strictly to the tideline and is not apt to call very often. As soon as the year has turned, however, there is an increase in numbers along the shore by day. Early in January it begins to come inland, but at night only. This is abundantly announced by its vigorous call notes as it skirmishes about the fields in the dark. Whenever two or three oystercatchers are gathered together they 'create' noise and thus advertise their excitement. Although it is too dark to see what the birds are doing, it is reasonable to suppose they are already marking out and taking up the territories they will occupy for nesting later. You may hear the loud shrill call note 'klee-eep' and you may also hear the same note run into the rapidly increasing trill known as the 'piping trill', which accompanies the extraordinary concerts carried on by two and often three birds.

It is not until March, however, that the paired adults come up from the rocks and occupy their territories by day on the island. As you have described in your paper, these 'territories' are widely ranged over the island. Some territories go down to the shore, others are 'locked' inland by surrounding territories, but all usually have the essential access to water – if not the sea, then some pool or spring of fresh water. Thus it is interesting to find that the most inland-nesting oystercatchers voluntarily shut themselves off from the sea for the whole of the breeding season, while others nest within a few feet of the tideline. This has some effect on the food of the inland birds, which must live on terrestrial mollusca, worms, insects, etc.

In March the excited (presumed male) oystercatcher begins a curious and rather beautiful butterfly-like flight over the territory in which the wingbeats are much slower and appear therefore more deliberate than normal. Another form, accompanied by shrill piping, is a rapid fluttering of the wings in flight, but with a progress as slow as the slow wingbeat flight. Coming to earth in a wide parabolic curve the bird's excitement is then often intensified by a piping concert with the female or even three or four other oystercatchers. The birds come close together, their necks thrust out but with their shoulders rather hunched, the beak is opened slightly and pointed to the ground (it may even rest momentarily on the ground) and each begins.

At first the notes are clear, 'klee-klee, klee,' but soon they run together and blend into a long quivering ripple, occasionally rising in loudness, but usually fading slowly to complete silence. During the height of this piping the group of two, three, or more birds may move together quite a considerable distance on an erratic course about the favourite performing ground.

You rightly consider this piping is rather a ceremony or sexual dance than a display directed against another bird, and is used in a variety of situations that call forth the emotions of joy, alarm, and anger and love. Certainly I have heard piping at all seasons of the year, even on winter nights, but, of course, it is more frequent and intense in the breeding season. The special display or ceremony of most species is indulged in when the bird is in high spirits and requires an outlet for its excitement.

That excitement is usually heightened by the presence of others of its kind, but at times the individual will perform alone, or will be so utterly absorbed in the performance as not to notice its mate at all. Thus I have a note of an oystercatcher which began piping alone, as if in response to a piping concert by a distant group of oystercatchers, and went on long after they had stopped. This individual was apparently absorbed in the enjoyment of its own performance! But this must be unusual and piping most usually begins when a pair is disturbed by the arrival of a third bird in the territory.

Actually fighting between males is rare. The emotion of jealousy is more often worked off by piping and pursuit flights. Usually the intruding male seems to be aware of his guilt and will seldom stand up in a rare kind of mock fight in which the (presumed) males jump about like timid domestic cocks afraid to come to grips.

I will not elaborate much further, as the most of the rest of this remarkable bird's life-history is covered by your paper. It is curious that coition occurs in almost a casual way, that is, that none of the elaborate excitement ceremony seems to lead directly to coition. This occurs repeatedly, when the hen is in a fit state just before egg laying; without any warning the cock may suddenly turn upon and tread the hen, who squats down immediately he advances upon her.

There are one or two observations which have accumulated over the twelve years in which I have lived with these birds. You have pointed out that the nest-scrape is invariably sited close to some vantage point such as an outcrop of rock, a stone, or mound of earth from which a look-out can be kept. There has always been a pair on the rocky knoll just beside the house and the same well-defined territories are taken up every year, though a new scrape is made. This scrape is lined with the nearest scraps of material to hand, even rabbit droppings. On the rock outcrops little chips of the red sandstone pave the nest like a mosaic, and provide a most attractive background to the richly coloured eggs, which are of a flat buff colour streaked and smeared with chocolate brown.

You confirm the incubation period at twenty-five to twenty-six days and that both sexes brood. And as soon as they are dry and rested from the effort of hatching, and once the yolk is absorbed after twenty-four hours, the chicks are ready to move off in the company of their zealous parents.

The young birds move from the island in their first autumn, but no oystercatchers ringed at Skokholm have yet been recovered abroad, and it is unlikely that they travel far from Wales and the south-western seaboards, while the adults, as I have shown, are largely sedentary and ever ready to return to their breeding ground, four and even five months before the eggs will be laid.

Yours.

24. PUFFIN

3rd April 1940

DEAR JOHN – All this intensive training must indeed be tiresome for you. I expect you are anxious to get away and have done with the job. I wish you good luck.

Today I am going to describe a bird you know very well, that extraordinary clown-like bird with the aldermanic air, the puffin, which has just returned for the summer. Although in great multitudes here, it has not been the easiest bird to study; for it deserts its burrow if this is examined too often. So the gathering of information about the incubation period has been difficult, but I have pieced it together at last.

The puffin rarely comes inshore during the winter. Those we see close to the rocks at that season are usually suffering with oil waste on their plumage. They feed far offshore, then, scattered over the sea some five hundred miles out. Probably the inshore waters in winter are devoid of the small marine organisms on which puffins feed.

In the latter half of March a few puffins with brilliant new-looking bills arrive in the sounds about Skokholm, and settle on the water close under the cliffs on which they will soon breed. These birds are always in flocks. The flocks rapidly increase in size, but are not to be seen every day. Nor do the puffins come to land immediately. It is usually a week and often longer before a landing is made. The flocks arrive in the forenoon and are generally gone a few hours later. They may remain away for several days, especially (but not invariably) in rough weather.

You could sit for a delightful hour or two or three watching these assembled puffins, and trying to interpret their movements. Most of them are doing something active, although the flock remains stationary on the water of the bay or cove. They scratch and bask, lying half on one side so that the white belly shows to the sun. They swim to and fro like toy boats within the pattern of the flock. The males, those with rather

larger heads and brighter false 'lips' and 'eyebrows', keep pursuing the females, sometimes two may pursue the same lady or one male may pursue one female after another as if, so to speak, 'trying his luck'. You may see a male successfully treading the fourth or fifth female which he has pursued within ten minutes. This suggests a promiscuity which, however, is not borne out by events at the nest.

When approaching its mate at pairing time on land as well as on the sea the puffin keeps jerking its head upwards and backwards – the movement suggests that of one human being bidding – by sign only – another approach. Perhaps the bird pursued will turn round and meet the pursuer face to face, swimming breast to breast and bill to bill. Then ensues the typical rubbing together of the bills with sideways, and often an up-and-down, shaking of the head. On land the loving male may approach with a kind of sailor's roll, a mincing exaggerated walk, one foot placed before the other with the deliberateness of a person not altogether sober; bill-rubbing is then indulged in. At other moments puffins can be seen yawning, when the yellow interior of the mouth shows up well, but I do not think this can be construed exactly as a 'threat' posture as some observers have suggested.

The puffin is one of the most sociable of birds, and it would not be difficult to interpret many of its yawning and preening and sleeping poses, and the visiting of neighbours, pattering and parading about, in the fight of our own human attitudes and habits. Brawls between neighbouring males are perhaps rather more common than they are at the tavern corners with us, but possibly less serious. Usually the puffin is quite a friendly fellow in his many gregarious hours, and a group standing and sitting about on a cliff-edge or an outcrop of rock of a fine evening in summer is most strongly reminiscent of a crowd of happy human beings by the seaside. Even to the end of the season, in late July, the puffins continue their bill-rubbing and sociable assemblies and visiting. Another activity which goes on throughout the summer is the gathering of nesting material. Bits of grass and feathers from the land and odd straws picked up at sea are carried into the burrow long before (and after) the egg is laid. Some puffins can be seen vigorously tearing up the withered stems and roots of last year's grasses on the cliff-edge, and carrying these to build quite a substantial lining to the burrow, but as often as not some of this material will be dropped along the passage to the burrow quite indiscriminately. So that nest-making seems to be no serious affair, but merely another outlet for superabundant energy.

All this activity on land is conducted during the hours of daylight. There is no movement at night, every puffin being then at sea or in its burrow.

The puffin lays its single egg usually at the end of a burrow dug in the soil either by itself or some other burrowing bird or rabbit. The egg is white with a faint zone of lilac freckling around the big end. Early in April the old burrows are cleared out, enlarged, and improved, the puffin working with its powerful bill as a pick, and shovelling the loose material back out of the burrow with its strong webbed feet, which have very sharp claws.

Examination of the puffin at egg laying time – end of April and early May – has proved to me that it has not one, but two, brood spots, suggesting that at one time during its evolution it used to brood two eggs. These brood spots are placed one each side of the body just forward of the 'thigh', so that the puffin holds its egg well against one side of its breast, almost under its wing. This is impossible to observe in a burrow-nesting species, but it can easily be studied in the razorbill (nesting in the open) which has two brood spots similarly placed.

In some eight burrows which I marked and kept under observation in 1933 the same bird, identified by a ring, was caught in each burrow. So that at first I concluded incubation was by the female alone, which led me to expect that the males were thoroughly promiscuous and took no deep interest in family affairs. But then this idea was not in harmony with the fact that you might often see a pair sitting affectionately close together in the mouth of a single burrow, or that you might see first a male and then a female carrying fish to a chick in a burrow. In the following years I kept a number of burrows under observation, and although the egg in each was invariably deserted before hatching time because of this inquisitiveness of mine, I secured enough data to prove that the male takes a regular part in the incubation, at least in the proportion of approximately one day in three.

These visits of mine also proved that the puffin frequently leaves the egg cold during the day, especially from noon onwards.

The aerial assemblies or flighting of the puffin begin in the afternoon and it seems both males and females join in this pleasant social event. The dark hole in the earth is temporarily abandoned for the joys of light and flight. But the egg hatches just the same.

Except on a few occasions these assemblies do not develop to any extent until early or mid May, by which time egg laying is completed. These flights are very engaging to watch for it is obvious that the puffins enjoy them. Why should not we admit that birds, whose intelligence is of a specialized and limited nature, are capable of enjoying their 'leisure'? The puffins fly round and round in a circle upwind over the cliffs and downwind over the sea without any other apparent object except pleasure. They alight near their holes or on rocky points, walls, and eminences from which they can take off into the wind. There they sit, apparently happy in this communion.

Apart from the bill-rubbing and the occasional exercising and stretching of the wings they stand or sit quietly in groups together. The low, throaty, comical-sounding 'ah-haa!' is uttered infrequently, and can more usually be heard from individuals deep in a burrow or on the sea. When excited, as in fighting, this note becomes a gruff, growling 'arr!' Every now and then the majority of the assembly will suddenly take flight, for no very apparent reason unless you are willing to imagine they are feeling rested and carefree and are stimulated to fresh aerial manoeuvres.

The following figures were secured on the identification from sixteen nests under observation:

Nest	Year	Egg laid	Egg hatched	Incubation period	Young bird left burrow	Fledgling period
A	1931	30th April	9th June	40 days	30th July	51 days
D	1931	6th May	18th June	43 days	4th Aug	47 days
F	1933	5th May	16th June	42 days	4th Aug	49 days

The incubation period in nest A is probably nearest the true period in undisturbed conditions. My inquiring into the other thirteen nests resulted in all sorts of calamities, such as desertion, disappearance of the egg, and collapse of the burrow. It is likely that in nests D and F (above) the brooding bird, disturbed by my handling it (in order to read its leg-ring number), may have left the egg cold for a day or so and thus retarded the development of the embryo and so delayed the hatching for two or three days.

The newly born chick is covered with a sooty down and is quite active immediately. It quickly learns to walk. It is fed on small fishes brought by both parents. Sand-eels and the fry of herring, mackerel, and pollack are numerous in the waters about Skokholm from mid-June onwards. When the high tide fills the bays and creeks with the deep-blue Atlantic water the abundant shoals of these rapidly growing young fish are brought up close to the cliffs and you may see their orderly regiments gleaming silver and green as they swim in columns close to the red rocks of the island. So twice each day the 'table' is spread for the puffins to gather food, and it is during the two high-water periods in each day during June and July that the adults are busiest in gathering food for their chick. As this grows the parents are able to bring in still larger catches of larger fry to match the appetite of the voracious young bird.

It is popularly supposed that the puffin holds its catch of fish nicely in its bill with the heads all one side and the tails the other. This is, however, just a pleasant fancy, for in fact the fish are carried irregularly. I cannot say how the puffin manages to catch and hold so many fish at one time, working as it does under the water, but perhaps its tongue and slightly serrated bill assist in this operation. I have counted as many as twenty-three small fish dropped from the beak of a single puffin which I disturbed.

These fish are devoured raw by the chick, who thus passes far more waste than that other burrow nester, the shearwater. The burrow would become thoroughly insanitary if the young puffin did not soon learn to walk down the passage, turn round, and squirt its waste with some force into the open. This semicircle of grey-white guano at the entrance to a burrow is a sure advertisement of the youngster within.

The young puffin grows fat rapidly. The feathers appear under the long straggling down in the third week, and in six weeks from the time of hatching it is ready for the unpleasant but salutary event which then occurs. The adults stop feeding it; it is deserted suddenly and completely.

When I first lived at Skokholm I was puzzled to find that during August the young puffin was always seen at sea alone and without any adults near; whereas the young razorbill and the young guillemot at that time were always convoyed by one or both adults, presumably its parents. Nothing in the reference books on birds referred to this fact; all I could read there informed me that the young razorbills and guillemots flutter down to the sea of their own accord or are carried down by the neck in the bill of the parent, but the way of the young puffin in reaching the sea was not mentioned. I became anxious about the young puffin at this stage.

It was soon clear to me that no young puffins left the burrows in daylight, in spite of the adult puffins being strictly diurnal in their activities on the land. One August morning I found a young puffin lodged within the confines of the little garden at Skokholm from which its feeble wings could not release it. Had it, I wondered, 'crashed' on a night passage to the sea? I spent the next few nights wandering about the cliff-tops and was rewarded by stumbling upon several young puffins moving, alone and quite untended by any adult, towards the sea. They walked or pattered along in the light of my torch, looking, with their dull, sooty faces, very forlorn and deserted and a little bewildered. Yet they seemed to know what to do – to keep going downhill, and to blunder onwards and downwards until they could at last flutter over the cliffs to the sea.

It was not difficult to realize now, from this and the appearance of the young birds alone at sea, that desertion of the young is a part of the life-history of the puffin. Nor was it difficult to realize that this desertion was useful in enabling the extremely fat young puffin to fast for a while and, like the young shearwater, slim and harden itself and mature its feathers ready for launching out into the world alone; while the night-passage to the sea was also essential to its survival, at least on an island inhabited by so many predatory gulls, hawks, and crows.

How long does the chick remain deserted? That I discovered by placing matchsticks upright in the mouths of marked burrows containing puffin chicks. The last visit of the adult was thus ascertained by the pushing inwards of the matchsticks. By this means I found that desertion of the chick occurs on or about the fortieth day of its existence. The abandoned chick may then remain several days (up to a week) alone and fasting. Its unanswered hunger call – a feeble 'chip-chip-chip' – gradually ceases. It walks almost to the entrance of the burrow and squats there, well inside and retiring fully within on the slightest alarm. It will not venture out until the force which it has so far resisted – the force which we can call hunger, or thirst, for lack of a better understanding of its nature – at last moves it to take the seaward plunge.

To observe the behaviour at sea it was only necessary to take some of those young birds which had fallen at night into the garden. When dropped into the sea these youngsters would paddle with their feet, their wings half open upon the surface of the water. They would dive swiftly, swimming rapidly underwater with easy, distinct strokes of their wings. They did not appear to use their feet when swimming thus, as far as I could see, but only used them in coming up to and swimming upon the surface. The average length of time spent underwater was twenty-one seconds, the extremes nine and twenty-seven, while the intervals of resting on the surface were much shorter, averaging less than ten seconds. They seemed a little bewildered at first, and often swam near the shore as if they meant to land, but they soon appeared to get their bearings and make off straight to sea, proceeding by a series of dives with increasingly longer intervals of swimming upon the surface.

The desire to get far out into the ocean is very strong. Each morning in late July and August the night's contingent of young puffins may be seen floating down with the currents in the sounds about the islands, but by the evening they have scattered and swum far out of sight offshore.

Until it has learned to fly with ease the fledgeling escapes the gulls, which frequently swoop at it, by diving, and no doubt in the more hospitable underwater world soon obtains small fish with which to break its recent fast.

All good wishes.

7th April 1940

DEAR J.B. – We have had quite an interesting selection of migrants in the bird-traps this year, and on the whole migrants have been early. The first chiffchaff – mentioned in a previous letter – was seen and chased into the Heligoland trap on 9th March. On the same day we caught and ringed two female black redstarts, and three more (one came voluntarily into the house for the night) on the 10th. Wheatears arrived in numbers on 12th March, on which day that delightful and exotic bird, a hoopoe, was watched for a considerable time; but it was just too shy to be persuaded into the traps. On the 21st a hoopoe was again seen. Puffins landed on the cliffs on the 31st. Willow warblers and sand martins were on passage on 1st April.

This morning the temperature rose to fifty degrees and it rained until noon, with the wind south about four strength, veering and dying down in the afternoon. It was quite hot in the sun as we collected driftwood in the island bays. In Crab Bay we found a forty-gallon barrel of turpentine washed up. This prize took a lot of manoeuvring with ropes to parbuckle it up the cliffs. Among those who helped in the last stages of this task was Sir William Rothenstein, who had landed from a pinnace belonging to the Royal Air Force, to which he is attached as official war artist.

It was a day of pleasant surprises. While we were sitting out of doors, giving tea to the distinguished visitor, a fieldfare flew into the garden-trap, the first we have ever caught here. This north European thrush is usually too wary to be caught in a trap, although from time to time we have caught a redwing, its smaller cousin.

West coast migration does not produce the great variety of rare birds associated with east coast migration. Thus our west coast island of Skokholm cannot compete in this respect with such east coast islands as Fair Isle, Isle of May, and Scolt Head. The list of uncommon birds is quickly written down.

A female crossbill alighted on the garden wall on 5th July 1929 and was pursued by meadow pipits until it flew away.

An ortolan-bunting was caught in the garden-trap by Mrs Dorrien-Smith, the wife of the governor of the Scilly Isles, on 19th May 1938. This bunting is occasionally seen here, on both migrations. Two immature Lapland buntings were seen during September 1936, from the 5th to the 12th, and one was caught for identification. The snow bunting is a regular visitor in October and November, but other buntings – reed, corn, and yellow – are only stragglers. I have mentioned before that bramblings visit us with the passing flocks of chaffinches. A male twite sang for a while from the peak of the house on 8th April 1933. The red-backed shrike is an uncertain passage migrant. No rare warblers have yet been recorded. The warbler which visits us least often is the lesser whitethroat, of which we have trapped one or two. Yellow wagtails commonly appear in autumn, but are scarcer in the spring. Ring ouzels and grey wagtails bring us a hint of the mountain glens when they drop in at infrequent intervals in the spring and autumn passages. White wagtails are often abundant, arriving mid-March to mid-April. In the autumn they are even more numerous, birds of the year preceding the adults, which usually pass in late September and October.

The Greenland wheatear is a regular passage migrant in late April and May. And so is the black redstart, which can be seen at any time from early March to the end of April, and from October to December.

Of the doves, the turtle dove is frequently flushed during May and June, and sometimes its murmurous note is heard from the shelter of the bracken. It does not breed.

One might expect the rock-dove to be found on these wild and cavernous coasts of Pembrokeshire, but I have not yet discovered any true-to-type rock-doves. There are a number of the particoloured gone-wild domestic pigeon (which is descended from the rock-dove) on these shores and breeding in caves. These visit Skokholm but do not nest. Many lost homing pigeons also alight with us during the summer months when the pigeon-racing season is on. These homing pigeons seem to have lost heart and cannot be persuaded to leave the island. Even when we have carried them ashore and released them on the mainland they will often return to the island, which they seem to have adopted as their permanent home. In this state, as I have already mentioned in an earlier letter, they are little use to their owners; it is no loss when the peregrine falcons sooner or later strike them down.

I remember when camping for a week in June on the twenty-two acre island of Grassholm how two lost racing pigeons came to feed on our crumbs. We had intended to catch them and take them to the mainland on leaving, but we failed to secure them. Later, during September, on a visit to Grassholm, I found the dried corpses of these two pigeons in a niche in the rocks. Presumably they had starved to death rather than fly the eleven miles to the mainland.

It might be expected that so good a flier and migrant as the wood pigeon would visit us often; but I have only seen it at very rare intervals in late spring. It is really interesting to note that there are birds like the wood pigeon which are quite common on the mainland opposite the island, but which never or rarely visit us: such woodland species as the magpie and jay, bullfinch and hawfinch, of course, are never seen. But the tree-creeper has been seen twice – rather remarkable for a bird of such feeble flight, and the goldcrest is almost a regular visitor.

The house-sparrow and the tree sparrow are very rare stragglers, and never stay longer than an hour or two. Tits never come here, if we except a coal tit that spent the winter of 1930-1 with us, from 8th November to 6th March. It lived principally in the shelter of the cliffs.

I have not yet seen a wood warbler here, nor a reed-warbler.

Herons are regular visitors at all seasons, but usually in late summer. A kingfisher has been watched fishing from the rocks of South Haven on 17th August 1936. Later it flew over the house. The nightjar may sometimes be heard crooning on June nights, and although I have found young nightjars scarcely able to fly, I think that they do not nest, but have come across from Skomer or the near mainland. Of course, woodpeckers are not to be expected, but a wryneck was once noted.

Of the falcon order, I have nothing exciting or rare to report, unless you except a Montagu's harrier which flew leisurely over the island on 5th August 1935. Kestrels and merlins, of course, are frequent visitors. And the peregrine falcon and the buzzard have already been described. The white owl is a casual winter visitor, especially in years when mice are numerous. The short-eared owl is more regular in winter. The little owl would be a regular resident if we allowed it, but since finding a nest with two grown chicks and a larder of nearly two hundred storm petrel corpses (14th July 1936), we have discouraged this owl, either by shooting or by deporting. Evidently at Skokholm it would live exclusively on storm petrels, catching them so easily that only the heads were devoured, and the bodies laid in a rabbit-hole store! We prefer the storm petrels to this stranger owl.

Wild geese occasionally visit us in winter, but are so shy it has so far been impossible to identify them accurately. Our ponds lie in the open and are difficult to approach without being seen by these voyagers. The same can be said of ducks and waders; a full list of those which we have identified on the island I will send you in due course. None of them is very rare.

That most graceful flier the fulmar petrel, in the course of its advance as a breeding bird down the coasts of the British Isles from its original home at St Kilda, has reached us. Its beautiful albatross-like movements in the air catch the eye as it glides through the flocks of gulls about the cliff-face. Yet, perhaps because our cliffs are so shelving and without many suitable ledges, it has never been seen to land here, as it has on the more sheer cliffs of Skomer and the mainland, where doubtless it will soon commence breeding. More than once it has flown inland, skimming and circling low over the white roof of our house, during the early spring mornings. This I regard as significant; in the northern islands, the fulmar is known to nest freely in or upon the roofs and walls of unfrequented (and more rarely of occupied) buildings. But I have no expectation of so new a colonist settling here in such a manner, so long as we maintain this bustle of our small island farm.

Yours.

26. SKYLARK

Dear J – Thank you for your letter. I am glad that you will soon be off on your north European expedition. I can guess your destination.

I think my subject today is the little brown bird of the earth, the cream-streaked skylark, which loves the wild open heathy nature of our island. You tread on him almost before he rises with a hovering wavering flight, unwilling to leave the earth; and he soon settles again. If you do not follow him immediately he is lost against the background of grey and brown grasses, heather, and dwarf vegetation. He walks quickly with a very easy graceful movement, not hopping in the least, and is swiftly hidden from sight.

We certainly are grateful for the residence of the lark here. His vehement song is heard at all times of the year over the island, excepting during the moult in August and September. Often it rises above the fury of wind and sea in the late autumn and midwinter gales – a strong stout bird he is and fit to face our hard conditions.

In some years we have had three and four pairs nesting, but of late only one. When there was more than one cock you might expect long and sustained singing in rivalry, but I find that even in years when only one pair bred the singing was as fine and sustained. Perhaps the lone lark can hear the songs of other larks three miles away on Skomer or on the mainland? I timed the island lark singing for 201, 183, and 159 seconds non-stop on three occasions from my bed early this morning, which began with a very beautiful clear sky – too clear in fact to last, for by midday the sky was overcast and it began to rain, with a hard wind from south-east, which raised rough water in the harbour. However, after we had taken all the trouble to haul our boat up on the slip, the wind suddenly veered to the west, and the sun came out again.

I have nothing remarkable to tell you about so common a bird. Here larks abound throughout the winter, and are continually on the move then, performing their local and general migrations. Vast numbers cross the island during October; sometimes they appear to fly westwards, if a west wind is blowing; and at other times, with an east wind, they fly east! They become fewer in March, and in April only the nesting birds are left. They are not easy to drive into ringing-traps, and as yet I have not tried out the spring or clap nets of the bird fancier, which could be conveniently used for the purpose of ringing heath-dwelling species such as larks, pipits, and plovers. So at present we ring very few skylarks. We never see the woodlark here, though it breeds in Pembrokeshire quite commonly.

Yours ever.

27. QUAIL, LAND AND WATER RAILS

5th May 1940

MY DEAR JOHN – This has been quite an interesting two weeks full of migrating birds. I would mention in particular that on 23rd April we caught and ringed a hoopoe, which – imagine our delight – stayed with us for a whole week; it was not too shy for us to enjoy its bright but harmonious colours, and chough-like feeding habits at close range. On 25th April I saw the first stone-curlew ever recorded here, feeding in the thrift on the peninsula of the Neck. On 29th a land-rail was trapped and ringed, together with that other creeping bird, a grasshopper warbler. Today I saw a quail.

There was a thick fog at first today, but it was warm, the temperature rising to sixty degrees. The song of our free-flying canaries (of which more in a later letter) mingled sweetly with that of a willow warbler as I walked in the garden. It is a pleasure to walk there at this time of year, and see how quickly the vegetables are growing between the little hedges (how little as yet!) of fuchsia, rosemary, and willow. Fortunately there has been no severe wind to hurt the young buds this spring, and all is flourishing with the moisture and sunshine. Our border of daffodils and narcissi has now given way to a mixture of forget-me-nots, daisies, and London pride.

As we were short of timber for some repair work, and as it was very calm, we made an expedition in the boat to a beach in Mad Bay where I had seen two good planks thrown up. A Breton fishing-smack had taken advantage of the mist to creep inshore and drop his *langouste* cages about our island. We boarded him and warned the captain (in a friendly way) that he was poaching. He was a Falstaffian-stomached fellow with a thunderous laugh, and was quite unmoved by any fears about being caught by a Fisheries Protection Patrol vessel. He scorned England for not calling up all able men between seventeen and forty-seven. His own crew were misfits and rejects from military duties. He gave us some crabs and we gave him a basket of gulls' eggs.

It was while I was climbing on the cliffs after getting the timber that I nearly stepped on the quail. It flew off like a bullet inland. This is the only member of the game-bird tribe that we see at Skokholm, where it is at best a stray and irregular summer migrant. We are indeed sadly lacking in these and other large running and covert-dwelling birds.

Even the corncrake or land-rail is an uncertain visitor, though one or two usually appear in the spring and autumn migrations. It has bred once – in 1930. In that year it was first heard calling on the bog on the night of 5th June. I seldom saw it. But I discovered the nest of six eggs just about to hatch in a rushy cover near North Haven on 15th July, quite half a mile from the scene of the adult's usual craking. How these chicks got on after hatching I do not know; the nest was empty on 18th July, and no corncrakes were seen again, nor were they heard after 31st July.

The water-rail is far more common here. It arrives regularly from mid August onwards when its loud screaming note is heard from the shelter of the bracken. This scream is not unlike the agonized yelp of a rabbit caught in a gin-trap, though more deliberate, and quite disturbing when first heard at close quarters. But I quickly got used to it at Skokholm where it is to be heard throughout the winter. I often saw it running through the bracken, or moving in unexpected places, sometimes on the garden wall, or climbing about the bramble bushes near the well. It would run into a rabbit-hole or bird-burrow when surprised. Water-rails moulted immediately on arrival in August and dropped their feathers so rapidly at times as to be quite incapable of flight, being for one week a mass of blue-sheathed young feathers – an extraordinary sight!

In 1929 a pair remained to breed. The sharp 'yip-yip-yip' or 'chip-chip-chip' went on throughout the summer day and night, but especially between 9 p.m. and 3 a.m. This was varied by an occasional typical scream. The young rails were first seen with one parent on 30th June near the covert of dropwort, nettles, and cow parsnip above South Haven where they had evidently been born.

They bred again in 1931 and 1934, but not since. The winter residents usually all depart by 17th April.

Yours.

NOTE. The land-rail ringed on 29th April 1940, mentioned in the above letter, was reported caught by a cat at Emly, Co. Tipperary, Eire, on 20th June 1940. A most interesting westerly migration.

28. TIDES AND CURRENTS

15th May 1940

DEAR JOHN – The movements of the great waters of the Atlantic Ocean under the influence of the moon, movements which we call tides, are particularly noticeable about the island.

It is to be expected that the pressure of the rising tide in the confined angle or bottle-neck of the Severn estuary and Bristol Channel causes a piling up of the sea against those shores. This is the case. The pressure is greatest where the Channel suddenly contracts at Barry, Glamorganshire, where high-water of the highest spring tides registers over thirty feet above low-water mark. The same tide, as measured at Milford Haven dock gate, has its greatest height recorded at slightly under twenty-six feet. (In the local tide tables another ten feet is added to all measurements which are made from the bottom of the dock gate, ten feet below low-water mark.)

In the harbour at Skokholm I find by measurement that the highest high tide is twenty-five feet from low-water mark of spring tides; this nearly covers the top platform of our landing-steps. (In rough weather waves splash another twenty to thirty feet above this as they dash against the rock and concrete there.) The slackest neap tides rise no more than twelve feet between their low- and high-water limits.

Many millions of tons of water must pass through the sounds to fill and empty this vast acreage twenty-five feet deep at spring tides. The configuration of this coast and the position of the islands cause this mass of water to move in a series of regular currents through the sounds here during each complete rise and fall of the tide. Each such complete movement occupies rather more than half a day, that is, approximately twelve and a half hours; or two tides in the lunar day of approximately twenty-five hours.

In the estuary of Milford Haven the current begins to flow upstream as

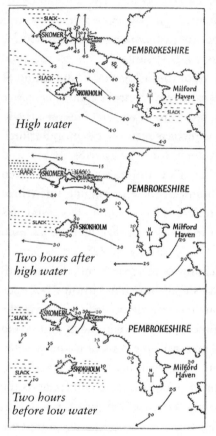

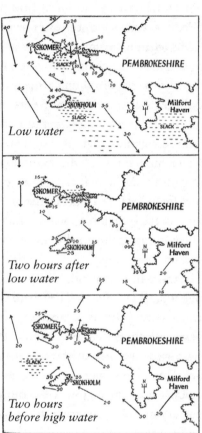

soon as the tide begins to rise, and begins to flow downstream as soon as the tide begins to fall; as might be expected where there is only one outlet to what is otherwise an enclosed lake receiving only a comparatively small contribution of fresh water. Here the water simply pours in and out of the narrow mouth of Milford Haven with the rise and fall of the tide, in obedience to the laws of gravity.

But outside the haven, and all about the islands, there is a considerable time-lag in the changes of the currents, presumably due to the tidal thrust or force of the main mass of water in the Bristol Channel and St George's Channel. Our currents, as a whole, do not change and move north until three hours after the tide begins to flow; and consequently do not reverse and move in a southerly direction until three hours after high water. So that it is usually most convenient for us to leave Skokholm and sail north through Jack Sound to our mainland base or supply haven of Martin's Haven during the six hours of the north-going tide (three hours each side of high water); and to return to Skokholm from Martin's Haven during the six hours of the south-going tide (three hours each side of low water). Actually our sailings are not regulated as simply as that. Much depends on the direction of the wind and the strength of the current. The local fishermen taught me what I know about the currents and they had a saying that 'the first of the tide is always the best'; meaning that you should launch your boat at slack water and start with the first of the current moving in the direction you wish to go. This is sensible, for the current is then gentle and it is possible to guide a boat through it with comfort, even against the wind. But as the current increases in strength it becomes more difficult to steer across it, and if there is any wind, blowing against the current a very rough sea is worked up. The north-going current is at its strongest here exactly at high water and the south-going current exactly at low water (in contrast with the inside of Milford Haven, when at those very times the current is slack and at turning point). At strong spring tides the current at high water (and at low water) reaches between five and six miles an hour in the narrow part of Jack Sound and off Skokholm Head, which is faster than the average small sea-fishing boat can sail even in a storm. Should the wind be against such a current the violence of the sea is very great, and Jack Sound at such moments is a mass of short white waves through which no small boat could pass without filling. But larger boats and ships with high freeboard can pass safely through then, provided their speed and steerage way is sufficient, and provided there is no swell coming in from the Atlantic. Storm swell, added to high wind and the full force of a contrary current, build up the worst kind of heavy broken seas, terrifying to the navigator but very beautiful and majestic to witness from the safety of Skokholm.

I am enclosing six sketch maps to illustrate six phases of the current between high and low water about these islands, which will perhaps give you a better idea of the regular changes in the direction of the tidal 'stream', as it is named on the charts. The figures attached to each arrow are knots (a knot is 6,080 feet) per hour, and are only approximations gathered from my own experience of sailing a small boat in these waters; they represent the maximum speeds of the stream at spring tide. At neap tides the stream is running at only half this speed.

Ever yours.

29. SWALLOW

26th May 1940

DEAR JOHN – I was happy to have your letter from Norway, dated 20th May, in which you say how pleased you were because you had seen a solitary swallow flying black-winged over the winter snow, and this spoke to you of an English village in spring time. This would be more than a month later than the average time of arrival of the swallow on this island, which I find to be invariably between the 4th and 11th April for the first main 'flight', though stragglers may appear in the last days of March.

> O swallow, sister, O fair swift swallow,
> Why wilt thou fly after spring?

wrote the poet in graceful words. Having had an adult male in my hand I can write feelingly about this fair beauty of the swallow, this splendour of the chestnut-red throat and forehead, the iridescent light of his rich metallic blue wings and breast and back, and the warm gold of his underparts. While the tail, with its four-inch-long outer feathers, and the eight white panels, gives the bird an exquisite balance and delicate grace. Nor is the fully adult female much less rich in colour. I have often had these birds in my hand, for during their migrations swallows will fly into the house on the island, and we try then to capture and ring them. When caught they are generally more composed than most wild birds, perhaps because of their close association 'with man and his herds and byres'. They struggle less, and seem less afraid – indeed they will peck the hand quite aggressively – and when released resume their feeding and daily business about the buildings as if nothing unusual had happened.

It is, I think, generally true that swallows are most plentiful on those farms and settlements where animals are grazed in numbers, and are scarcest on the arable lands devoid of cattle and sheep, because of the abundance of flies and winged insects attendant upon animals and the ordure of animals.

When I first settled here in 1928 one pair nested, although the only animals on the island were a donkey and half a dozen goats. But I noticed that this pair of swallows seemed to get a fairly good living from the winged insect life which found cover and a breeding ground amid the considerable growth of annual vegetation – chiefly nettles, hogweed, hemlock, ragwort, and other tall-growing, rank-smelling plant life about the buildings; and also about the rushes and hemlock water-dropwort

which filled the hollow below the well. Their feeding range was quite limited to this small area of about twelve acres during the many rough days which are found in the island summer. In fine weather they hunted a little farther afield, making trips as far as the north pond and down along the cliffs of the harbour, but in general they seldom ventured over the western half of the island or along the southern side.

In the next year, 1929, I began to reduce this unsightly growth of weeds about the buildings in favour of a green sward which I endeavoured to encourage. The swallows – or rather some swallows – came to the house and buildings in April and May and flew up to the rafters where the 1928 nest still lay intact. But they did not stay. It may be that the bare grass around the settlement was too sterile of winged prey.

The swallows did not nest again at Skokholm until 1932. I like to think that they came back to us because by that year we had accumulated a sufficiently large flock of sheep to provide them with a fresh source of dipterous food. We started with twenty-six sheep in the autumn of 1929, increasing these to a hundred breeding ewes and their lambs by

1932. One pair of swallows nested with us as long as the sheep were at this maximum figure, during 1932, 1933, and 1934. It was noticeable now that they fed on a wider radius, on fine days following the sheep flock all over the island, and most usefully devouring the sheep fly (the greenbottle, *Lucilia sericata*) whose maggots, if allowed to develop in the wool, are fatal to the sheep. In September 1934, as the island was rather overgrazed and sheepsick, I sold the entire flock. The swallows visited the island in 1935 but did not breed, nor have they done so since.

I made some notes on the nesting of these swallows. In 1933 the first egg was laid in a nest built on a collar of the roof-tree of a store shed on 13th June. The fourth and last egg was laid on the 16th. They began hatching on 1st July and were all out by the 2nd: that is, after sixteen days of incubation, for the hen, who appeared to incubate alone, did not sit until 16th June. The nestlings were all fledged by 22nd July; period in nest: twenty to twenty-one days. A second brood was raised.

In the spring swallows usually fly in a north-easterly direction over the island and the surrounding channels, and this migration lasts until mid May. There are stragglers to be seen all through the summer (I hope to have occasion in a future letter to refer to this straggling midsummer migration of swallows and other small birds) and until the autumn migration begins in earnest in mid September. This lasts for a month and is usually in a south-easterly direction. The last swallows of summer may be seen during the first days of November.

What I have said of the swallow on migration applies in lesser degree to its cousins, the house- and sand martins. Both are less numerous at these moments than the swallow, and they never stay more than a few hours on the island. Even this is rare and occurs only on fine windless days when they gather on the stay wires of the flagstaff and rest and preen for a short time. But in windy weather they fly past very rapidly, 'leaning on the wings of the breeze,' impelled by the intense migration fever in their slender bodies.

Yours.

30. THE ISLAND POND

1st June 1940

DEAR JOHN – The little white blossoms of the water crowfoot (*Ranunculus aquatilis*) star our pond today, on the edge of the low growth of the amphibious persicaria, whose rich bottle-brush flowers stand like an army of soldiers in red-and-white uniform on the green-and-purple field of the lanceolate leaves. In this cover skulks one pair of moorhens or water-hens. We see very little of this pair, though it is resident throughout each summer. On mainland ponds the moorhen is quite tame and so fearless of man at times that it will feed with domestic poultry. But in our wild environment moorhens, and other birds too (such as robins and blackbirds) are excessively shy. So that we hardly ever see the moorhens unless we can surprise them by creeping up to the pond unseen by them. And often the first sign we have of them is a typical platform nest in the persicaria.

What causes this timidity in the moorhen and certain other birds on the island it would be hard to say. Especially when we find wheatears, meadow pipits, and rock pipits so tame. But I believe moorhens, blackbirds, and robins are equally as wild in some parts of the Continent.

Only by building beside the pond a small hide of stones, boards, and sacking were we able to observe some of the details of the life of our moorhens. They both took turns to incubate the four to six eggs, and during the day, the bird off duty would spend its time walking and swimming about not far from the nest, plucking insects and plant food from among the persicaria. There are at least six kinds of water-beetle in this pond, especially *Ccelarabiis inoequalis* which swarms there in late summer. Mr Gerald A. Walton, who visited us in August 1933, also found specimens of *Haliplus ruficollis* and *lineatocollis*, *Hydroporus palustris*, and *Hydrobius fuscipes* and *Helophenous griseus*. While in our freshwater spring he found as well *Agabus bipustulatus*, *Colymbetes fuscus*, *Anacoena limbata* and *ovata*. And Dr W. S. Bristowe in August 1934 found the marshy areas rich in spiders – seventeen species plus four phalangids or harvest spiders, one of them, *Nelima silvatica*, new to Britain.

The moorhens are the only birds actually nesting on the pond, and they are obliged to lay their eggs late in May, for the persicaria does not become thick enough to provide cover earlier. The persicaria grows rapidly then, and as the rainfall diminishes the water shrinks, exposing more of the vegetation. As mentioned in my previous letter on the flora, a few other plants are found mixed with the persicaria: the minute *Apium inundatum* is abundant though inconspicuous, and the usual floating pondweed (*Potamogeton natans*), water purslane (*Peplis portula*), the lesser duckweed, and the water crowfoot, with the rushes and sedges which I have already identified for you.

As the pond grows smaller under the summer sun a margin of mud is exposed, attractive to such wading birds as visit us on migration. Dunlins are so tame that we can walk them into wire-netting funnels placed half in and half out of the water, and we have caught and ringed a number each summer in this way. They are always in very small parties, rarely as many as ten, often only one. We also see stray individuals of such waders as ringed plover, turnstone, sanderling, knot, ruff, little stint, redshank, greenshank, bar-tailed godwit, and black-tailed godwit. Many of these individuals are, in contrast with our moorhen, often very tame indeed, so much so that one would suppose they were tired or partly lost on migration. The redshank, of course, excepted – it is the sentinel, and, with its desperate shrieking alarm-note, greatly cursed by the observer for betraying his presence to other birds.

Near the pond in July assemble great packs of curlew. I have then seen five to six hundred together – a noble and exciting moment to watch this multitude rise with mournful musical concert. They feed little, resting until their full moult is completed. Their feathers and quills cover the rough surface of the nearby moor.

We endeavour to conserve the winter flood water of the pond by damming, and so raising, the height of the outlet. As a result there is as much as an acre underwater in early spring or after heavy rains. This is a considerable attraction to migrating wild fowl. During most of the winter the enlarged pond is alive with the calls and splashings of large flocks of wigeon, mallard, and teal. They are resting, washing, preening, and flirting. They find perfect sanctuary with us during the day. We enjoy this trust they place in us. Some remain all night, but the majority fly off to feed on the mainland at dusk, as, of course, we have no corn or cultivated land, and our grass is short and overgrazed by rabbits. They return in the morning.

As our pond is very shallow, even when flooded, we never see any true diving ducks and coots are very rare. A few shovellers associate with the mallard and wigeon, and occasionally a pintail turns up. Common scoter and shelduck pass by, but over the sea only. Wild geese find our grazing too bare, but from time to time a few white-fronted geese drop in on their way to and from their Severn estuary haunts. When I hear their gaggling notes and see their dark chevrons against the sky, there rises in me a rich exhilarating feeling. The mind is excited by the knowledge that these grand birds are travellers from Novaya Zemlya and the uninhabited northern Siberian coasts. They bring an air of mystery and majesty and power which is heightened by their clanging cries. So might you feel at sight of a Bedouin caravan on the rim of some far desert.

There are no fish in the pond, excepting eels which, incredible as it may seem, manage somehow – when in the elver stage – to wriggle up the mossy waterfalls where our island streams fall over the cliff into the sea. And presumably it is the eel which the heron hunts when for a few hours in late summer or autumn he ungainly flaps over the island. The gulls mob him with loud screams, instinctively fearing the power of so large a bird; they make aerial plunges upon his slow-moving form, forcing a loud 'fronk' out of the heron. But once he has alighted and is standing immobile by the pond's edge, the gulls soon lose interest.

Oystercatchers nest in the vicinity of the pond, on the soft thick cushions of sea pinks which rise above the damp perimeter where the green discs of marsh pennywort cover the ground, and the pale-pink cups of the bog pimpernel make a delicate carpet. And here, too, within three hundred yards' radius of the pond is the breeding ground of lapwings, which are ever present at Skokholm.

On fine days in March the lapwings begin their beautiful courtship song-flights on this territory. The cock, with his long black crest waving over his head, runs forward and sweeps into the air, rising at a steeper angle until he appears to shoot skywards; then as suddenly throws himself downwards with wings swaying gustily as if he was caught in a whirlwind, zigzagging, even appearing to turn a somersault, and calling wildly 'Pee-weet-weet!' he screams and upwards and onwards he twirls and twists, producing a loud 'hoo-hoo', a throbbing note, with his broad wings. Others may join him until the air is filled with the humming of the heavy wings and the beautiful, mournful notes of the peewits.

In April the male begins making scrapes on the dry tops of the thrift tussocks while the hollows between are still glistening with the spring rainwater. He lifts his tail and lowers his wings and in a kind of bowing display turns round and round, scraping with his sharp clawed feet, and mewing gruffly. Sometimes he plucks at the thrift stems and grass and picks up stones and dirt, throwing them backwards so that they slide off his burnished plumage and drop down on the edge of the scrape. The female may or may not be witness of this invitation to nest, but sooner or later she is drawn to one of the excited males, and when she is ready he quietly alights upon her back and the marriage is consummated.

She immediately flies to the nest-scrape and settles down to the job of enlarging and finishing it. Late in April the four black-splotched brown eggs (sometimes three and once seven – probably the product of two females) are laid.

They are a loving pair, taking turns to incubate and stand guard. On my approach within a hundred yards the watching bird would rise, screaming, and come swooping in my direction with humming wings. The head of the sitting bird could be seen peering out of the thrift flowers, and if I continued to advance it would slip off the nest and run away, dodging and hiding behind the clumps of sea pinks until it was far enough to rise in the air and join its mate without betraying the nest site.

In twenty-seven days the eggs hatch and the chicks leave the nest soon after. In another month, if they survive the attacks of gulls, against which their parents vigorously defend them, they are on the wing. Their first plumage is like that of the adult, but they have a white throat and hardly any crest.

We have had as many as twelve pairs of lapwing nesting in the marshy central plain of the island, but usually four pairs only are resident. At the end of the breeding season in June some thirty natives, young and old, gather in one flock. This is augmented by mainland parties and by October there are often several hundred. These moult with us, as the curlews do; and some are with us all through the winter. The lapwing is sensitive to temperature changes. It migrates locally according to the degree of cold, seeking the coast when the land becomes frozen. In hard weather (as in February 1929) they become very weak and tame for lack of food. They creep up to the island buildings as if seeking protection. They die or are killed by gulls and buzzards, being too feeble to fly. On 17th December 1927 vast flocks were crossing high over the island, flying at great speed due west before a bitterly cold south-east wind. A few days later many lapwings were taken in Newfoundland, one of them bearing a ring showing that it had been marked in England.

Yours.

31. GRASSHOLM

DEAR J – We have just returned from a visit to Grassholm. We started in the *Storm Petrel* at eight-thirty this morning, Ann and I and four friends. This is the last visit we shall make to Grassholm perhaps for many years. It was the hottest day of the year so far – seventy-four degrees in the shade, a high temperature for our small sea-cooled island plateau. A very slight north breeze filled the sails most of the way out and back. There was no swell and we made an easy progress – one and a half hours each way.

It is this calm warm weather with light mists which has helped us clear the beaches of Dunkirk in the last week. The wonderful but terrible scenes of the evacuation by sea off Flanders are over and now our tormented minds must settle down to the hard work ahead. But our normal life is no longer normal. It has become a strange thing, this dwelling here in peace and beauty, while the world reels in the gathering battle. All nature here seems to have taken on a new and poignant loveliness. Our garden seems especially rich with flowers, and the thrift, once more covering acres of the island with its vivid soft pink heads, has an unremembered power to delight the senses of sight and smell and touch.

Soon we shall all be dispersed. This solemn thought gave our visit to Grassholm an added interest, so that we seemed to notice everything in more particular detail than usual. The outward voyage was made memorable by the appearance of a school of grey dolphins, which kept about us for at least ten minutes. Three or four of them kept diving under the boat, appearing now one side and now the other, and twice slightly grazing the boat's keel. It would have been easy to strike them with a harpoon. But you can imagine we were content merely to take photographs. I judged them to be individuals of the common species (*Delphinus delphis*).

As usual we moored the *Storm Petrel* in the little south-east gut, where, fifty years ago, the local fishermen used to moor their open sailing boats. And first a swallow flew by, and then a small flock of six turtle doves rose from the long rich green grass of the eastern slope. This was a most pleasant greeting on this bare rock; to find these gentle birds, dwellers in the sheltered farmlands and the secluded coppice, paying a summer visit like ourselves. Though we, of course, were deliberate visitors and they were accidental wanderers, delayed or lost on migration. Nearly every visit to Grassholm produces a few such strays, so that in the forty-four visits I have paid to Grassholm a list of sixty-four birds has been recorded.

On this occasion we were pleased to find that the gannetry is still on the increase. When you visited Grassholm with me on 31st May last year you will remember we estimated that the number of gannets was round about 6,000 breeding pairs. There is slightly more ground occupied by nests this year, which would argue a further increase.

This great assemblage of gannets, and the large colony of Atlantic seals, make Grassholm of special interest. But its fauna and flora are naturally very limited, owing to its size – twenty-two acres. Even its geology is plain and straightforward. The rock is entirely a tough basalt, which, in quite recent times, must have been under the sea – there is a raised beach suggesting this. There is little or no soil. We can imagine how vegetation, from seeds dropped or washed ashore, sprang up in the fissures of the rock and gradually spread over the crown of the island, growing up and dying down each year until at last only a huge haystack of the principal plant – sea fescue grass – existed. No other grasses could compete with this hardy wind and drought-resisting grass; save in the wetter hollows where a few plants of Yorkshire fog grass are now established where the fescue has died. This natural bed of live grass growing on dead grass over the otherwise bare rock was two or three feet thick when it was colonized by puffins. These birds found the weathered haystack, with its protective green crown, an easy site in which to excavate homes. They came to Grassholm in hundreds and then in thousands. One observer estimated 250,000 pairs in 1890! That is approximately 12,500 per acre or roughly three pairs to the square yard!

Fifty years later we find that this great puffin city is almost a complete ruin, the haystack has been burrowed until it has collapsed in a jumbled ruin of ceiling-less passages into which the visitor stumbles as he crosses the surface. And only some two or three score puffins haunt this puffin Pompeii today. The local fishermen believe that most of the puffins moved to Skokholm, which had only a small puffin population at that time.

Other rapid changes have taken place in the natural population of Grassholm. The observer who recorded the 250,000 pairs of puffins in 1890 saw only one seal there and some 200 pairs of gannets. As far as I can trace gannets did not always exist on Grassholm, or if they did then they were in insignificant numbers. There is no record of them at Grassholm previous to 1820, as there is of the gannetry at Lundy or Bass Rock or Ailsa Craig. They suffered persecution by fishermen who stole their eggs and used their carcases as bait for lobster-pots. There were only twenty pairs in 1883, but in 1890 they were protected by their new owner, Mr J.J. Neale of Cardiff. From that date onwards they have flourished both as a result of protection and of the cessation of the lobster-fishing about the island.

The increase was slow at first, but became accelerated during the first world war, probably because no one had time to molest them during those four years. Before 1914 there were only 300 pairs. In 1922 there were some 1,000 pairs. Two years later Mr Morrey Salmon and Miss Acland found nearly 2,000 pairs breeding, an increase of fifty per cent per annum which can only be explained by a considerable colonization. In 1933 Morrey Salmon and I made a very careful photographic census, each working separately; his estimate was 5,181 adults, and mine was 5,045, a difference of less than three per cent. The mean total was therefore 5,113. We found it necessary to allow seven per cent from this to account for the proportion of cases in which a pair of birds was at the nest together, and our total thus became 4,750 breeding pairs.

Today, as you know, there are over 6,000 pairs, and what an amazing sight this great colony is! Each bird or pair of birds standing guard on a cup-shaped hummock of seaweed and dried grass matted with guano, and each nest within a yard of its neighbours. Each individual adult beautiful in its Chinese white plumage, the head with a rich yellow-gold tinge, the powerful dagger-bill plumbeous, the eye cold with a pale silver like that of the squid's eye, the wing-tips a velvet black, the leaden-coloured feet with surprising longitudinal stripes of bluish-green.

Perhaps the Atlantic seals have increased for the same reason. Up to 150 of them, of all ages and both sexes – to say nothing of many colours – can be seen lolling and basking on the rocks about Grassholm on a fine summer's day. But curiously enough few, if any, breed there. Salmon and I made a special pilgrimage to ascertain this on 27th November 1936, going out in one of those smart, efficient, and safe little Breton smacks which happened to be in our waters at the time. We could only count twelve seals all told and not a sign of a young one. You might have thought so lonely a place was ideal for breeding seals, but in spite of suitable rocks shelving up on a gentle slope from the sea on the eastern half of Grassholm, it seems these seals prefer the pebble beaches and caves of the mainland of Pembrokeshire, and of Skomer, Ramsey, and Skokholm, on which to drop their calves.

It might be thought that the ecology of a little island is easily surveyed. But even on so small a rock and where exposure must limit the number of living things, it is a formidable task to make a *complete* list of all. When camping for a week here in June 1934, when making a film of the life of the gannet with Julian Huxley, we surveyed the breeding population of birds and were able to count with some accuracy the following number of breeding pairs: gannets, 5,000; great black-backed gulls, 67; herring gulls, 104; kittiwakes, 115; puffins, 130; razorbills, 43; guillemots, 188; oystercatchers, 5; rock pipits, 6; raven, 1.

The non-breeding birds (i.e. the visitors) recorded on various visits between April and November are jackdaw, starling, greenfinch, chaffinch, skylark, meadow pipit, white and yellow and grey wagtails, goldcrest, spotted and pied flycatchers, chiff-chaff, willow and wood and grasshopper and sedge warblers, whitethroat, song thrush, blackbird, ring ouzel, common and Greenland wheatears, whinchat, robin, wren, swallow, house and sand martins, swift, peregrine falcon, heron, cormorant, shag, Manx and sooty shearwaters (seen close offshore), fulmar-petrel, wood pigeon, turtle dove, ringed and grey plovers, turnstone, purple and common sandpipers, redshank, curlew, whimbrel, common and little and Arctic and Sandwich terns, lesser black-backed gull, Arctic skua, coot (three-quarters of a mile offshore).

The invertebrate fauna of the island has been surveyed also, by various friends who have accompanied me on these expeditions. F.W. Edwards has made lists of the Diptera (37 species) and Hymenoptera (10) and Coleoptera (6) and Lepidoptera (3). W. S. Bristowe collected eleven species of spider there on 9th June 1930.

We found the silver Y moth was particularly abundant while we were filming the gannets from 7th to 14th June 1934.

Often I used to sit for a while on the high point of the island during those lovely midsummer nights, watching the sleeping gannetry spread like a snowdrift beneath. It was then – at midnight – usually very calm, and the migrating silver Y moths would congregate about me, fluttering and chasing each other about this high peak of Grassholm. This was a year of their special abundance, according to Mrs K Grant who has collated the evidence of their migrations from 1932 to 1937. I have also seen red admiral, peacock, and painted lady butterflies flying over the sea near Grassholm, drifting on the light easterly and northerly winds which must drive them either to Ireland or to the open Atlantic.

Under and in our tents at Grassholm, hiding in the bed of long trampled fescue grass, were other forms of life. The common sand-flea or hopper, *Orchestia gammarella* (Pallas), was found abundantly wherever the grass was damp. There was also a *Porcellia* isopod, the common earwig (*Forficula auricula*), and one of the cicada (*Ecocephalus albifrons*). There is only one species of ant, the minute *Myrmica scabrinodis*.

This by no means exhausts our faunal list, but it is high time to conclude this letter. I have scarcely mentioned the lesser biology of the tideline – limpets, dog-whelks, barnacles, seaweeds, and so on. Nor is our survey complete without reference to the mosses and lichens growing on the rocks.

The flora is, as I have hinted, quite limited: the two grasses *Festuca rubra* and *Holcus lanatus*, the tree mallow, the goose-foot (*Atriplex glabriuscula*), English stonecrop, a few sea pinks, scurvy grass (*Cochlearia officinalis*), rock spurrey (*Spergularia marina*), and common chickweed.

Like our visits to Grassholm, our picture of this lonely but fascinating islet must perforce be all too brief and hurried.

Yours ever.

32. SWALLOW

Friday, 14th June 1940

THIS NIGHTMARE WAR! I was sitting down to write you a letter about migration when the fishing-boat arrived in the harbour with a letter from Marjorie with the message that you are reported missing in Norway. I was stunned with the news, and for a while, my dear John, I must confess I sat with a mist of tears before my eyes. The letter had been difficult to read, for it was already beautifully stained with the tears of the anguished woman who wrote it. But there it was, on re-reading it the letter told me without any doubt that you were reported missing.

And now I want to tell you how, though the letter was so tragic in its contents, I was quite suddenly convinced that you were safe somewhere, either as a prisoner of war or in hiding with good Norwegian patriots. One day when you read this you will be able to smile at the curious way in which I was convinced.

This is how it happened. One moment I was sitting in utter gloom of mind trying to convince myself that so good a friend and one with so rich a comprehension of life could not have perished so soon. And I tried to picture you from the account in your last letter, written from Norway, gliding over the snow on your allotted secret mission and watching the solitary swallow that spoke to you of an English spring. Mark how the swallow came into it! The next moment, as if in direct answer to my inward prayer, a swallow flew quietly into the study and alighted first on my right arm as it lay against the window, and next upon my hand as I raised it in my surprise!

You know I am not a superstitious person, as a student of real nature cannot readily believe in the *super*natural. But it was impossible not to be moved and very greatly comforted by this omen. I could not even rid my mind of the absurd notion that this was the selfsame swallow you had seen in the snow in Norway, even that you had sent the bird as a sign to me that you were safe! This feeling was heightened by the fact that the swallow was very tired, as if exhausted by a long journey; and so tame that I could handle it easily. Indeed it fell asleep in the sunlight on my desk when I put it down in order to fetch a ring to mark it with. There it slept for nearly half an hour after I had ringed it. Then quietly – as I was writing a letter to your wife to tell her of this omen and to comfort her – as quietly as it had come, the swallow flew away, Its ring number, in case it ever reaches you, is DW 910! The whole incident of the swallow alighting on my arm happened to coincide with the message about you, and my last picture of you, which was of you watching a swallow. Of course, I am well aware that a swallow in Norway in May would not fly south to Wales in June. But such is the way of the human mind that it will cling to any good omen, and I must admit I am still profoundly moved by what has happened today. The letter has gone to Marjorie, and now I feel I must complete this to you, and although I may not be able to post it for a while I shall hold it until I get your new address. Today the Germans entered Paris, and nothing it seems now can save France, with Italy stabbing her in the back at the same time. It can't be long now before we shall have to leave Skokholm, too. By this post came an official letter that we must be prepared to evacuate the island at short notice, and advising us to leave while there is time to move out in comfort. But one day all this agony and separation will be over and we shall meet you again on island soil. Meanwhile, from the calm June weather and quiet sea and the air full of the soft island summer, murmurous with nesting birds, I send you a message of hope, and my faith that soon we shall hear of your safe recovery.

Ever yours, dear John.

33. SWIFT

right19th June 1940

JOHN! – The omen of the swallow was a good and true one! This is a very happy day for me in the middle of the world's anxieties. For Marjorie telegraphs that she has a wire from friends in Norway – via Sweden – that you are a prisoner of war and unwounded. The chain of omens held to the last: it was on the day that she got my letter about the swallow that the telegram arrived from Sweden!

You will no doubt deeply regret the circumstances that have resulted in your imprisonment. But these were beyond your control, and must be accepted with the philosophy with which your mind, as I well know, is fully equipped. To us the prospect of a long separation – for it will surely take a year or so for unprepared Britain to recover from this impact of the highly armed and prepared Nazi machine – grim as it is, is offset by the thought that you are safe.

It is my intention to conclude this series of letters to you, and send them on to you as opportunity allows me to write them. For in your prison camp you will no doubt, as an officer, have some if not much leisure in which to think and read and write. You will in a sense be as enisled as we are, and your observations will be limited to the fauna of that entity of your camp and its perimeter. This should give you the chance of concentrating particularly on one or two species as I have done here, and making a study of great interest. I shall therefore look forward with special excitement to your letters from your place of internment.

I confess to feeling rather too moved about your safe recovery to make a lengthy letter of this.

Perhaps I can finish with a note about the swift, a bird which has been flying over the island today. It is a regular passage-migrant over Skokholm, from late April up to the second week in September, generally in very small numbers; often we might see only one in a day. A great deal of this migration seems to be in a westerly direction, towards Ireland. I have never seen this scythe-winged beauty alight or rest in any way on the island. It is the most aerial and tireless of all birds on the wing. Systematists place it in the order Apodiformes, along with the humming-birds, also an aerial family; but humming-birds perch whereas swifts never do, at least not voluntarily, and they are said to find difficulty in rising from the ground if they fall down accidentally. This last is true. I have occasionally found swifts on the ground beneath their nesting holes. With their legs so far back on their bodies they do have difficulty in getting up again, but as it is usually the weak or sick that fall to the ground this is not surprising. I have no doubt that a fully active swift, taken from the nest and placed on a flat surface, would take wing much more easily.

A friend of mine once marked a number (to be precise, nineteen: thirteen adults and six young birds in the nest) of swifts for me in the town of Pembroke. Of these one adult was recovered two years later in the nest where it had been ringed. Another, ringed as a nestling on 25th July 1933, was recovered on 16th May this year, that is, in its seventh year, by a boy who picked it up on the asphalt playground of East End School, Pembroke. The bird seemed a bit tired and was put in a box overnight. The ring was removed for examination next day and while this was in progress the swift suddenly gathered its wings and flew screaming into the sky, free of both man and ring.

Seven years is, I imagine, a good age for a small bird, but the swift must be a longer-lived bird than the swallow, since it is single-brooded, rearing only two (or three) squabs in one year, whereas the swallow may rear eight to twelve young in one summer.

There are many curious facts about the swift which need further investigation. It is so well developed as to be almost completely aerial. Perhaps, as swifts are so common everywhere, it may be possible for you from your camp to try to elucidate some of these problems. As you know it feeds in the air, mates in the air, and even collects all its nesting material in the air. If it could only suspend its salivary bed of agglutinated straws, feathers, and grasses in mid air no doubt it would nidify there!

I have often watched swifts circling in a small flock high in the sky at dusk on quiet evenings of summer, ever gyrating upwards until voice and form were quite lost in the darkening blue vault, but I have never yet read of a proof that swifts do spend the night on the wing at a great height. As a boy I used to watch at dusk in June and July under the eaves of a chapel in Glamorganshire, and invariably as the twilight gave way to night some at least of the swifts would return and sweep silently over my head up into the eave-crannies where they nested. But I always felt uncertain that the whole flock had returned in this stealthy manner.

Again, where do swifts sleep on their migrations and in their winter quarters? In sea cliffs or mountain precipices? This is a question I would wish to see properly investigated. Does the swift, like the seal and the seabird overtaken by the long winter gale, live without true sleep for days on the wing, tirelessly?

In places where the swift is a permanent resident, presumably it continues to roost all the year round in the crannies where it breeds. When in Madeira last summer I used to watch at dawn the small dark Madeiran swifts issue from the great cliffs of the Deserta Islands, and begin their day's business. This was the signal to cease my own – for I had been occupied all night in a study of the nocturnal shearwaters and petrels of that wild and grand region.

Our very best wishes to you in your new environment.

34. CANARIES

29th June 1940

Dear J.B. – You will be interested in the behaviour of birds which, bred in captivity for centuries, have been released and allowed to return to a free and wild existence. I refer to the canaries here, in the study of which you took a share last year.

For this experiment we introduced six pairs of canaries into an aviary twelve feet square by eight feet high which I had built in the corner of the enclosed yard here. The high walls gave shelter from the cold north and east winds, the aviary facing south. It was planted with two small cypresses and a few deciduous shrubs. Known to the bird fancier as Border canaries, the subjects of this experiment were of several colours, some fawn, some green, some blue, some cinnamon, and one nearly white. Each bird was identified by a differently coloured ring or rings. They made a brave show, but what pleased us most, I think, was their singing. The six cocks were first placed in the aviary (on 7th April 1939) and the six hens a few minutes later, when vigorous singing began, each cock seeming to try to out sing the others. The rippling, bubbling, rolling, trilling notes were poured out in a joyous medley most pleasing to ears more attuned to the roar of the sea and the endless soughing of the wind.

The cocks soon began to pursue the hens and fight each other for them, but no real damage was inflicted, and much of the pursuit and fighting was done to the accompaniment of song. The cocks showed great interest in nesting material and struggled for possession of a stray feather discovered in the aviary. The twelve birds roosted that night in the cypress-trees.

Next day I fixed nesting boxes and opened holes in the walls for them to build in. In five days time there were three nests built and the first egg laid. The cocks were monogamous; each zealous in driving his hen back to the nest when she came off to feed. We trained them to take food from our hands and they soon learned to perch upon our heads and shoulders. They became especially tame with Ann.

As soon as the first young were hatched I opened the large doors of the aviary one sunny morning in May and drove one cock out. He seemed bewildered and tried to get back, but could not find the door again. Then the other cocks and one hen flew out and, finding themselves free, began to call to each other, using the typical 'twhy!' note. They only flew short distances and seemed quickly exhausted by a flight of more than twenty yards. They eagerly picked at the weeds on the walls. During the day they learned the way in and out of the aviary doors, and were back voluntarily to roost in the aviary that night.

May and June were busy and happy months for the canaries, and we too enjoyed their obvious pleasure in their freedom and endless singing about the house and buildings. They would fly down to us and alight upon our heads, or shoulders, or open hands. They began to build their second and third nests outside the aviary, but all within the boundaries of our garden and grouped buildings. Soon there were flights or 'charms' of young canaries on the wing. These groups of juveniles began to roam farther about the island than the breeding adults had. But never ventured out over the sea.

The sitting hens came off their nests to exercise and drink – usually twice a day, at 8 a.m. and 8 p.m. – and were then anxiously followed by the cocks, who seemed much agitated by this regular interruption of incubation. The cocks fed them at the nest during the day. Some promiscuous feeding of newly fledged young was noticed, where a hungry fledgeling waylaid an adult carrying food in its crop, and coaxed it to regurgitate.

The young canaries proved to be better fliers than their parents, which seemed unable to rise more than about eight feet above the ground, and moved through the air with a laboured beating of the wings. They were incomparably heavy in flight compared with the pipits and other wild birds with which they mingled. Most of their food was gathered from the seeds of wild plants such as dandelion, sand-spurrey, plantain, groundsel, and garden weeds, supplemented by the supply of rape, canary, hemp and millet seeds which we kept in the aviary for them. When handled these free-flying canaries were always in a fat condition, with plump bellies. Island life certainly seemed to suit them, and so far, enjoying the protection of our presence and of our homestead, they had no enemies.

The plumage of the old birds was becoming very worn and bleached by the end of June. But nesting went on without a break until August, when the moult came on with great suddenness; so quickly in fact that some of the adults showed bare patches in a few days. Those with eggs and young suddenly and completely deserted them, leaving the new-born or half-grown chicks to die from cold and hunger.

Then with the autumn migration of the wild birds the first serious tragedies occurred. One or two migrating sparrowhawks, as usual, took up residence and began to prey on the charms of canaries. The slow heavy flight of the canary, whose aerial powers have so diminished in the centuries of its restriction in captivity, made the bird an easy victim; and the bright colours attracted attention. Soon the sparrowhawks seemed to be killing for the wanton pleasure of it.

If we had not made haste to capture the remnant of the canaries in the aviary and bird-traps we should not have saved a nucleus of breeders for 1940, as we did. As it was we saved only seven out of some fifty canaries flying free on the island.

In 1940 the same chain of events is taking place. The canaries, locked up all winter and their numbers in the spring made up to twelve by the addition of five new birds purchased, began to breed in the aviary in March and were released in April. They are increasing rapidly. We shall have to catch as many as possible to take with us to our mainland home; but this year we shall have abandoned Skokholm before the sparrowhawks migrate here.

Yours.

5th July 1940

M Y DEAR J – It is a matter of interest, but also of some regret, that certain species find Skokholm too circumscribed to make it their nesting-ground year after year without a break. I would like to mention here some of the small birds which from time to time have nested with us. You will doubtless appreciate my pleasure as well as my anxiety when I find a new species preparing to nest here, and will understand the encouragement which I try to give it, for every such occurrence is an enrichment for the islander ornithologist, who is bound to miss the voices and ways of the small birds of the mainland countryside which he knew so well in youth.

Every year certain birds visit us in the spring, and remain about until nesting time has arrived, only to disappear at the last moment when I am preparing to congratulate myself that they would breed with us. That has happened so many times with the pied wagtail. It nested in our garden wall in 1928 and was a source of joy to me as, in that busy first year, I saw the pair at the nest from time to time, during my labours on the roof of my house. Its plain but sweet twittering song lasted throughout the summer, for it reared two broods and was silent only during the time when the young were growing in the nest.

Each year male pied wagtails would arrive (generally singly) in March and April, and call loudly from the top of a roof or wall. A pair nested again in 1929 and 1932, but not after that until this year, when I was delighted to find a pair settling down to a nest in Boar's Bay. This was successful, and a second nest was built in a roofless building here and so far they have safely reared four youngsters. My daughter and I ringed these in the nest today.

Another bird which nested in 1928 and 1929 (and also 1930), but not since, was the sedge warbler, a species which is only seen here on migration in the first weeks of May and in August. Its vigorous sweet polyglot song was most welcome to us day and night, once it had established nesting quarters in the dropwort and cow parsnip below the freshwater spring. I say 'night' because it would sing very loudly as soon as the first homecoming shearwaters interrupted its sleep. It would now chatter harshly in a scolding way, then give out some quite rich musical notes, and would then inextricably mix the soft with the strident in its song and continue for half a minute without pause. One brood was successfully fledged in June each year.

In 1931, in place of our sedge warbler, which only sang for a short day in May, a male whitethroat occupied the dropwort-hogweed cover, and with his vigorous singing and song-flight soon attracted a mate from among the hundreds of whitethroats which used this sheltered corner on their spring passage. One day I watched the female plucking fine white rootlets from the earth of a hedge where the turf had been kicked off by my foot.

I followed her to the nest, a deep cup nearly completed in the long grass at the base of a bramble bush. And here, too, a pair of whitethroats nested in 1932. But as I did not ring the 1931 adults I am unable to say if they were the same individuals. None has nested since 1932, and I think the reason is that in 1933 the rich growth of hemlock dropwort and hogweed was eaten down (I think by a plague of slugs) and it has never recovered since. Also we have established in this spot the main Heligoland-type ringing-trap, and our activities in driving birds by beating the bushes and cover is not conducive to the successful nesting of any bird therein.

Of other casual nesting birds we have for the first time a pair of starlings. They built an untidy nest in between the matchboard lining and the corrugated iron roof of a store shed near the landing place. Access to this well-hidden nest was by way of a hole in the rusted iron. The cock wheezed away many a fine half-hour in imitative song from his perch on the ridge of this building in April and May. I cannot account for this whim of the starling in nesting here. It does not nest at Skomer, and is quite absent from many parts of the mainland of Pembrokeshire, where it is common only during the winter. Starlings are supposed to breed freely where there are sheep and cattle present, but in the years 1930-4 when we had over two hundred domestic sheep and lambs at Skokholm no starlings remained to breed.

Why should the starling breed casually here? It has even bred casually on remote Bear Island, in the region of the Arctic Ocean! It breeds on North Rona, forty miles from Cape Wrath. Yet it fails to breed in many of the most suitable situations, such as the well-watered and stocked meadows, and in the villages composed of old houses, of Pembrokeshire.

Yours ever.

Sunday, 7th July

DEAR JOHN – These last three days have been very beautiful, very 'soft' as they say here, with glorious cloud effects. We have been ringing razorbills and guillemots.

Approximately one thousand pairs of razorbills breed at Skokholm, wherever the red sandstone cliffs are sufficiently broken above the reach of the sea to provide the cover which this handsome auk seeks. Where the cliffs are crumbling down with great boulders and large stones resting haphazard is the favourite haunt of the razorbill. Here it may hide its large decorated egg from the attentions of the gulls, particularly that great egg thief the herring gull. It will also nest close to the mouth of a rabbit- or puffin-burrow. More open situations, almost as open as those favoured by the guillemot, are freely adopted, in fact it will often lay its egg in a guillemot colony or at least on the same ledge.

It is always a delight to go 'razorbilling', a pastime which requires a thorough exploration of these broken parts of our cliffs. Armed with packets of special rings, pieces of wire of different lengths for hooking the birds from their holes, and a notebook, we have spent these fine afternoons in July very happily indeed. With two friends we have ringed over five hundred razorbills, by climbing over and in and about the tumbled wilderness of the sea's fringe. These have been vivid hours for us – for they are among the last we may spend here – while the strife in Europe increases and the British fleet seizes the French ships in the 'most melancholy battle in naval history'. In the wild rock garden of the red cliffs we have momentarily set aside this agony.

You yourself know what mental and physical satisfaction there is in the intelligent and *active* study of nature. And for this razorbill study you have as your working environment the green-blue sea below you, the warm sun above, a wide horizon zoned with rich cloud colours, and birds and flowers everywhere.

The long bamboo with a wire hook at the end is a useful implement on these occasions. Razorbills and guillemots, like puffins, allow themselves to be hooked with this if you approach carefully, keeping yourself steady in a crouching position, and slowly pushing the hook along until you can slip it over the leg of the bird. The natives of St Kilda, Outer Hebrides, used to slip hair-nooses over the necks of seabirds, but our experience suggests that the wire hook over the leg is less frightening for the bird and more efficacious. You can hook a puffin or razor-bill and pull it quietly into your hands, ring it and release it, without its neighbours, standing within a few inches of where the captive was standing, taking flight! The foolish birds are unable to associate the slowly advancing wire with any danger to themselves.

By visiting the cliffs annually in July for this purpose we have been able to recapture many razorbills ringed in previous years. At first we had some difficulty with the rings; the razorbill shuffles along the rock surface of its breeding-places with the tarsus flat on the ground. The ring becomes quickly scratched and defaced. However, we eventually hit on the idea of using rings with duplicate inscriptions and of a length which enables them to be overlapped sufficiently to cover and protect the inner inscription.

Seventeen adult razorbills have been re-caught in the year following their first ringing, nine two years later, four after three years, and one after four years. These are the adults which we meet year after year inhabiting certain crevices and holes most easy of access by our inquiring hand or hook. Their recapture merely confirms an obvious truth (holding good for birds generally): that the adult returns to its familiar nesting site of the previous year. These figures also give us a glimpse into the vital statistics of the razorbill; although a much more extended survey over several years by the ringing method is necessary to get a complete picture. This ought to be attempted in the future. As it is we find the rate of recoveries drops by about thirty per cent per annum, and this might well be a rough guide to the death-rate in adult razorbills.

Of young birds returning to the island after ringing, at present we have none recorded in the year following birth, but nine have been found breeding two years after ringing, seven three years, and two four years later. Figures which help to show that young birds – as one would expect – supply the gaps caused by death in the ranks of the old ones on the ledges of their birthplace.

A very pretty incident occurred while we were ringing today. A young razorbill that had tumbled off a ledge just after the adult had flown off was immediately followed by its parent, who, with anxious growling notes, timed its flight to parallel the feebler fluttering of the fledgeling. They alighted together on the sea and the adult conducted the baby away from the rocks with gestures of fondness, swimming around it and driving away other curious adults.

Usually when we see a fledged chick going down to the sea – sometimes disturbed by our presence into taking the flight it has so long premeditated – it flies down alone, but calling loudly, and it is then surrounded by an excited group of adults who press upon it, as if all desired to answer its anxious squeaking by offering their protection. This seems to alarm the chick, which dives to escape the crowd. But at last it seems to find its parents – for in the end it always swims away with one and sometimes two adults to convoy it to sea.

Razorbills form distinct patterns when assembled on the sea, even at this time of year, but more so in early spring, in April and May, when they first come and are conducting their love affairs. They gather in regular close lines, swimming in single file; then they may turn about and meet in a circle, facing each other, swaying close enough to touch bills, and nibble at each other's faces, as puffins do, tails elevated stiffly at right angles to the body and bills upraised and opened slightly to show the yellow mouth. They look like a lot of smart black-and-white painted toy boats, for they swim with great buoyancy. These 'nuptial' dances on the sea are very charming and greatly endear this pretty bird to me.

As far as I know it has never yet been remarked that the razorbill carries two brood patches, though she very rarely lays more than one egg. These patches are situated high up each side of the breast, above the thigh, so that the razorbill is obliged to brood with its body on one or the other side and the wing is drooped slightly over the outside of the egg. After thirty days the egg is hatched. The chick grows rapidly, being tenderly fed with small fish carried crosswise in the parent's bill. In two weeks time it is fully feathered, though only half-grown, and takes to the sea in the manner I have already described. I have never seen the adult carry it down as suggested in some of the older reference books.

The chick follows its parent at sea until it is full-grown and able to feed for itself. The ringing of these nestlings at Skokholm has brought to light a surprising migration, and our efforts at 'razorbilling' have been well rewarded on this account. It seems that young razorbills from Skokholm travel south, passing down the Bay of Biscay during September; they enter the Mediterranean and work up the east coast of Spain, the south coast of France, and finally reach the Gulf of Genoa, where our ringed birds have been taken by Italian fishermen during late November to early February. In late February they have been taken in the Bay of Biscay on their way home. Some winter all along this route, and some adults go with the young birds into the Mediterranean.

Razorbills ringed by other observers at Handa, Sutherland, have moved in quite a different direction, travelling north and east to reach Norwegian and Danish coasts in the autumn. Occasionally some of our birds get caught in this stream, and are recovered north of Skokholm in October, and one reached Kristiansund, Nordinov, Norway, on 2nd October 1938; this bird was ringed as a chick on 19th July 1937.

All good wishes.

37. GUILLEMOT

21st July 1940

DEAR J – We ringed forty guillemots, chicks and adults, in Little Bay today.

On fine summer evenings I love to lie in the sun's rays where they warm the top of an inverted buttress of the sandstone of the cliffs of Little Bay on the north side of the island. From this flat-topped perch a hundred and twenty feet above the sea I can watch the affairs of our largest colony of guillemots, set out on three ledges, one above the other. The two lowermost hold some thirty each, and the top ledges ten adults. And all about and above are other holes and niches occupied by puffins and razorbills and herring gulls, and hung with the flowers of sea-campion and beet. I can hear storm petrels crooning in the rock-crannies, and the reedy song of the rock pipit mingles with the beat of the wave in the channel below. Truly it is a grand site for study. I am half hidden on this buttress and the birds soon forget the silent, unmoving watcher.

Almost first to arrive of the seabirds, the guillemot is, next to the storm petrel, last to lay its egg. The November rains and gales have hardly cleaned the ledges of the stinking guano of last summer before the guillemots pay their first visits.

Some time before Christmas, on a fine, quiet, early morning, they appear in 'rafts' on the sea under the ledges. After flying around for a while they may settle for an hour or two, crowding on their favourite narrow ledges; but they are all gone again long before noon. Are these early visits prompted by the urge to stake a claim to nesting territory in the overcrowded communities?

The guillemot spends a great deal of its life on land in ducking its head up and down and grunting – an 'endless obeisance' – which is its typical way of expressing emotion. It is possible that the guillemot is promiscuous. It mates usually on land, but it is impossible to say whether, in such congested communities, the pair is faithful. From its behaviour later one would suspect not. The female is probably faithful only to the nest site where she lays a huge pyriform egg which varies greatly in its ground colour and markings. Simple experiments with the egg prove that although the pyriform egg is better than the oval it still needs a wider area in which to spin round than is provided by the narrow breeding-ledges. And many eggs are rolled over the cliff by the clumsy movements of the guillemots crowded on the ledges.

The bereaved adults cling to the space occupied by the egg, however, and as fresh eggs appear up to the end of June, we can surmise a second egg is laid. You will find that there is always a surplus of adults in relation to eggs or chicks surviving in any guillemot colony. These adults – some of them are probably those which have lost their eggs earlier – are ready to pirate and assume control of the egg or chick of a neighbour. This is obvious to anyone who observes a guillemot colony containing upwards of a dozen adults.

In the case of my colony of the buttress I can count at least seventy adults on the three ledges, which contain only fifteen young ones and four eggs. All these adults appear deeply interested in these eggs and chicks. Those which are not brooding stand close to those which are, and the reason is obvious. They are waiting to take control of any egg or

chick that they can seize either by force or in the absence of the previous 'tenant'. Idle birds can be watched suddenly taking off, circling round in the air, and crash-landing on top of a brooding bird. This manoeuvre, whether deliberate or not, often has the effect of displacing the brooding bird, or drives the chick away, and the new arrival thereupon waddles upon the egg or chick with complacent-sounding grunts. But the adult in possession may as often resist the new arrival. A battle develops and the fighters may scramble hither and thither through the community until they suddenly fall over the edge. Meanwhile the egg or chick is immediately adopted by a third guillemot which has hitherto stood idle, apparently awaiting this very chance.

Squabbling and pirating of this kind is part of the economy of the guillemot's life as it is of other sociable nesting birds, e.g. certain penguins. It is useful in that if a parent is killed or dies at sea there is always another eager to take on the job of nurserymaid, of incubating, of brooding, and of feeding of young.

The egg hatches in one month and the chick is ready to fly in less than three weeks, usually after fourteen days.

The guillemot's slender pointed bill seems less adapted than the razorbill's for gripping fish crosswise, and the fish is usually a single large one, carried lengthwise in the bill, tail outwards. Communal feeding seems to be the rule even in quite small colonies; this may account for the fact that an adult may hold the fish patiently for as much as half an hour before a chick is hungry enough to take it. The fish may even be dropped by the owner, when another adult may seize it and do the feeding instead; or occasionally one adult may snatch a fish from the bill of a neighbour who, tired of holding it, is unwary enough to shuffle the fish into a new position and so for a moment leave it hanging loosely and invitingly from the tip of its bill.

Today a number of the chicks we ringed flew down to the sea, which was in an angry mood with a swell beating on the red shelves beneath us. It was fine to watch the young guillemot master the waves. It beats its half-grown wings rapidly, descending on a long oblique plane – since it cannot fly properly at first. Some fell into the open sea, on touching which they continued to fly downwards, and from the height of our cliff perch we could watch them exploring the deep with wings half closed and beating more slowly in a tougher medium.

Momentum thus checked, the chick rose to the surface, only to dive under the next breaking wave. It rapidly worked seawards, followed – in answer to the shrill 'willou! willou!' – by a party of excited squawking adults. You might imagine these adults, from their behaviour, were deciding who should take charge! But one cannot say whether it is one of the parents which actually succeeds in convoying the chick finally. Perhaps the strongest or at least the most determined individual gets possession? Or, as I believe most likely, the adult which has done most of the feeding, recognizing the individual cry (its individuality is distinct even to the dull human ear) of its protégé, is most assertive in mothering the chick and finally, by driving away others, takes it to sea in all parental triumph.

Some chicks fail to make the open water on the first flight and plunge into an advancing wave which throws them among the great red boulders. Or if they hit the rocks they bounce off unhurt into the sea. I watched one of these rolling in the shallow channels between the rocks as the water sucked backwards. I saw it rise in the lap of the next wave and be carried onwards, to be battered against the red walls and between the grinding rocks. It vanished in the flood of water, only to reappear in the ebb, struggling, piping, swimming outwards with the white rushing water. Again and again it was buried in that heavy mass of broken water advancing on the shore, but each time it was seen, dragged roughly but buoyantly in the outgoing surf. It was swimming vigorously and diving as soon as the wave advanced again. Twenty times the wave lifted it inwards, but the young bird battled outwards and at last I saw it was gaining seawards, encouraged in the direction of a group of adults at sea who were answering its calls.

The young bird seems to be very thirsty. It sips the salt water, holding up its head to let it run down its throat. Perhaps thirst, among other considerations, helps to drive the young guillemot to the sea?

At the end of the season, in a few days time, only one or two chicks will be left on the ledges, but these will have a large bodyguard of adults to feed them and fight for the 'convoying rights' when they go down to the sea. And for many weeks longer, even into November, the adult guillemot, with chick swimming and squeaking close behind, may be seen far at sea, an affectionate pair.

Ringed guillemots do not show such a surprising migration as razorbills. They evidently do not invade the Mediterranean. Two ringed as nestlings reached Norway during their first October; in the same month a third youngster was recovered near Morbihan, Bay of Biscay. On 31st January 1936 one ringed as a chick in 1934 was recovered at Biscarosse, Landes, France.

The adults are faithful to the same ledges. Five ringed adults have returned to the same ledge when they were breeding the year before and two have returned after two years and two after three years. So far only one guillemot ringed as a nestling has been recaptured (a year later) on the island. But as we have only a small colony of guillemots, round about two hundred pairs, many of which are inaccessible for study by ringing, our material is limited.

In the whole of this Skokholm colony, by the way, there are only two individuals with the white ring around the eye and the 'bridle' behind which give the appearance of wearing spectacles. That is to say, 0-5 per cent of our guillemots are of the bridled variety, which as you know is not even a subspecies but merely an example of polymorphism, such as the 'dutch' blaze in our wild rabbit here.

Yours.

38. SHEARWATERS

DEAR JOHN – The last word of the monograph on the Manx shearwater was written today. I'm very glad this is finished, as I feared I would never do it in time. We have to leave Skokholm by the end of August. I am looking out for a place where I can transport my family and the animals. If I can find a farm I shall be able to settle my possessions, leaving all in charge of my wife and the Baron. I expect to be sent away on Naval Intelligence work fairly soon. So this may be one of the last letters I shall be able to write for some time.

Whether any publisher will consider it possible during the war to put this monograph into print is quite another matter, but I intend to post it to our friend H.F. Witherby for his comments.* As I have deliberately written it in the plainest English possible, avoiding the use of those technical and scientific terms which are not in common use, I am hoping it will be acceptable to the general public. So much of interesting new information on birds is buried in the scientific journals under a mass of ugly statistics and modern tautology. The tendency is to write of birds as complete automatons, and to be terrified of ascribing to them one thought or action which can be interpreted as akin to human thought or action, whether instinctive or reasoned. Such writing is dead, and is soon buried in the archives of ornithological libraries. Surely we need to present our discoveries in a more living way, in the way of Jean Henri Fabre and Maurice Maeterlinck? I think you will agree wholeheartedly.

When you were staying with me at Skokholm we had many pleasant nights together watching this astonishing bird the Manx shearwater. And, therefore, you will not object if I refresh your memory by a very brief synopsis of the monograph I have just completed.

* *Shearwaters* was published in 1942.

In the first place the Manx shearwater proved, in spite of its nocturnal activities, an easy bird to handle and therefore to study. Its long wings and legs placed far back on its body make it rather helpless on land, and it is killed by gulls and hawks at every opportunity if discovered there in the day or by moonlight. For this reason it only comes to and leaves the land on sufficiently dark nights, and for the same reason it nests in the safety of burrows in the ground.

You will remember that it was only on dark moonless nights that our shearwaters held their greatest island concerts. Then they arrived in thousands, about two hours after sunset, each incoming bird giving out its unearthly crowing scream as it circled about the colony before alighting. And many of the birds which had been hidden underground all day replied, making a more muffled contribution to the general uproar. Some ten thousand pairs are estimated to nest on the 242 acres of Skokholm.

This coming to land, meeting of mates, mating, and nesting contacts are all concluded in the few hours (about midnight to 2.30 a.m.) of the summer night, and then one bird departs, leaving the other on the egg or brooding the very young chick.

The shearwater nests in a hole in the ground, sometimes deep in a rabbit-hole, but it will also excavate a hole for itself in soft ground. A small colony nested in shallow burrows within a few yards of my back door. So it was not difficult for me to trace with a stick the winding of each burrow to the nesting recess at the end, and to cut out a turf immediately above the nest and then to use that turf as a convenient inspection lid. I wish I could tell you how much pleasure I got out of this acquaintance with the individual bird. In successive seasons individuals returning to the same burrows became almost tame and quite used to handling. Of course, I had to lift them out of the nest very frequently in order to note the ring-number by which I identified them as individuals.

By degrees I was able to work out something of the Manx shearwater's life-history. The burrow would be inhabited as early in the year as February, the paired birds meeting each dark night as if they were determined to make sure of their nesting territory in good time for another season, although laying does not take place until late April and May. Ringing has since told us that the old breeders arrive first, and secure the best burrows.

There was a shortage of desirable burrows. In the absence of the legitimate pair, their burrow might be seized by a new, younger home-hunting couple. I ringed these wandering couples, of course, and found that they were moving from hole to hole like the newly married in search of the ideal home. This spring hunting was not without its comedies. I would surprise lovesick couples trying to convince each other with much crooning – for that is not an unfair description of the bird's powers of conversation – that the shelter of an old box, a plant, or some other inadequate recess was the real thing. But the light of morning would prove that these places were not dark enough and the lovers would fly out to sea before the predatory gulls and hawks discovered them. Sometimes too I would find a bird of one pair, which I had registered in our books as an established married couple, sitting in its burrow with a strange bird, an unringed bird, or at least a bird recently ringed as a newcomer to the colony. It was easy to interpret this new bird as an interloper enterprisingly on the look-out for a ready-made home, if not also a ready-made mate. This promiscuity or 'visiting' is known to exist in the fulmar petrel also. It was frequent up to the time the egg was laid. I found that after that date the pair which was properly registered, the pair which had done the donkey work, if I may use the term, the digging and enlarging and the nest-lining, and performed the evening concert of crooning, this pair settled down to incubate. The occasional visitor now seldom or never intruded upon the domestic scene. Sexes are indistinguishable in the field, but in most cases we knew the female by finding her on a new-laid egg. Only one egg is laid and incubation is equally shared. Thus, for instance, the male would spend two, three, or four days on the egg without quitting the burrow then the female would take over. On dark nights the bird at sea would return and converse with the sitting bird for an hour or two and would usually (but not necessarily) relieve it. Nor could I get any evidence that it fed its sitting mate. I came to the conclusion that the sitting bird stuck to the egg as long as hunger permitted, or as long as it could retain possession of the egg against its mate's determination to brood it.

On moonlit nights, however, this ardour to incubate was cooled by what I presume must be the bird's fear of being seen and killed by the predatory gulls and hawks which frequent the island, as already mentioned. So when a period of moonlit nights intervened the bird at sea never visited the bird on the nest at all. Thus for five, six, seven, and more rarely up to ten nights and days, when the moon happened to be near or at the full and the skies cloud-free, the sitting bird remained brooding but starving at the nest. I even weighed some of these starving birds and proved an average loss of a very small fraction of an ounce every twenty-four hours. Starving is really the wrong word, though at the time it seemed appropriate in our view. Now I have learned that a seabird can easily endure long fasts and no doubt this fact will help us to understand how the seabird survives long storms at sea, when the weather conditions are such that feeding may be impossible and the bird's energies may be entirely directed to fighting the storm.

The incubation period of the shearwater must be a record for a British breeding bird – fifty to fifty-four days. One parent remained in the burrow by day to brood the downy chick for the first week of its existence, but afterwards it was only visited by night. When the moon was bright at night the same thing happened as during incubation – the burrow was not visited at all. The young chick thus early had its first lesson in fasting. However, it was fat from the day of its birth, and showed no perceptible sign of going back during the occasional enforced fasts, in fact it seemed simply to sleep and, so to speak, consolidate the position already gained. At any rate this programme of cramming, interspersed with an occasional fast, results in the chick becoming enormously fat by the time it is sixty days old.

To our surprise we now found that the parents deserted the chick. They had spent sixty days busily gathering fish for it and many nights feeding it from the supply of semi-digested food stored in the parental crop. Now suddenly and completely they gave up all this, and stopped visiting the burrow, and probably the island, since the burrow, after all, is the only point on the island that has ever attracted them. They went off to sea and certainly would not appear on the island again until the following spring. Probably, in their winter quarters at sea they would soon be plunged deep in their moult, which takes place in the autumn. We can surmise, if we like, that the physiological state immediately preceding the moult has something to do with this, to us, rather unnatural desertion of the tender nestling.

And yet if it seems unnatural, it is at least not improvident. At this age the chick is so fat that it could scarcely waddle to the sea. If it did so and plunged over the cliffs it would drop like a pound of butter and go to pieces on the rocks below.

The chick has never been out of its burrow yet. Since its parents vanished the match-sticks which I placed at the entrance to the burrow have remained upright. (I used match-sticks a great deal in these experiments to enable me to prove whether a burrow had been visited by night, for, of course, it was impossible for me to remain watching every night.) After about six days the fledgling is beginning to thin down, and, probably feeling hungry and cramped, it now comes out of its burrow for an hour or two each dark night. It not only proves this exit by pushing over the match-sticks, but it leaves additional evidence in a trail of the natural down which it has lately moulted. These deserted chicks, sitting outside their homes at night, are a regular, if rather pathetic, feature of the island on dark nights in August and September. In the open air they can try their wings at last. They flap their wings a great deal, but do not move from near the entrance to the burrow, into which they retire before dawn. After a week of this fasting and a week of this combined fasting and exercising, the fledgeling is fully feathered and has very little down visible. It takes off for the sea at night, blundering along on all fours, using wings and legs and beak to scramble over rough ground, for it cannot fly yet. When it reaches the cliffs, over it goes and flaps down on a long plane to avoid the rocks below.

Once in the sea the young bird is safe. I have taken shearwaters at this stage and put them in the sea by day. How thirsty they are! I wonder if thirst may not be for them an important factor in drawing them to the sea, the sound of which they must hear before they leave the nest. At any rate their first action is to drink, then to wash, then suddenly they discover that they can dive. They half open their wings so that the quills remain partly spread, like a half opened fan, and with these strong paddles they swim underwater with the agility of penguins. They come up for air, and dive again, and so gradually work off to sea, making haste to leave behind the land, of which they have perhaps unpleasant memories of hunger and thirst. When a gull has swooped at a young shearwater so released by us, the shearwater has simply dived deep and swum away underwater.

The young bird is now comparatively safe, but it is quite alone, and must learn for itself how to fish, how to fly, and at last how to link up with others of its kind so that in due course it may become a successful adult.

It was a disappointment to me that of the ninety-three nestling shearwaters ringed in the colony outside our backdoor during the past eleven years none returned to their birthplace during the time – two and a half years – in which their leg-rings remained attached. Unfortunately the slender aluminium rings supplied in the earlier years were easily worn out in this short period. I have now got the Ringing Committee to supply a tougher ring and one which bears two identical inscriptions, the inner one of which is covered and protected by the overlapping of the outer end of the ring; so that if the outer inscription wears away with the attrition of salt water the inner one will still be legible as long as the ring remains on the bird's leg.

Eventually the young bird must return to the island to breed if the numbers of the shearwaters are to be maintained. That these young birds did not return to their actual birthplace in the first two years suggests that they do not remember the site with any exactness, although in their nightly vigils at fledging time there seems to have been a good opportunity to memorize the surroundings. Also it is unlikely that the shearwater breeds until it is two years old. I find that in summer

(early July especially) many 'new' shearwaters arrive on dark nights and perform courtship rites, often in situations inadequate for nesting purposes, and these birds are obviously youngsters (probably yearlings) and non-breeders, familiarizing themselves with the terrain in readiness for an earlier and genuine attempt to breed in the following year. These shearwaters, when examined, prove to have their breeding organs small and undeveloped. Probably they are stimulated to make their first return to the island of their birth on dark nights when the experienced breeders are sweeping in from the sea with their usual grand clamour. Like the adolescents in a human crowd at a race-meeting or a dance, the younger shearwaters become excited enough to want to join in the revelry. The young birds are swept up with the old ones, and find themselves screaming as they circle over the great metropolis of shearwater burrows round and about the west end of Skokholm. But when they have landed they find every burrow occupied by the breeders. Competition for a home in the shearwater city is keen, and a place can only be secured as a result of the death of an adult, or by the energetic digging of a new burrow. This competition probably drives the inexperienced bird to the perimeter, to the less crowded suburbs, even to the comparatively uninhabited wilderness where the ground is harder and a lot of pioneering necessary. Here, on its first return to land, it can play at house-making with another shearwater, on dark nights enlarging some scrape started by a rabbit, or excavating an entirely new site.

During the years 1935-8 we determined to ring as many young shearwaters as possible in order to find out how soon they returned to the island. With the help of friends 2,746 young shearwaters were ringed in these four summers at the western metropolis. Sixteen were subsequently recovered there in the following years. Of these only one was recovered within a year of its birth – that is on 22nd April 1939 following the year, 1938, of its hatching from the egg. The rest were recovered: one in the June following, four in the July following, nine in the second year, and one in the third year following birth.

It is only by extensive ringing of large numbers of seabirds that we can uncover something of their life-histories. During the years of our occupation of Skokholm up to the end of 1939, with the help of visiting friends, 17,761 shearwaters have been ringed here, including the 2,746 young birds mentioned above.

I wish I had room here to give you the details of the several interesting recoveries that have resulted from this ringing, but I must be patient and wait until I can send you the monograph in book form, by which time, however, I hope you will be free again.

There is only space here to refer to the group of shearwaters that were recovered in the south part of the Bay of Biscay, and by their recovery there proved beyond doubt that the adult shearwater may leave the egg or the young chick and fly six hundred miles south to feed in Basque and north Spanish waters, while its mate takes up the brooding for a spell of a few days. The first record was of a shearwater ringed on 15th April as an active breeder at Skokholm; it was washed up on the shore near Bordeaux on 5th June. Another adult ringed at Skokholm on 7th May was taken at sea off Lequeitio (N. Spain) seven days later! A third was first ringed at Skokholm on 29th April 1937. It was recovered at Skokholm in 1938 and again on 25th April 1939. In May 1939 it was taken off the coast of Landes, and its ring is now in the Biarritz museum. These recoveries were followed – and are still being followed – by similar evidence: tried breeders at Skokholm being found during the nesting season in the Bay of Biscay. Most of these recoveries are due to the guns and nets of Biscayan fishermen, who shoot seabirds for food, for bait, and for the sake of discovering if the birds are feeding on sardines, and if so, where to set their nets.

This remarkable flow of shearwaters between the Pembrokeshire islands and the Bay of Biscay during the summer months, by the way, has since been measured by observers on the cliffs at Land's End. One watcher estimated that 43,200 shearwaters passed southwards in three hours on one April morning. This migration is found to be intense only in the morning. No obvious northward movement is recorded; presumably the birds return on a broad front farther to sea.

Yours ever.

27th July 1940

MY DEAR JOHN – Marjorie has sent me your delightful *Prisoner to the Singing Bird* of 16th May, written from your internment camp in Norway, on hearing a chiffchaff:

Sing on, sing on, beyond the walls,
That I within may know
Spring is in the woods again,
Where you may go.

Sing, sing on, then in my cage
I shall delight to hear
That you are glad and free out there
So near, so near!

What pleasant memories of the past and what hope for the future the song must have brought to you! As it brings to us on this desolate storm-swept island each March, when we first see the slender small greenish-brown form actively hunting for insects in the garden or the heather or the cliffs, or leaping into the air to snatch a fly, or more rarely hear it singing from some vantage point such as the stay-wires of our flagstaff.

I told you in an earlier letter that the first chiffchaff arrived here on 9th March this year, but usually it is in the last two weeks of March that we get them, and they are then frequent up to the middle of April, with odd birds in May, June, and July. The autumn migration sets in during the latter half of August and continues for two months, ending in mid October.

The other *Phylloscopus* which we find quite abundantly here on passage is, of course, the willow warbler, larger and yellower than the chiffchaff, which arrives as a rule about 6th April (this year 1st April), and is then seen almost daily until early June. You will remember that when you were staying here you drew up some graphs from our records showing the rise and fall in the numbers of migrating warblers at Skokholm in the years 1933-8. That for the willow warbler rose sharply from the early part to the end of April when it was at its height, and there were 'rushes' of willow warblers also in the first days of May. The island swarms with them on certain days in spring and in autumn. On 23rd August last year, for instance, there were at least 700 present, of which we trapped 130. (But the next day they were almost all gone, and we only ringed two.) 23rd August was in fact a record day for trapping small birds. Our total was 252, including 105 common whitethroats, 9 spotted flycatchers, 4 sedge warblers, 1 garden warbler, and 3 wheatears.

The common whitethroat, excepting that it arrives two weeks later than the willow warbler, has a similar migration, and is almost as numerous with us on passage. Odd birds (not counting the nesting pair in 1931 and 1932) may be seen here during midsummer, and until the autumn passage begins early in August. The last whitethroats leave us in mid September and the last willow warblers about the same time or slightly later (one was here on 9th October last year).

I have been puzzled to account for the considerable passage migration of these two common *Sylviidae* during late May, at a time when nest-building and egg laying is in full swing among the mature adults of these species. But after handling many of them, caught in our cages here, I feel sure that the majority of these individuals are birds which were hatched only a year before; that is to say they have never bred before and they have only experienced one migration – the southward one. They are in fact novices, lacking the experience of the travelled breeding bird of two years of age and above, and they are largely 'feeling' their way back north in the direction of the land of their birth. Lacking experience, with their sexual organs less developed than the older birds, these yearlings are in fact in no hurry to breed, and are inexpertly moving north. They have partly lost their way, you might say, or are meandering with the idleness of youth, having time seeming illimitable before them.

This view is encouraged by the obviously young appearance of these migrating warblers both spring and autumn. In the willow warbler the yellow is most pronounced in the late migrants, so that they appear almost a distinct race from the duller, more olive-green adults seen in April. And the late-arriving whitethroat has almost a dull-brown head compared with the rich grey of the head of the early migrant.

I suppose the majority of our 'rushes' of migrants – which commonly occur after the mature adults of these species are already established and have started breeding in their mainland summer quarters – are composed of young and inexperienced birds, and if we reflect this seems a reasonable supposition. For the travelled adult of two or three summers is likely to bound on ahead with strength and confidence, his maturity urging him to get to the breeding ground with the least delay, and his experience guiding him surely to the very site of last year's nest. Whereas the yearling, flying without confidence or guidance, is impelled only by an inherited instinct (the same blind instinct which taught him to struggle out of the egg and respond to the feeding pattern of his parents while still a sightless chick), is more easily disturbed by those natural phenomena of storms and fogs which result in their appearance on remote islands, in what we call 'rushes' of migrants.

It is not only these large 'rushes' of common migrants that are composed principally of (in the spring) yearling and (in autumn) juvenile birds. Rarer birds visiting here such as red-backed shrike, nightjar, black redstart, cuckoo, Lapland bunting and ortolan, garden warbler and blackcap – to name a few at random – are usually juveniles or yearlings: confirming that they have lost their way because of their inexperience as migrants.

If all birds were to fly with the assuredness of the fully-adult we should, I venture to think, see very little migration of the small woodland and bush warblers on remote islands, so far out of their natural sheltered breeding habitat, except occasionally in or after the severest storms. And something of the charm and pleasure of studying birds here would be lost; for we should not be able to handle them so freely as we do now.

In order of abundance on migration here the willow warbler is first, then the common whitethroat, followed by the chiffchaff and sedge warbler. The grasshopper warbler is a regular spring visitor, creeping tamely about the buildings, even entering the house. Blackcap and garden warbler occur only in very small numbers, late each spring and very rarely in the autumn, the garden warbler more often than the blackcap. Still more rare is the lesser whitethroat; one stray individual appeared here on 3rd November 1927 after a severe storm.

I wish I could give you a fuller list of the soft-billed birds, but, situated as we are to the west of the mainland mass of Britain, we do not get any of those warblers which nest principally in the south-east of England, such as the reed-warbler and the marsh-warbler. And we never see the nightingale here.

The best I can do is to send to you some time a complete list of all the birds recorded here, placing them in two categories: a census of pairs of breeding birds (over thirteen years), and a list of all birds seen. The compiling of such local lists is usually the first step in bird study; I remember it as a great joy when I became an observer at an early age, and before I began to find the study of the individual bird more satisfying than the collecting of mere lists of birds.

Ever yours.

40. THE PHENOMENON OF MIGRATION

4th August 1940

DEAR J.B. – The migration of animals, including whales, seals, caribou and other deer, lemmings, birds, butterflies and other insects, has excited the wonder and admiration of centuries of observers. In olden times these movements were attributed to the supernatural and were put down as portents and auguries of significance to the human community and individual. Today we know a little better, but there are still problems of migration unsolved. We now believe that migration was encouraged by the movement of the polar ice cap. At one time luxurant forests grew as far north as Spitzbergen, where now only dwarf plants and mosses greet the brief Arctic summer. Since then ice has moved south and for a while covered all Britain, and now once more it has retreated. With the slow exposure of new lands by the melting ice the animals have learned to migrate to follow the summer, up to the land of the midnight sun. Thus caribou move north in vast herds with the spring, and those that prey on caribou follow – men and wolves.

Birds, with their superior mobility, have been most able to take advantage of this new territory, and have flown to the edge of the ice in the summer. The swift melting of the snows uncovers the wild fruits which the early winter preserved in its refrigerating grasp. Billions of insects hatch out to enjoy the long hours of sunlight, and there is abundant food for the short period during which the migrants are able to nest and rear their young. Then winter swiftly returns and the birds fly south again.

It is generally true, I think, that the farther north a migratory bird breeds, the farther south it winters. Competition for breeding places and food drove the bird to migrate in the first place; and in flying south it passed over the central and equatorial areas already occupied by less mobile species, to winter far south in conditions similar to those of its breeding grounds. Familiar examples are the golden plover and the tern; while the British-breeding swallow is an example of migration between two temperate areas: our isles and South Africa. There are, of course, many degrees of migration between, from seasonal movements within the British Isles, or within Europe and north Africa, down to the limited movements of more resident birds, and some birds do not migrate at all.

In Spitzbergen and Greenland and on Scottish mountains, ptarmigan are resident, even through the severest winter. On Skokholm the raven and some of our rock pipits and a few great black-backed and herring gulls are also sedentary throughout the year. Plainly they are dominant species and get enough food to enable them to live satisfactorily without migrating.

But if food and competition for nesting sites are the main incentives to the migration of less dominant and hardy species, this explanation only tells us why birds migrate. It does not tell us *how* birds are able to migrate, or what guides the bird on migration.

How does the young petrel or shearwater or puffin, deserted by its parents, find its way to the wintering ground of its species alone?

How does the young warbler, living alone after its parents have started another brood or gone into moult, find its way unaided to its winter quarters in Africa? Most young birds move south before their parents, with the exception of the young cuckoo which leaves the country some time in August and September, the adult cuckoos having departed in July.

There is a plausible fable, still regarded as true in the minds of the average person one questions on the subject, that the old birds lead the way on migration. But as far back as Temminck there were ornithologists who knew otherwise. Temminck says that 'the young birds migrate apart from the old ones'. While Gatke of Heligoland wrote that he agreed with Temminck, but that 'the last ten to fifteen years have amply taught me what an almost hopeless task it is at first sight to oppose an opinion which has remained uncontested for centuries.'

You cannot live long on a small island like mine without being aware that the young bird needs no adult to guide it along the traditional migration route, and that it actually initiates the first move southwards in the autumn. In fact it is safe to say that, always excepting that exceptional bird the cuckoo, and seabirds, the old fully adult breeding bird is the last to leave the nesting area in the autumn just as it is the first to return to it in the spring.

Thus, as early as June, and until the end of July, considerable flocks of young starlings in their conspicuously drab grey-brown plumage arrive on Skokholm. The adults do not arrive until three months later. Young willow warblers in bright yellow dress are to be seen from the end of June to the end of August, at which time the paler adults are caught in our migratory bird-traps. And juvenile white wagtails precede the adults in autumn.

Young wheatears and young meadow pipits, with a sprinkling of young rock pipits, are on the move then, though it is not easy to distinguish the true migrants from the island-bred youngsters. And in fact we often catch in the traps young birds of these species which have already been ringed in the nest on the island. The adult wheatears and pipits remain with us until after the majority of young birds of these species have moved on during August and September.

From these few observations it is clear that the young bird in migrating is acting as blindly, or shall we say – to cover up our ignorance – as instinctively, as the brainless caterpillar that lays a silk thread across a leaf and waits for the thread to dry and shrink and roll up the leaf so that it has a shelter in which to pupate, or as instinctively as the wasp which paralyses the living grub by stinging the nervous ganglia, and then places two such living but helpless grubs in a cell along with her egg – the egg and the living food are sealed up in a chamber of salivated dust or pulp and the wasp goes away to die.

There is no satisfactory answer to this problem of how the young bird migrates without an experienced leader. We only recognize that it does and that therefore it is an inherited ability, unreasoned and as natural as the act of a baby sucking at the breast. It is as automatically begun or 'released' by certain stimuli. In the case of birds the annual moult is an important factor. Most adult birds are in perfect plumage during migration: most young birds are in their first full plumage which they retain until midwinter. Adults (of landbirds) usually moult after nesting at their breeding grounds and are thus unable to migrate until their new plumage is acquired. But seabirds – whose habits are so different from landbirds – usually moult in their wintering grounds, e.g. petrels and shearwaters, gannets and puffins desert their young and go off to moult at sea in the autumn. Guillemots and razorbills take their young with them to sea.

When I visited the bird observatory at Heligoland in the autumn of 1936 I was shown newly caught redstarts in cages with perches electrically sensitized so that any activity of the bird was recorded on a tape which registered both the time and the amount of the activity. In this way it was found that during the migratory season the redstarts were restless and beat their wings for a certain number of hours during the night. This illustrated for me vividly the powerful and automatic nature of the impulse to migrate. Other workers have successfully induced birds to sing and migrate at the wrong time of year by artificially stimulating them with light, food, and exercise.

Is this ability to migrate at certain times of the year inherited in birds which are hatched and reared artificially by man entirely without sight of their parents? It would be interesting but rather difficult to find this out by an experiment with aviary-reared birds. There is a theory that much of the birds' natural wisdom is somehow 'imprinted' during the first few hours of its life in contact with its parents and nest mates.

I could go on almost indefinitely 'thinking aloud' about migration but, apart from the above observations, would only conclude in the end that migration is a very interesting phenomenon indeed, and that, in spite of all experiments so far, it remains as much a riddle as life itself.

Yours.

41. THE HOMING OF BIRDS

DEAR JOHN – In my last letter I outlined the present knowledge of the migration of birds, only to prove to you how little is really known of the nature or mechanism of this most useful phenomenon.

When you stayed here in 1939 you helped me to carry out some experiments with the object of testing the power of orientation in seabirds, a power which is an essential part of the migratory function. You will therefore be glad to have a brief sketch of these experiments and their results.

Most spectacular was the first return, that of a Manx shearwater released at Start Point, South Devon, and which homed in some ten hours. It had been taken by boat from Skokholm to the mainland of Pembrokeshire and thence by train to South Devon. On its return this bird must have travelled two hundred miles in ten hours in order to get around the Land's End to Skokholm. This would represent a speed of at least twenty miles an hour, not allowing any deviation in flight, or pause to drink, feed, and bathe. The normal flight of a shearwater is a fast swinging glide, at a speed perhaps of thirty to forty miles an hour. It would appear at first that the Start Point shearwater, therefore, had only a small margin of time for natural deviation of flight, and for recuperative feeding and resting. But this presupposes that the shearwater knew instantly and exactly where it was, and wasted no hours in considering the direction it had to travel to get to its nest on Skokholm.

There is, of course, the possibility that the bird returned in a direct line between the two places, involving only half the distance of the sea journey, if it crossed the Devon peninsula. The experiment raised all these questions, but proved beyond doubt only one: that *the shearwater was able to get home quickly to Skokholm from Start Point.*

It was a step to have proved this. Subsequently shearwaters safely homed to Skokholm from the Firth of Forth, and from the mist-wrapped Faroe Islands, half way between Scotland and Iceland. A storm petrel homed from the Isle of May, while both storm petrels and puffins homed from Start Point. Finally a shearwater, taken from its nest on a Faroe bird-cliff and released near Edinburgh, returned to the Faroes, where its arrival was being watched for by a Faroe bird-fowler.

Now all these releases were made within the known geographical range of these seabirds. We desired, however, to proceed slowly and, by testing their homing capacities gradually, to avoid as far as possible undue distress to the birds. One test we wished and yet were reluctant to make was of their homing power from inland localities. We felt that such an oceanic bird would be confused without sight of the sea within its view. We have always been sceptical of the late T.A. Coward's theory, expounded in his well-known *Birds of the British Isles*, that Manx shearwaters regularly migrate in a southerly direction across England in the autumn. He deduced this from the records of shearwaters which, over a period of more than a hundred years, have been picked up dead inland from August to October. Now this season is just the period when the young shearwaters are leaving for the first time the burrows on Welsh and Scillonian islets where they were hatched. Deserted by their parents, and driven by hunger to scramble by night to the sea, they are for weeks after in a thin and weak condition. Equinoctial storms sweep many of them inland when they at last get on the wing, and in our opinion it is almost entirely young birds of the year that fall by the English inland wayside.

Thanks to the researches carried out by my friend Mr W.E. Kenrick of Birmingham, and the kindness of the Meteorological Office, it has been proved that these records of shearwaters inland are all associated with spells of south-westerly gales, or violent storms from the direction of the Atlantic.

In 1936 we chose two adult shearwaters from nest-burrows which contained no egg or chick. In the spirit of scientific inquiry into Coward's theory, W.E. Kenrick released one of these at Birmingham, and A.J.

Harthan a second at Evesham. It was these releases which brought a mild protest from – curiously enough – a submarine flotilla commander. We ourselves were uneasy about them, although we did not expect them to return to Skokholm again in 1936. It has been with mixed feelings then that we recovered the Evesham bird in its burrow early in 1937, mixed because we were delighted to know that it was safe and sound, and startled to realize that after all the homing power of this seabird is not impaired by the presence of land mass between it and its seagirt home. This success led us to repeat the experiment in 1937. The same observers each released one of another pair of shearwaters (again with no nesting cares) at Evesham and Birmingham. Both birds safely returned, this time within a few days.

We were making progress. We had established an important fact, that the shearwater can home over land as well as over sea. This point was proved further by sending a Skokholm shearwater to Manchester and another to Limerick, Ireland. Both were recaptured on Skokholm within a few days.

More brilliant was the homing of two adults (from separate nests) which were released over Frensham Ponds, Surrey, at dusk on 8th June. Both circled round at a height of about five hundred feet, then setting off between south and west. Were they trying to orientate themselves, perhaps to find the English Channel – sure guide, to a human way of thinking, to the home seas of the west? Both birds must have travelled fast and surely with little pause, for both were the very first of many thousands of shearwaters to land on the island on the next evening, 9th June. We found each brooding its egg shortly before midnight.

The moment had now arrived for the greatest test of all, that of the ability of the shearwater to return home when released well outside the limits of the known geographical range of its species. But first some shearwaters were released in the southern and western parts of the North Atlantic, which however, is within their winter range. All these distant Atlantic releases were made later in the year when the birds had finished family cares for the season. We did not expect to recover them in 1936.

On 8th May 1937 we recovered the first of these Atlantic released birds, one that had been set free in lat. 43° N, long. 9° W, that is, off Cape Finisterre. This is the only recovery of that particular batch of releases, but it is possible that others may have returned and slipped into the depths of their burrows in the many nights during the breeding season when we were unable to maintain a watch. There is a limit to human endurance and it has, of course, been impossible to keep anything like a regular midnight vigil. The element of luck must necessarily figure largely in future recoveries of birds which have failed to turn up after the first week or so of vigil kept for them immediately following their release.

The non-recoveries and the deterioration in the health of the birds

during the voyage of several days deterred us from sending further seabirds across the Atlantic. Instead two shearwaters were sent by air to Venice, both crates arriving at their destination within twenty-four hours of leaving Skokholm.

Of these shearwaters one had already homed from Frensham, Surrey, in a day. It was released with the other on a lagoon in the Adriatic south of Venice on 9th July 1937 by the kindness of the British consul there, Mr Alan Napier, who later wrote that 'the birds, which were first dipped in the water, and then thrown simultaneously into the air, flew off strongly in a southerly direction, but one of them had wheeled off towards the west when last seen.' Both shearwaters had left behind them on Skokholm mates, each engaged in hatching a well-incubated egg. Two weeks passed, during which one sitter deserted the egg; the other sitter did not leave its burrow until it had brought off its chick. Even then it did not go off to gather fish-food, but brooded the youngster and kept it warm and dry for the first few days.

The Manx shearwater does not, as far as I know, wander as far as the Mediterranean at any season of the year. Therefore, imagine our delight when exactly a fortnight later we found one of the Venice birds – the Frensham homer – in its burrow, engaged in a noisy discussion with its stay-at-home mate and week-old chick (which it was greeting for the first time)!

How did this shearwater find her way home from Venice? She had taken 14 days, 5 hours, and 10 minutes to (1) negotiate 3,700 miles by sea, or (2) cross Europe direct in 930 straight miles. In terms of plain arithmetic if she had negotiated (1) a sea-passage by the Straits of Messina and Gibraltar, she had travelled at a speed of nearly eleven miles an hour day and night, without food, rest, or deviation. However, it is safe to double the bee-line speed in order to arrive at the actual average surface speed of a shearwater. This gives us twenty-two miles an hour for the journey. If we allow six hours a day for resting and feeding, we must increase this speed by one-quarter, and so we get a speed of nearly thirty miles an hour. This is nearer the true flight speed of the Manx shearwater; but even so it presupposes that the bird had a comprehensive knowledge of the topography of the Mediterranean – and this we cannot grant to a bird that had never been there. It argues that she was capable of flying south-east for five hundred miles down the Adriatic, directly away from Skokholm, with the knowledge that once through the Strait of Otranto she could fly south-west for the Strait of Messina, and thence due west for Gibraltar. Then, and then only, once clear of Cape St Vincent in Portugal, could she head directly north for Skokholm.

Could she do all this? There is a small margin of time and speed to account for. We can allow her to waste one-quarter of her time in finding her way by sea; that would increase her speed to forty miles an hour, about the average speed of a bird in good condition. There is just the possibility, then, that, given the above allowances, she did find her way by sea. But for myself I find it hard to believe that she resisted the mysterious 'pull' of home so far as to fly directly away from it in unknown waters, or that she could ever find her way so quickly by sea. I feel that the probability is she took some shorter cut, perhaps over the Italian Apennines to the Gulf of Genoa (Mr Napier noticed that one bird flew west, landwards, after release), and then across France to the Bay of Biscay, which, as we have seen, is the haunt of Skokholm shearwaters nearest to the Mediterranean. This course is more in line with whatever influence Skokholm might exercise at that distance.

Of course, if this 'pull' exists and can act strongly, then the bird should have flown directly across Europe to Skokholm, that is to say, right across the High Alps and France, 930 miles as the crow flies. In that case, at a surface speed of ten miles an hour, she ought to have been home in four days. Did she reach home waters, perhaps, in that time, and then rest and feed for ten days? This seems too long a period of recuperation.

No; I incline to the belief that she, by some sense, some physical mechanism unknown to man, aware that Skokholm lay approximately just so (in our language, north-west) from Venice, flew in that direction, but after crossing Italy she was diverted by the sight of the Gulf of Genoa. After resting and feeding there, she continued her westerly flight, which brought her into the Gulf of Lyons. Here she was embayed, and found herself obliged to strike homewards over the south of France. This course would bring her to the Bay of Biscay. Here, in the sardine-filled waters, she could rest and feed among other Skokholm shearwaters. And here, perhaps, she acquired that fat and glossy appearance which we noted on finding her home at the nest with mate and chick.

The other Venice-released shearwater did not return – or at least I failed to find her – until 30th March next year.

These two successes told us that the shearwater is able to return when released in distant, almost land-locked seas previously unknown to

them, hundreds of miles from home. They had, to quote a definition by
B.B. Riviere, who has experimented with homing pigeons, a very strong
'sense of geographical position'.

The experiments were completed by those releases of shearwaters
in the High Alps in which you assisted, John, in 1939. Twelve adults
were sent by air to Switzerland. Three were released on a little hill near
Basle, nearest point in Switzerland to Skokholm; three were released
at Lugano, farthest point in Switzerland from Skokholm; three were
released at Andermatt, near the St Gothard Pass; and three were released
on a snow-covered hillside near Berne.

Of these twelve, one released near Berne returned to Skokholm
in thirteen days; two released near Andermatt were recovered to the
westward, dead, in the valley; and, surprisingly, of the three released
furthest from Skokholm, at Lugano, two returned safely, one in ten days,
the other in fifteen days. These were rather hard tests, and evidently
some birds have a stronger homing-sense than others, but too many
factors operate as potential 'hazards' for us to say much more about
the few failures. We have only proved that this wonderful power of
returning home from alien inland country as well as from unknown
Mediterranean seas is very strong in the Manx shearwater, a bird which
is usually never out of sight or hearing of the Atlantic.

Yours.

42. CORMORANT AND SHAG

D EAR JOHN – Cormorants and shags, like the poor, we always have with us. And these rather dull, heavy, and reptilian birds do not excite much admiration. They are to be seen every day here, fishing in the sea or flying past the cliffs (shags rarely and cormorants often fly across the island) or resting on the rocks, especially on the Stack.

Yet though numerous they do not nest with us, above one and sometimes two pairs of shags. There are, however, colonies of these birds on the Pembrokeshire islands of Skomer and Ramsey, and on St Margaret's and Cardigan Island. The cormorants invariably choose a south-facing aspect, but the shags seem to prefer either a north-facing site or the darkness of some ledge high up within a cave.

They are much alike in their habits, diving for fish and swimming sinuously and rapidly underwater with great oared feet thrusting like propellers but with wings closed. Both usually take a little leap out of the water and dive in to give them an impetus, but I have also watched both dive without a splash merely by sinking down as if pulled from below by some submerged force. They seem to feed largely on the coarse inshore fish such as small conger eels, pollack, wrasse, and whiting which are not of any value commercially. I believe that you have studied the diving of the shag, and will agree that their dives are much shorter than those of their fishing rivals, the seals, averaging under a minute, although you record an individual dive of 170 seconds. I think that the fish if small is gulped down underwater, for it is only the larger fish that seem to require raising to the surface for beating and shuffling into the head-first position for swallowing.

I have had few opportunities of studying the courtship and breeding of the cormorant, but I believe it very similar to that of the shag. The cormorant wears then a panoply of black with a shiny blue tinge, a clear white throat and thigh patch; and the feathers of the back and sides are a rich bronze each margined with iridescent blue. It is truly resplendent then – a royal bird of the netherworld. A fisherman once told me that the shag was the cormorant's maidservant, and pointed to the crest which the shag wears in the spring as suggestive of a maid's serving cap. This fancy is a not unpleasing one, for if you know these birds well enough you can imagine the cormorants, dressed in their royal blue and black and bronze and with white panels, airing themselves in the best sun-parlours of the cliffs, while the sombre brown-black shag lives in the dark holes and sunless back regions and corners and caves.

Shags nest here in a cranny in Mad Bay which only receives the sun for an hour as it dips down into the north-west sea. They have afforded me many a half-hour of pleasant observation as I gazed down on them from the cliff top, eighty feet above their ledge. Here minute ferns grow where the surface water from the island seeps through the dark red stone; razorbills nest in the broken part of the cliff, and opposite, where a high shoulder of rock turns its lichened side to the sun, is the crevice where the ravens usually nest. I have cautiously shown my head only above the cliff edge, and unnoticed by the shags have watched their serpentine courtship on April days. The hen would sometimes be alone in the nest. Presently the cock would arrive with some twig or piece of flotsam picked up at sea. The hen would 'make faces' at him by darting her head towards the male, opening the mouth to show the warm yellow interior (which stands out vividly against the black plumage and the dark rocks). She would vibrate the pouchy skin hanging about her throat at the same time, and throw her tail up. Then she might seize the twig and amuse herself placing it in the nest and pressing it in with breast and feet: thus was the nest made. The hen might then resume the gaping and darting and vibrating display, growing more and more excited if the cock waddled nearer to her. He would raise his head and gape back at her in the same extraordinary reptilian fashion. She appears most excited, and ends by erecting her tail over her back as the male springs upon her.

Cormorants are greater wanderers than shags, which are practically

sedentary: of 81 shags which I ringed on Lambay Island, near Dublin, in June 1939, 7 have been recovered, all in Irish waters, some as far west as Co. Kerry and Galway, and 1 as far east as Anglesey in the Irish Sea.

Of 200 cormorants ringed at the same time on Lambay, 40 have subsequently been recovered on Irish shores, 2 in south-west Scotland, 2 in Wales, 9 in Devon and Cornwall, 3 in France, and 1 in Asturias, north Spain. Thus the majority of Irish breeding cormorants are stay-at-homes. It is curious that of 131 cormorants ringed in various years in Pembrokeshire only 1 has reached Ireland; 8 others have been reported from England (chiefly Devon and Cornwall) and the rest – 24 – have been recovered along the shores of the Bay of Biscay.

From these figures it will be seen that nearly one-third of the ringed cormorants, but less than ten per cent of the ringed shags, have been recovered by man, and we can safely say that the majority have been shot by jealous fishermen. The cormorant has suffered most simply because it is less strictly marine and is often found fishing in fresh water. It may even risk a visit to trout hatcheries where several of our ringed cormorants have been shot by angry keepers. Cormorants will take trout gluttonously, in fact one cormorant ringed in Pembrokeshire in 1934 was found dead at Llanelly five and a half years later, choked by a fine three-quarter-pound trout.

Yours.

43 · MIGRATION OF THE GANNET

17th August 1940

MY DEAR J – I was interested to see in the fourth volume of the *Handbook of British Birds*, just issued by the publishers, some details of the migration of the gannet, including two maps which show the localities of winter recoveries of gannets ringed in summer at breeding stations in the British Isles. The majority of the recoveries marked on these maps are the result of our ringing work at Grassholm, where in ten years we have ringed 3,700 gannets. I exhibited similar maps when giving a lecture at the Royal Institution in November 1938.

Out of this total of 3,700 ringed, 170 have been recovered, that is 4·3 per cent. 18 of these were recovered where ringed, at the nest; 60 in home waters, on or near the shores of England, Ireland, Wales, and Scotland; and 92 abroad, principally from Brittany south to Capes Blanco and Ghir, West Africa.

Analysis of these recoveries abroad bring to light an interesting truth about their migration: it is that the young bird of the year migrates farthest south during the winter. Thus, taking the recoveries of young birds reported from 1st November to the end of February, none of the Grassholm juveniles is found in home waters. Seven of these under-one-year-olds are as far south as the tropic of Capricorn in the region of Mauretania and Cape Blanco, two are off western Morocco, two near Cadiz in Spain, and two in the Bay of Biscay.

Now look at the recoveries of birds a year older, that is the under-two-year-old birds. Of eleven reported all are in or near the Bay of Biscay and English Channel in the four winter months, except for two which are reported on the seas between Cornwall and Ireland. While of ten birds above this age all are in home waters from Dover south-westwards to the Severn and Irish seas. (Saving one reported off north-west Portugal.)

This is a pleasant reward for many days of effort at Grassholm with good friends, laboriously walking over the stinking debris of rotted seaweed and decaying fish, the whole warmed by the summer sun, amid the white glare of six thousand adult gannets sitting determinedly on six thousand nests containing altogether six thousand (or rather fewer) eggs or young! This labour we look back upon with pleasure now, and its results are most interesting, as they form a complete picture of the migration of the gannet.

We can now visualize the young gannet, deserted by its parents, awaiting at the nest the moment when hunger shall have thinned it down sufficiently for it to be light enough to flap, with wings which have been very much exercised during the last few days, downwards to the sea. The fledgeling gannet cannot fly, but it can beat its wings and steer a course to avoid the rocks as it slants downwards to the sea. Once on the sea it is a swimmer of some power, using its great webbed feet to drive itself forward at least as fast as the fastest human swimmer. At first, as far as I have been able to observe in following these young gannets in a boat, it does not dive. It is probably a long time before it learns to feed in the traditional gannet manner, by plunging from a height. For to do this it must learn to fly. How soon it learns to fly must depend much on the weather. If fresh breezes greet it soon after it leaves the gannetry it is doubtless encouraged to take off into the air from a wave-top fairly quickly. If the gales are very severe (as they sometimes are towards the equinox in September, about the time of the mass fledging of the gannets) the young bird is often too inexperienced to face this trial, and if the gales blow it on to a lee shore it may be battered to death. I have found many young gannets killed in this manner on the mainland beaches of Pembrokeshire after severe autumnal gales blowing from the direction of Grassholm.

The power of flight and of diving for food comes to the young gannet, and it moves southwards to warmer seas in company with others of its age. There is none to guide them; they are impelled, we must suppose, by that same subconscious inherited vision or 'wisdom' which secured for other young untried migrants their visas for the winter route. Nor do we know what 'subconscious' barriers determine the halting point when they reach the limit (known to us by ringing to be the Senegal coast) of their winter range. This actually touches the winter range of the black-tailed or Cape gannet (*Sula capensis*); but as our winter season is the summer season of the Cape gannet, they probably meet only accidentally.

After its first winter the year-old gannet seems to move north again, but not necessarily back to its birthplace. One sees extremely few gannets in the dark-backed, white-breasted yearling plumage at Grassholm, and very few in the mottled two-year-old plumage either. They are more frequent at sea. Thus we find one of our ringed gannets just over two years old recovered in the North Sea in its second July and another Grassholm gannet also just two years old reported from the Faroe Islands in July.

It seems clear that as the gannet matures it is less inclined to migrate in the winter, and finally as an adult it seems to remain permanently within a few hundred miles of its breeding ground. As it is a colonial nester, it is jealous of nesting sites, and like other community nesters, such as guillemots and gulls, will assemble at the breeding-place long before the egg is laid. Grassholm is occupied from mid-February to the early part of October, and once nest building begins in March the pair seem to take it in turn to guard the home; if they did not do this the nesting material of grass and seaweed would quickly be pilfered by neighbours.

This competition may be an added incentive to the adult to remain near home.

How near home do they remain in the summer? Again ringing helps us to answer this interesting question. Adult gannets ringed at Grassholm as breeders have been killed in fishermen's nets at sea, 80 miles (on three occasions), 140 miles, and 160 miles from home. This may seem a fair distance to go fishing, but in terms of the direct powerful flight of the gannet it is just an hour or two away.

Many of the recoveries of gannets abroad are due to their being accidently caught by fishermen, in nets and on lines and sometimes by shooting, especially in the Bay of Biscay. One ringed gannet was caught on board a warship. If I had more space I could tell you of many curious recoveries of ringed wild birds, but much of this and other information about our recoveries has been published in scientific journals. I am so glad to hear that some of these are now reaching your library in the prison camp, and these I hope will be of some intellectual solace.

I will end this letter with yet another fact which ringing has given us. The adult gannet returns to the same nest year after year; that is to say, we have recovered in subsequent years several adults in or near the same nesting site where they were first ringed. The record so far is held by an adult first ringed six years previous to its latest recovery. Of course, one would expect adults to return to the familiar nesting site, as I have proved to be the case with so many other species mentioned in these letters. But the expected, as you know, does not always happen!

Very best wishes.

19th August 1940

DEAR JOHN – As I have had a special opportunity of making a film of this bird, I cannot very well leave the gannet without completing my notes on its interesting life-history. What we have learned from ringing I have already set down, and the years ahead will doubtless provide more recoveries of ringed birds to complete our knowledge of its migration and longevity.

Gannets begin laying in April. But as far back as February they gather at the gannetry. Many other colonial-nesting seabirds assemble thus early on their breeding ground. It is the experienced old gannets that are the first to assemble – the young birds being still in Mauretanian and West African waters. They do so apparently because their breeding organs become enlarged early in the year, and also there is a genuine need to be early at the colony so as to secure a site for the nest.

Once the gannets come to settle at the gannetry, the nest is occupied continuously until the young are ready to fly. I gave you a good reason for this. If one or other of the mated pair did not always stand guard at the nest it would be quickly seized by a pair without a nest. And once on the nest the bird in possession seems to be filled with a fury to defend it that is usually successful even against the 'lawful' owners. Moreover, if the gannet leaves its nest unprotected, all the hard-won nest-lining of grass and seaweed is instantly thieved by one or other of the adjoining circle of nesting gannets, who by craning their necks can just touch the perimeter of neighbouring nests. For although nesting in close community the gannet is a quarrelsome bird, ever ready to peck and steal from its neighbours.

At Grassholm the nests are composed largely of grass and seaweed. The grass is plucked from the green eastern side of the island. During March and April this side of the island, viewed from Skokholm, shows

at times a white patch. A powerful telescope reveals that this is due to a large group of gannets plucking grass, a whole steady stream from the 12,000 individuals of the gannetry flying down, settling, plucking grass, and going back to their nesting pedestals along the western cliff of the island.

On the nest, which year by year becomes more and more raised by constant additions plastered down by voidings and refuse, is performed the ceremony or dance of the gannet which is the expression of the birds' emotion not only during the courtship or pre-egg stage, but also long after the chick is hatched. A lone bird when thus excited, raises but does not unfold the wings, throws the neck up with a graceful movement, and then bows three or more times, the bright steely bill being thrust each time under one or other of the raised wings with an odd nodding, twisting, snake-like movement of the head. The movements end with a stately, almost a smug, drawing up of the head and neck to the normal slightly arched position, and a final shaking of the pointed tail.

When the pair are together this ceremony is also attempted, the birds facing each other, breast to breast. The excitement is greater, the wings are much wider open, but there is no room for the bowing movements although these are attempted. They result in what is almost an intertwining of their necks. The bills come together, pointing heavenwards, and the nodding and twisting of the head begins. As a result bill strikes upon bill with quite a sharp clatter and at the same time the birds utter their strident 'urrah' note. This bill-beating may go on for two or three minutes without pause.

Another interesting attitude seems not to be associated with joyous excitement, but is, or looks as if it were, induced by fear. The bill is pointed rigidly upwards as the bird turns slowly round on the nest, seeming to look warily at the neighbours, as if saying to itself: 'I'm taking off now. Hope it won't be a crash, but if so, may I be spared the worst.' And suddenly with a loud groan the performer leaps into the air. If the nest is near the cliff edge it usually gets away easily, but in taking off from the more level ground, unless there is a high wind to help, the bird usually fails to fly clear, and crashes through the assembled ranks of nesting adults. These stab it mercilessly, inflicting only very minor wounds, however, or merely pulling a few feathers out.

One wonders indeed that the gannet should be so sociable in the breeding season, for it is thoroughly anti-social in most other ways. It will make no attempt to defend its neighbour's egg or chick from the thieving herring- and great black-backed gulls or human beings. Its attention is directed solely on its own affairs. There it sits, incubating the single greenish-white egg by laying its webbed feet, overlapped, *on top of the egg*. There it sits and thinks, or if undisturbed perhaps it just sits and does not think! How little we really know of the mind of a bird. But at least it will resist man if he walks quietly up to the nest; but if an abrupt approach is made only a few braver individuals will stay to fight it out. It is these individuals that we have been able to seize – by a swift manoeuvre to avoid the stabbing bill – and ring and release, and recover in later years at the same nest.

We see then that one or other of the adults remains at the nest from the first days of building it with grass and flotsam and through the courtship and mating stage (coition takes place on the nest), throughout the incubation period of six weeks, and until the white down of the solitary chick is hidden by the 'pepper-and-salt' feathers of its first plumage. Then only does it become safe for the nest and the nestling to be left.

Once again we see that the nest is the focal point, the only meeting and mating place. Probably at sea the gannet never sees (or recognizes) its mate. Even at night the guard remains, and sometimes the pair will remain sleeping together then. The gannetry at night is almost silent, becoming quiet soon after sunset, a pleasing contrast to the clatter and uproar and flighting of the daylight hours. Thousands of gannets asleep, evenly spaced over two acres of grassland, is surely one of the most wonderful sights in nature, spread as they are against the rosy tints of the summer night sky. Around the end of the colony many 'off duty' birds, and some in immature plumage, are also dozing, bills tucked into the feathers of the back. A few score are resting on the sea below, drifting by on the fast-moving currents.

Towards dawn there is more activity. Many birds seem to have come in at night, probably with full crops ready to feed their young, and not daring to land, have settled on the sea.

This, as the eastern light grows, is found to be dotted with resting gannets. The gannets sleeping on the nests begin to move a little uneasily, and a new faint undercurrent of sound at first puzzles the watcher. But this turns out to be the minute combined voices of scores, and soon hundreds, of nestling gannets hungry for breakfast. Individually it is a moderately high note sounding somewhat like 'uk-uk'. The young bird calls jerkily and lifts its head towards the adult. This reacts with pumping movements of the neck as the fish, partly digested in the adult's paunch all night, is worked into the gullet. The adult then reaches down as if about to be sick, but at the last moment the young chick's head is scooped up into the wide open bill, and disappears well into the gullet of its parent where it gropes for a part of the warm mass of softened fish. As it withdraws the chick swallows down the food while the parent throws back its own head and swallows back what remains in its throat.

Feeding thus usually takes place in the morning and the chick seems to thrive and get very fat on one good feed a day. The guard is changed during the day and the adult on duty one night might well be, I suspect, away fishing on the next night.

As the young gannet grows up this regularity of feeding slackens. When it is about two months old the adults feed it more and more irregularly and at last abandon it altogether. This is really a kindly provision, for the young gannet is at first almost too fat and heavy to walk. A period of starvation changes this – the fledgeling becomes light and its wings grow strong enough, by frequent flapping exercises in the nest, to bear it down to the sea at last. At least it achieves a long fluttering glide during which it manages to steer clear of the rocks.

For some days it cannot fly, but sooner or later the wind assists it to take off from a wave top, and then its inborn wisdom teaches it to dive for fish and to fly southwards for the winter.

I have seen seals sporting among newly flown gannets and even swimming up to nose the bewildered fledgelings, but the seal's interest seems to be one of curiosity only, and if the gannet beats its wings in alarm, the seal will dive with a vehement splash.

Much nonsense has been written about the diving of gannets. In my observation and that of fishermen I have met they seldom dive from great heights and never reach great depths. They rarely stay under for more than a few seconds. They are caught on lines and in nets, but always within a few fathoms of the surface. They are sometimes hauled up in trawl-nets which have been working on a bottom 100 fathoms deep, but in these instances they are entangled and drowned while diving after fish in, or escaping from, the trawl as it comes to the surface. Many dives are made only a few feet from the water as the gannet, skimming low, suddenly sees its food and starts down to it almost without hesitation. Usually diving takes place at from 10 to 100 feet above the water. The gannet, deliberately searching, suddenly sights fish, checks in flight, half closes its wings and drops perpendicularly (or on a slant if the fish is moving rapidly). Just before striking the water – as our slow-motion film showed – the wings are completely folded and the bird has the appearance of making a half-turn as it arrows downwards. The fish is not 'speared'; it is gathered between the mandibles in the normal way, and usually swallowed underwater, probably because the gannet fears to be robbed by gulls and skuas above water. If you have seen – and what a grand sight! – that pirate, the great skua, catch a gannet by the tail and force it to disgorge in the air you will understand why the gannet gulps its prey down underwater! But when the fish is very large the gannet has to come to the surface to finish choking it down.

The closing scenes of our film were devoted to the diving of the gannet. For this we had to go out on a steam trawler and photograph the follow-up of gannets diving upon the small fishes that escaped from the meshes of the trawl as it was being hauled to the surface. Like so many white meteors they plunged downwards, a fountain of spray rising and a ring of foam marking the spot.

In the hand the living gannet is a beautiful creature and its structure is seen to be completely adapted to its diving habit. The external nostrils of the young chick close up before it leaves the nest – otherwise these would incommode it in its violent diving by allowing water to be forced through them. It has also practically no tongue and there is a network of cellular tissue beneath the skin, especially of the neck region, which can be inflated and which is believed to act as a cushion to absorb the shock of diving (though I have not yet met with any *proof* that this structure is so used).

The last world census of the gannet shows it is an increasing species. It is pleasant to realize that the persecution it formerly suffered at the hands of fishermen and primitive outlying communities has now practically ceased. At one time gannets were largely used for food, the oily fat of the young being used for lighting, heating, and greasing purposes, and the feathers for beds, etc. At St Kilda a hundred years ago the stomachs of the gannets killed for food used to furnish sufficient hooks for the natives to use on their hand-lines; these steel hooks had evidently been swallowed (with the fish bait or capture) by gannets following sea-going fishing fleets in other waters.

Yours.

30th August 1940

My DEAR J.B. – In these last August days we have been ferrying over our farm animals and our small store of material wealth. I am reminded by the swarms of flying ants and the abundance of insects that, in August 1934, we had two entomologists staying with us. W.S. Bristowe collected altogether fifty-one spiders and four harvest spiders, one of the last new to Britain. He found the island had many unexpected absentees, of which he lists the ceiling spider (*Pholcus phalangioides*) and the common *Zygiella* as notable. As these depend on humans for transport they may never have inhabited Skokholm. But since Dr Bristowe's visit the ceiling spider has made its appearance: in 1936, when it was evidently imported with some furniture we ferried across. It is now common in the living quarters, where you may see its long legs and attenuated body resting gracefully on almost invisible webs in the rafters and ceilings.

The webs of *Araneus diadematus* are found everywhere in the autumn, on walls, in bracken, on the cliffs. It is probably the commonest spider, taking the place of the absentees, *Areneus umbraticus* and *Zygiella x-notata*, usually predominant in such situations. In our driest caves lives *Meta menardi*, whose white globular cocoons hang like mothballs. And in wet caves *Halorates reprobus* is abundant, finding food in the flies which feed on decayed seaweed and the minute Crustacea which haunt the pitted red sandstone walls. The harvest spider (then) new to Britain was *Nelima silvatica*, hitherto recorded in France and southern Europe.

F.W. Edwards collected flies at Skokholm when he visited us from the 25th–27th August. Owing to the large numbers of dead puffins, shearwaters, and rabbits – slain by the gulls – in the summer and autumn the common bluebottle fly as well as the greenbottle or sheepfly are numerous, and, if we do not look after our sheep and dip them often in a bath containing arsenic we should lose many. As you know, the greenbottle deposits its eggs in the wool and these hatch out in moist warm weather. The larvae feed first on the cutaneous waste or grease of the sheep but bore into the flesh as they grow larger and ultimately eat the sheep alive.

Smoke flies (*Microsania*) have also appeared at Skokholm. On 9th July 1934, after the visit on the previous day of the Eighth International Ornithological Congress to Skokholm (this was a great occasion for us: to be visited by ornithologists from all over the world, and, as it happened, on such a perfect calm warm day when even the two destroyers – HMS *Windsor* and HMS *Wolfhound* which conveyed the excursionists, maintained a level keel through the tide races!), several fires were found burning in dry peaty ground on the island. When trying to put these fires out swarms of little black flies clustered around my head. With the idea of driving them away I moved into the thickest part of the smoke, only to find them increase in density! They seemed to enjoy the most pungent parts of the smoke and heat! Dr Edwards tells me this is typical of *Microsania*, whose life-history is still a mystery, and little is known except that they are resistant to oxygen deficiency, and take twice as long to succumb in a killing bottle (cyanide fumes) as other flies do.

We have five species of ant: *Acanthomyops niger*, L., A. *alienus*, Forst., A. *flavus*, F., *Tetramorium coespitum*, L., and *Myrmica scabrinodis*, Nyl. The last is a very small ant and extremely hardy, living in exposed situations on rocks with very little vegetation. I have found it on our isolated Stack Rock (0.320 acres!) and it is the only ant at Grassholm Island. Ants are numerous on Skokholm, found under almost every large stone in the driest places. Their nuptial swarms are thrown into the sky on the first calm days of late summer, from mid July onwards – they are pursued by almost every species of our birds. As there are usually light airs even on the calmest days, the fecundated ant-queens – as they drop pendicularly down again – are freely drifted and are just as likely to fall into the sea as upon the island. The sea to the lee of the island on these days is usually plastered with drowned ants, on which the gulls eagerly feed.

Ever yours.

46. HERRING GULL

D EAR J – I was very glad to have your letter dated a month ago in which you said you had found in your prison-camp library and had read Goethe's admirable account of a herring gull colony in the *Journal für Ornithologie*. As you know we have three kinds of gulls nesting with us, the herring, the great, and the lesser black-backed gulls. All three are migratory in varying degree, but the lesser black-backed gull the most. Some at least of the other two species remain with us the whole year, though probably few single individuals are completely resident. At the lighthouse here they had for several years a herring gull with one leg broken off above the foot; it became tame enough to feed out of the hand, and could be called to the door of the lighthouse at any time throughout the year by offering it food. In the same way we had an adult herring gull as a kind of pet bird for two winters; it lived on the house scraps and other food thrown to our chickens. At first we discouraged it because it was so voracious, but refusing to leave us, it retired to explore and exploit the heap or midden of refuse and compost which we were storing for the garden. In the end we admired its courage and became quite fond of the impudent bird.

About three hundred pairs of herring gulls nest on Skokholm. After the breeding season is over in September they gradually move from the island, leaving behind a few immature birds and a remnant of adults. In October they are very scarce. During November there are rare days without a herring gull on Skokholm. Then early in December, if the weather be mild and spring-like with a high temperature, as frequently happens, there is an increase in the number of adults. If the warm spell continues the herring gulls begin to settle in their nesting territories for a few hours in the morning. So that you might say the herring gulls are the earliest to think of nesting, earlier even than the guillemots. Of course, they are not actually building nests so early, but merely standing about near the usual nesting sites. Here the pair conduct the curious posturing performances which typically include a bowing of the head and distension of the throat to the accompaniment of a loud wail followed by a special reiterated note. Or, if alone, the male may pick up bits of grass and thrift, only to drop them again in an ostentatious manner as if calling the attention of females to the desirable spot he occupies, or as if he would challenge any other male to dispute the site. Mostly they are in pairs, even before the new year – suggesting that they pair for life, which I think is likely. They spend the few hours of early morning sunshine at this standing site. Cliff sites are occupied first, and first of the cliff sites to be occupied are those where there is a group nesting close together on some favourite shelf or terrace in the rocks. Many pairs nest in more isolated positions where each nest is well out of sight of its neighbour. And a number of herring gulls nest among the lesser black-back gulleries on the plateau of the island: but these, without exception, adopt some outcrop of rock or large stone in the colony against which to build the nest, thus seeming to acknowledge in this new situation an ancient hereditary preference in the choice of their nesting environment.

There is a full description of their courtship in the article by Goethe in the *Journal für Ornithologie*, 1937, which you have just been reading, and although it describes a colony nesting on sand-dunes, I find the behaviour of our nesting herring gulls differs in no way from that of the north German representatives so ably observed by Goethe.

This displaying and posturing is intensified at Skokholm on fine January mornings, but much depends on the daily temperature.

When we get a cold spell in February it is interrupted. In the afternoons the gulls leave their 'standing sites' on the cliffs and as the sun sets they fly to their roosting places on the remoter parts of the island. Some fly to the uninhabited islet of Middleholm, some resort to our Stack Rock at the north-east point, some to a commanding spot on the peninsula of the Neck, where nothing can surprise them easily, and sometimes a group will settle for the night on the red shelves of the Devil's Teeth.

On calm nights many will roost on the sea in the tideless part of South
Haven. The numbers increase daily in February and March.

The male treads the female during late March and early April, using
a very distinct deep ululating note and flapping his wings to maintain
balance. He leads the way in preparing one and sometimes two nest
sites, on one of which coition takes place. The favourite nesting material
appears to be the nearest vegetation, usually thrift, which is torn up and
used to line the scrape which the birds prepare between them, pushing
and shuffling round and round, one taking the place of the other with
pretty enticing actions which suggests, as Goethe writes, a full connubial
harmony. In fact these cold-looking rapacious birds give the appearance
of great tenderness and affection in their nesting affairs. You will see the
male respond to his mate's begging attitudes by nibbling and caressing
her bill and even appearing to feed her. They will sit quietly side by side
for long periods, or he will stand upon her back or rest in a possessive
attitude upon or against her. The male also brings leaves, flowers, and
limpet shells to the nest, the real nest as well as, if he has one, the 'play
nest'. But the play nest is abandoned once the serious business of egg
laying begins.

Three eggs are usually laid, a pretty olive, or brown, much splashed
with darker markings. We eagerly look out for the first eggs from mid-
April onwards. They are delicious fresh, fried with butter. And we have
no compunction about taking all we can find freshly laid, since they
make such a welcome contribution to our larder and, in any case, these
gulls go on laying as long as we go on taking them – up to the middle
of June, by which time we have usually collected enough to put down
– with the eggs of the black-backed gulls as well – between two and
three thousand in water-glass. These we are able to consume during the
autumn and winter, and the surplus is fed to our livestock – as I have
already mentioned.

When undisturbed the herring gull begins to sit with the laying of the
first egg, so that the three eggs normally hatch in the order of laying
(usually two eggs in the case of the first clutch being taken). I give

below ten records of the incubation period of the herring gull, made in 1931, from second clutches, the first clutches having been taken for the house:

Nest	DATES OF LAYING			DATES OF HATCHING			INCUBATION PERIOD
	1st egg	2nd egg	3rd egg	1st egg	2nd egg	3rd egg	
No.	May	May	May	June	June	June	Days
1	15	17	—	11	12	—	(27), 26
2	15	17	—	11	13	—	(27), 26
3	18	20	23	15	16	18	(28, 27), 26
4	25	27	29	(bad)	23	(bad)	27
5	25	27	—	21	23	—	(27), 27
6	26	28	31	22	24	26	(27, 27), 26
7	27	29	—	22	24	—	(26), 26
8	29	31	2 June	24	26	28	(27), 27
9	29	31	2 June	24	26	28	(26, 26), 26
10	31	2	—	26	28	—	(26), 26

Average incubation after 26.4 days.

The downy protectively coloured chicks leave the nest in a few days if disturbed, and crouch in corners and crevices where they are not conspicuous – if there is room for them to do so. But on narrow ledges of steep cliffs they have to remain at the nest until they are able to fly, which they can do in about five weeks. At the stage of three weeks, when they can walk rapidly but not fly, if approached by man they will stumble over the cliff edge in an apparently stupid fashion, often killing themselves on the rocks or in the surf. A little later, with their feathers more advanced, they seem to fall more circumspectly to the sea when disturbed, and will then swim back to the rocks and endeavour to climb up above high-water mark by using legs, wings, and bill to hook themselves up with.

The young birds are fed at first on partly digested fish and other material which the all too omnivorous adult regurgitates. All too omnivorous because nothing much comes amiss to the herring gull. Its normal food at Skokholm includes the small life of the shore at low tide: crabs and starfish, sea-urchins, prawns, and shrimps are hunted in the pools and under the Folds of the laminaria; and any small, defenceless, or wounded or dead creature that can be found on the surface of the land, from worms and beetles and ants to eggs, nestling birds, mice, small rabbits and sick large rabbits, and birds, garbage, and even garden produce. The older adults develop 'rogue' habits and will prey on our guillemot colonies, or at Grassholm the gannet colony, constantly patrolling, ready to pounce on egg or newly hatched young (even of its own species) or fish (dropped from the bill of the parent guillemot or gannet) left only partly guarded by the owner. For this reason we try to avoid disturbing breeding guillemots and gannets early in the season, for this robber gull is swifter in getting to the nest than the legitimate owners whom we have disturbed. He is in fact swifter, or shall I say bolder, than the great black-backed gull in taking advantage of this disturbance.

So, too, although he cannot kill adult puffins, as does the great black-back, the herring gull is adept at molesting them, and will stand about on the cliff terraces of the puffin colonies, ready to run at a puffin landing with a beak full of small fishes, and is often, but not always, successful in intimidating the puffin so that the little fishes are dropped on the ground before the puffin can reach the burrow in which its hungry chick is awaiting the next meal.

As the young herring gulls grow bigger they snatch the food from the parents' bill raw, and early show their rapacious nature. They have a whining hunger cry which is a characteristic sound of our cliffs in June and July. This whine develops into a loud and plaintive note at fledging time and for much longer after – in fact you can hear it uttered by birds at least a year old, who follow the adults and seem to beg for food without results. The young gull seems to be a long time in growing to vigorous adult habits and appearance: the full adult plumage is not acquired until the third year.

The breeding adults begin to moult in June, July, and August; their quills are then lying everywhere about the island. They are becoming comparatively dull and listless, very silent, standing about in groups, preening and dozing, and losing interest in their importuning young. The adults gradually leave us, taking with them only a few of their chicks. So that by September there are perhaps about sixty immature birds and four or five adults left on the whole of Skokholm.

Many of these immature birds grow feeble with hunger before they have learned to feed themselves – so feeble that they have almost lost the power of flight and I have been able to run them down in the centre of the island where they collect, whining in vain for food. This seems to be especially the case when the weather is rough and heavy seas are breaking over the rocks where they have begun, in their amateurish way, to hunt for food.

I am no longer surprised that so predatory a bird as the herring gull, and indeed the great and lesser black-backs, need to lay two or three eggs to keep up their numbers, in contrast with the preyed-upon puffin, guillemot, razorbill, or shearwater which only lay one egg (and you would think should lay four or five, to allow for the appetite of the gulls). For the mortality among gull chicks is very heavy. Failing other sources of food adult gulls freely kill chicks of their own and other gulls. In a large gull colony there is an orgy of cannibalism soon after the general hatching time and while the chicks are un-feathered. I suppose, at a guess, much less than one hundred herring gull chicks reach the fledged state out of the eight or nine hundred eggs annually laid and incubated at Skokholm. And then more die off in the autumn before they can feed themselves independently.

None of our ringed herring gulls, young or adult, wanders far from Pembrokeshire coasts. Our recoveries are all within these waters excepting one adult, ringed here on 18th August 1938, which was reported from Launceston, Cornwall, on 2nd January 1939.

Yours ever.

14th September 1940

DEAR JOHN – What I wrote in my last letter about the herring gull applies in some degree to the great black-backed gull. It is just as sedentary, a few old birds remaining even in the depths of winter. We have sixty pairs nesting here, of which seven pairs use our insulated Stack Rock, where in the last century, it is reported, common and roseate terns nested, but were ousted by this great gull.

In general this majestic bird selects a commanding position for its nest: some rocky pinnacle or ridge on the coast or inland, or some single large stone against which it builds a circle of thrift, heather twigs, and other vegetation collected close at hand. When studying the incubation period of this gull early in 1931 I found I could encourage it to build a nest in a spot chosen by me for its convenience of observation: I had only to place a good rock or stone (about half a hundredweight) in an area frequented by these gulls, and they obligingly nested against it.

Out of six nests thus marked I obtained the following complete records:

Nest	DATES OF LAYING			DATES OF HATCHING			INCUBATION PERIOD
No.	1st egg May	2nd egg May	3rd egg May	1st egg June	2nd egg June	3rd egg June	Days
1	14	16	18	11	—	14	(28, 27), 27
2	13	15	17	(bad)	(bad)	13	(28) 27
3	13	15	—	10	(lost)	—	(28) 27

Excepting its voice, which is much stronger and deeper and more hound-like or baying, this gull has a spring display like that of the herring gull in almost every respect of the posturing, courtship, and mating actions and attitudes.

Its food, however, is in proportion to its size, and consequently it is far more rapacious than its smaller cousin. It does great slaughter to our puffin and shearwater colonies. It has a trick of standing and watching above a puffin burrow during the day; then seizing the adult as it walks out. Very rarely does the puffin wriggle out of that death grip of the cruel-looking red-spotted yellow bill. The victim may be worried to death on the spot, but if disturbed the gull carries the puffin down to the sea, where it is half drowned, half slain before life leaves its mutilated body. One's sympathies are with the puffin, but no amount of shouting and stone-throwing puts the gull off its horrible feast. The victim is eviscerated; all the flesh gradually torn off, leaving the skin everted with the head sometimes left, but often swallowed whole. You can pick up a food casting of the great black-backed gull consisting of a whole puffin's head.

Shearwaters are even more frequently killed, either at night, if it is not too dark, or early in the morning, when this gull hunts for those shearwaters which have – stupidly as we think – not taken cover for the day, but lie, like the proverbial ostrich, with head tucked under some herbage or in some crevice, leaving the body exposed. Young shearwaters, on their way to the sea, are very commonly taken. They, too, are reduced to everted skins.

This gull is not a great egg thief, but it is an inveterate hunter of the small chicks of the gannet, guillemot, and razorbill, and to some extent of its own and other gull chicks. It will persecute a colony of guillemots on an exposed ledge and take all the chicks by degrees, making a breakfast of one or two each day. Thus guillemot chicks we have ringed have disappeared day by day; and by searching the food pellets of great black-backed gulls nesting close by we have recovered many of the rings. These small chicks are swallowed whole, and often still alive.

You can imagine that, although we do not care to upset the so-called 'balance of nature' on the island, we are not very favourably disposed towards this savage gull, noble though it is in flight and appearance. We endeavour to collect all its eggs, and so prevent its increase, and short of constantly shooting it – which would cause too great a disturbance to other birds – we can do no more. Yet it continues slowly to multiply, and this it must do, since we allow so few of the eggs to hatch, by colonization from outside. There were thirty-one pairs here in 1928; there are sixty pairs today. This unwelcome increase may be part of a cycle, perhaps partly due (in the Pembrokeshire islands at least) to the protection given to nesting auks and shearwaters. If this increase continues it will have a serious effect on the guillemot colonies – noticeably dwindling in this area – and on the puffin population. There are, however, signs that it is at its peak – I take it that the increasing cannibalism exhibited by this gull today is one of these signs.

Great black-backed gulls ringed as nestlings at Skokholm are more migratory than our herring gull; one reached Guilvinac, Finistere, on 17th November 1939. Another reached Lastres, Asturias, Spain, on 25th November. A third was recovered at Sables d'Olonne (Vendée), France, on 21st January in the year after ringing. It is during January, rather later than the herring gulls, that our slender winter population of one or two pairs of great black-backed gulls begins to increase. Sometimes there are more than sixty pairs present here then, and some of these are obviously moving north to the higher latitudes to which this species extends its breeding range.

Yours.

48. LESSER BLACK-BACKED GULL

MY DEAR JOHN – As a rule the lesser black-backed gull arrives on Skokholm in the first week of March, when I usually find a small group together in their main breeding ground, the central bog. But in mild winters they may arrive in February. The earliest date I have is 17th February.

This gull I regard with more affection than the other two breeding gulls; possibly I am influenced by the fact that it provides us with some two thousand eggs annually, gathered from the nests of some eight hundred pairs breeding here! But it is, in my observation, much less of a murderer and egg thief, feeding on the carcases and carrion rather than killing live birds. In fact the food of this gull is a good deal of a mystery to me, as of this goodly host on Skokholm very few are seen collecting food. You may see them pecking at the turf, evidently picking up insects, and in July and August they fish with other birds on the shoals of sand-eels and small fry which are swept close to the shore by the tides. But evidence of larger prey there is little. It is less of a rock feeder than the herring gull. It does not patrol the cliffs in search of other seabirds' eggs. Some of the stomachs of lesser black-backed gulls taken at the nest have been quite empty; like most seabirds it is able, it seems, to fast for

several days. It may therefore feed much at sea, where it is always ready to follow a passing ship and seize the refuse from it.

As we take so many eggs, the number of chicks reared is not very large; but this gull continues to increase. It now covers the whole of the wetter part of the central bog or plain of the island with eight principal outlying colonies about Spy Rock, Frank's Point, the Neck, North Park, West Park, Mad Bay, Windmill Gully, and Bread Rock. In this general preference for a level plateau for nesting it differs from the other two gulls, but in places it encroaches on the territory of the herring gulls and nests among them on the less steep cliff slopes; just as the herring gull nests here and there on the plateau of the lesser black-backs, as already noted. When the bluebells are in flower the plateau is a beautiful scene, with nesting gulls, slate-blue and white, against the purple bells of the wild hyacinths, the blue of the sky, and the red and grey of the rock outcrops.

I found the incubation period of this gull, from nine nests marked, to be 26 to 27 days:

Nest	DATES OF LAYING			DATES OF HATCHING			INCUBATION PERIOD
No.	1st egg	2nd egg	3rd egg	1st egg	2nd egg	3rd egg	
	May	May	May	June	June	June	Days
1	16	—	—	11	—	—	26
2	17	19	21	13	(bad)	16	(27), 26
3	16	18	21	12	(lost)	16	(27), 26
4	16	18	21	15	15	16	(30, 28), 26
5	14	16	—	11	11	—	(28), 26
6	17	19	21	13	14	16	(27, 27), 26
7	23	25	27	18	(lost)	(lost)	26
8	16	18	25	11	13	(lost)	(26), 27
9	15	17	—	11	13	—	(27), 27

Looking at this table it is evident that incubation may or may not begin with the first egg laid. Both sexes incubate, as in other gulls. There is nothing worthy of remark in the difference between the breeding habits and emotional posturing and displays of this gull and those of the herring gull already quoted in my letter on that bird, to which it is so closely allied in all respects save colouring and migration. Even the voice is similar, though deeper. The usual expression of emotion, including that of alarm, might be put as: 'Oo-ka-ka-ka-ka-kee-ar-kee-ar-kee-ar'; but this will convey very little to any one who has not heard it and compared it with the 'kee-ow' notes of the herring gull. And I am sure you will excuse me if I do not further embark upon the difficult task of making phonetic renderings of the unhuman notes of birds, which the human ear interprets so differently, according to the pitch it is keyed to.

By mid March the arrival parties have split up into pairs and are performing the typical gull display in their real and 'play' nests. Eggs are not laid until early in May and, because we continue to take them, egg laying goes on to the end of June. Some of the adults, prevented from breeding in this way, begin to group together from mid June onwards. These 'disappointed' birds are the first to moult and the first to move on, in late July and August. Then in August the general exodus south begins. On some days the island is covered by great armies of these gulls, old and young, resting for a while on their migration. On any calm sunlit August day the ants may send forth into the air their swarms of queens and drones for the great annual nuptial flight, and this event is eagerly attended by the migrating gulls, which pursue the virgin queens in the air, or pick them up as they reach the ground fertilized (the drones perished in the act of consummation, the wings of the queens deliberately sheared off in preparation for the winter nest underground).

September sees the last of our lesser black-backs. Some of our ringed birds are reported from Spain and Portugal, and one has reached Dakar, in Senegal. The Dakar recovery, by the way, was a bird ringed as an adult on 18th August 1938. It was recovered on 5th May 1940, when it was reported as settling in the harbour and collapsing; evidently a bird too ill to make the northward migration.

Ever yours.

49. BUTTERFLIES AND MOTHS

20th September 1940

D EAR JOHN – I am reminded by your notes on butterflies seen in your prisoner-of-war camp that I have hardly mentioned the Lepidoptera in these letters. But that is simply because I am only a very amateur entomologist and have less than the average observer's knowledge of these creatures. In any case the island is not rich in the larger, more easily identified butterflies and moths.

Of butterflies we have, in fact, identified for certain only fifteen species, all common ones. Apart from a few stray individual red admirals and peacock butterflies which may hibernate (or attempt to – they are usually in very poor condition by April) in the buildings, the first butterflies to appear outdoors in fine spring weather are the small white, the green-veined white, and the small tortoiseshell. These appear as a rule by mid April, soon to be followed, early in May, by the large white, small copper, red admiral, painted lady, and peacock butterflies.

A month later, early in June, we get the small heath, the common blue, and the wall brown. Fritillaries do not turn up until July, when the silver-washed, the high brown, and the large pearl-bordered are not uncommon for a period of about four weeks, that is, if the weather is fine and warm. The dark green is, however, the most numerous of the fritillaries. Finally, the meadow brown is numerous in July and August.

Warm easterly winds bring us butterflies and moths in summer; both migratory, and what are usually considered non-migratory, butterflies begin to cross to us when these winds prevail for several days, and the movement is heightened if they blow for still longer periods. When great rushes of butterflies are reported in the English Channel at such times, we can safely expect a share to reach us. The three whites, the red admiral, the painted lady, and the peacock butterflies are then to be seen crossing the Broad Sound here, wind-drifted towards the island, and, perhaps missing it altogether, fluttering westwards in the direction of Ireland and America. Many must perish in the open Atlantic at such times.

It is in these good years that we find the silken feeding tents of the red admiral and the peacock spun about the leaves of nettles in the summer; and later, if the weather is favourable and the sea winds not too cold, one generation is raised, and the imago can be seen drying its wings in the late summer sunlight.

Flights of the large white, sometimes in vast numbers, pass over the island in late May, June, and July. Our cabbages are then visited and great numbers of their eggs are found glued to the leaves; these quickly hatch into voracious caterpillars, which attack the plants. The cabbages become mere skeletons of leaf-stalk. When the caterpillars are full-fed they march towards the house and buildings and walls, seeking dry niches in which to pupate and lie up for the winter. Fortunately for our garden these migratory hosts of the large white are always followed by a parasite – a kind of ichneumon fly known as *Apanteles glomeratus*, which deposits its eggs in the body of the growing caterpillar. The apanteles grubs live on the fat and non-vital body tissues of the caterpillar. On reaching the site selected for pupation the parasited caterpillar dies, and the apanteles grubs leave its body, and themselves pupate, spinning a little heap of golden cocoons beside the shrivelled body of the caterpillar. I find that roughly about seventy-five per cent of the large white caterpillars here fail to pupate, owing to the attentions of apanteles.

The small copper finds a plentiful food supply for its larvae in the amount of sorrel present on the island. It is numerous on the island from May to August, and is not infrequently seen crossing the sea. The common blue is nearly as plentiful, though later in appearing and later in disappearing – it is present until well on into September. These two, with the meadow brown, are the only species which we may count on finding with any regularity; even in cold, wet summers they can be relied upon to cheer you if you seek them in the more sheltered places on this wind swept plateau.

Since I am no entomologist I have little to say about moths, beyond attaching a list of those identified, at the end of this letter. In some years we receive large immigrations of moths, notably the silver Y (June to August). The hummingbird hawk-moth is a July visitor, usually observed feeding on marsh thistle. I once caught a convolvulus-hawk moth feeding at nasturtium flowers in the garden; when released it flew up almost vertically into the sky, with a pleasant humming note.

The cinnabar moth is perhaps our most useful moth. It seems to follow the numerical fluctuations of the ragwort, which in some years is all too abundant on Skokholm. Cinnabar caterpillars strip the ragwort of its leaves, and check the plant severely. I quote a note which you yourself made in our island diary for 23rd July 1938: 'Cinnabar caterpillars on almost all the ragwort, feasting and doing much good work.'

Yours.

MOTHS RECORDED AT SKOKHOLM: Cinnabar, garden carpet, ruby tiger, fox moth, gold tail, antler, drinker, angle shade, broom, knotgrass, rosy rustic, vapourer, dark arches, gatekeeper, yellow shell, convolvulus hawk, humming bird hawk, sweet gale, silver Y, five-spot burnet, six-spot burnet, ermine, lattice heath.

50. WEATHER

North Pembrokeshire
24th September 1940

MY DEAR JOHN – There was a fresh north-west wind today, but we made three journeys between the island and Martins Haven. After this, alas, we shall not regard the weather any more with such a deep interest. These are the last trips we shall make to the island. We brought back with us three cargoes of sheep and lambs – the last of our island farm. There was little time to be sad about this farewell. For the past month we have been busy ferrying our household goods and farming implements and gear, ponies, two hundred sheep and lambs, poultry, and so on. The moving out has been a gradual process, and on the whole the weather has been very kind. The authorities who ordered the removal have been helpful and have agreed to defray our expenses in getting the road transport to our new farm beyond the Preseli Mountains.

Our new situation is in quite a charming place, with native oak woods (now, alas, being cut for timber) surrounding this dilapidated Welsh manor house, with a large rookery almost over the roof. I was delighted to hear woodlarks singing in this mild September air. The size of the farm is that of Skokholm, about 240 acres, including 60 acres of a steep wooded valley or *cwm* which partly, so to speak, ensiles us from neighbours; but this valley is unfit for cultivation though full of wild creatures. Badgers are numerous, and otters in the river Nevern below. The leaves of the oaks, elms, beeches, chestnuts, hazels, and brambles are beautiful just now. The farm is in a bad state, and needs much pioneering. But it is a very pleasant retreat full of beauty and repose. Sometimes, especially on very calm days, it seems too much enclosed and shut in, and lacking air to us, accustomed to the wild weather of Skokholm. I shall like it best here when a strong west wind is blowing from the sea, which is only three miles away and can be seen from our higher fields.

As this is the last letter I shall be able to write about Skokholm I will give you a sketch of the meteorological conditions on the island. In the year ending last month I find our average mean temperature was 50·38° Fahrenheit. Particulars for each month are as follows:

		Mean
1939	September	56.75°
	October	51.98°
	November	50.00°
	December	48.93°
1940	January	35.55°
	February	39.28°
	March	43.04°
	April	47.26°
	May	52.40°
	June	59.80°
	July	58.96°
	August	60.65°

The highest recorded temperature in this year was 74.50° on 15th June 1940 and the lowest 22.00° on 21st January 1940. No frosts occurred in the autumn and until the cold spell in January, which lasted for about five weeks, until the middle of February. This is typical of Atlantic weather, which maintains a mild temperature with neither frost nor heat. Our air is naturally saline and cool, influenced by the temperature of the surrounding sea which does not rise much above 15° or fall below 8° Centigrade.

On this plateau of Skokholm we were susceptible to every wind that blew. Our records of wind show that the general belief that westerly winds are predominant is true here, but only by a narrow margin. There are more south-easterly winds than south-westerly. Taking the wind readings (to the nearest of the eight main compass points) at noon each day I find that the south-east wind blew most often, then the north wind; west and north-west winds were equal in number, south winds came next in prevalence, then north-east, then calms, then south-west, with the east wind last of all.

June provided the most (eight) calm days; November, December, and January had no really still days. May and June are the finest and calmest months, with the wind chiefly in a northerly direction. West winds with rain increase in number in July and August, but give way again to north winds and fine days in September and October. November and December bring rain and wind from the south half of the compass. South-east winds prevail during January and February, bringing either rain or cold weather. In March winds are often more southerly but switch to the north towards the end of the month. In April north-east winds alternate with south winds, bringing the traditional light showers and dry intervals which are so blessed by the cultivator of the soil.

We had no anemometer, rain gauge, or sunshine recorder at Skokholm. Wind strength was estimated on the Beaufort scale. Once or twice in each winter here the anemometer at St Ann's Head, opposite us, recorded speeds of above 100 miles per hour. On 16th November 1928 in a gale reaching 110 miles per hour some solid stone walls here were blown down, and the long grass was torn out of the ground in the boggy area here and blown out over the sea, which was perfectly white.

As to rainfall, we have the least in Wales. At St Ann's Head the average annual precipitation is thirty-five inches. And of fogs I suppose we have rather more than the average of mist, as in all coastal parts, but it is at least clean stuff and as it usually brings calm weather and migrant birds we do not greatly mind it.

There is little more of interest to add to these few plain observations on the island weather, and with them I must conclude these notes gathered at Skokholm. I shall be posting news to you from time to time as my mainland life and work allow, but for the moment, John, I write *au revoir*, with many thanks for your patience and for your interesting letters. We send you every good wish for your speedy deliverance from imprisonment. Our thoughts are always with you.

Yours ever, R.M.L.

List of birds recorded at Skokholm 1927–1940
(B. = breeding or has bred)

Raven (*Corvus c. corax* L.). B.
Hooded crow (*Corvus c. comix* L.).
Carrion-crow (*Corvus c. corone* L.). B.
Rook (*Corvus f. frugilegus* L.).
Jackdaw (*Corvus monedula spermologus Vieill.*).
Chough (*Pyrrhocorax p. pyrrhocorax* L.). B.
Starling (*Sturnus v. vulgaris* L.). B.
Greenfinch (*Chloris ch. chloris* L.).
British goldfinch (*Carduelis c. britannica* Hart.).
Twite (*Carduelis flavirostris pipilans* Latham).
Linnet (*Carduelis c. cannabina* L.). B.
Crossbill (*Loxia c. curvirostra* L.).
Chaffinch (*Fringilla coelebs gengleri* Kleinschmidt).
Brambling (*Fringilla montifringilla* L.).
Corn bunting (*Emberiza calandra* L.).
Yellow bunting (*Emberiza c. citrinella* L.).
Ortolan bunting (*Emberiza hortulana* L.).
Reed bunting (*Emberiza s. schoeniclus* L.).
Lapland bunting (*Calcarius l. lapponicus* L.).
Snow bunting (*Plectrophenax n. nivalis* L.).
House sparrow (*Passer d. domesticus* L.).
Tree sparrow (*Passer m. montanus* L.).
Skylark (*Alauda a. arvensis* L.). B.
Tree pipit (*Anthus t. trivialis* L.).
Meadow pipit (*Anthus pratensis* L.). B.
Water pipit (*Anthus s. spinoletta* L.).
Rock pipit (*Anthus spinoletta petrosus* Mont.). B.
Yellow wagtail (*Motacilla flava flavissima* Blyth).
Grey wagtail (*Motacilla c. cinerea* Tunst.).
Pied wagtail (*Motacilla alba yarrellii* Gould). B.
White wagtail (*Motacilla a. alba* L.).
British tree-creeper (*Certhia familiaris britannica* Ridgw.).
Coal tit (*Parus ater britannicus* Sharpe and Dress.).

Red-backed shrike (*Lanius c. collurio* L.).

Spotted flycatcher (*Muscicapa s. striata* Pall.).

Pied flycatcher (*Muscicapa h. hypoleuca* Pall.).

Goldcrest (*Regulus regulus anglorum* Hart.).

Chiffchaff (*Phylloscopus c. collybita* Vieill.).

Willow warbler (*Phylloscopus t. trochilus* L.).

Northern willow warbler (*Phylloscopus trochilus acredula* L.).

Grasshopper warbler (*Locustella n. ncevia* Bodd.).

Sedge warbler (*Acrocephalus schoznobcenus* L.). B.

Garden warbler (*Sylvia borin* Bodd.).

Blackcap (*Sylvia a. atricapilla* L.).

Whitethroat (*Sylvia c. communis* Latham). B.

Lesser whitethroat (*Sylvia c. curruca* L.).

Fieldfare (*Turdus pilaris* L.).

Mistle thrush (*Turdus v. viscivorus* L.).

British song thrush (*Turdus e. ericetorum* Turton).

Continental song thrush (*Turdus ericetorum philomelus* Brehm).

Redwing (*Turdus m. musicus* L.).

Ring ouzel (*Turdus t. torquatus* L.).

Blackbird (*Turdus m. merula* L.). B.

Wheatear (*Oenanthe ce. amanthe* L.). B.

Greenland wheatear (*Oenanthe oenanthe leucorrhoa* Gm.).

Whinchat (*Saxicola rubetra* L.).

Stonechat (*Saxicola torquata hibernans* Hart.). B.

Redstart (*Phoenicurus ph. phoenicurus* L.).

Black redstart (*Phoenicurus ochrurus gibraltariensis* Gm.).

Robin (*Erithacus rubecula melophilus* Hart.). B.

Hedge sparrow (*Prunella modularis occidentalis* Hart.). B.

Wren (*Troglodytes t. troglodytes* L.).

Swallow (*Hirundo r. rustica* L.). B.

House martin (*Delichon u. urbica* L.).

Sand-martin (*Riparia r. riparia* L.).

Swift (*Apus a. apus* L.).

Nightjar (*Caprimulgus e. europceus* L.).

Hoopoe (*Upupa e. epops* L.).

Kingfisher (*Alcedo atthis ispida* L.).

Wryneck (*Jynx t. torquilla* L.).

Cuckoo (*Cuculus c. canorus* L.). B.

Little owl (*Athene noctua vidalii* A. E. Brehm). B.

Short-eared owl (*Asio f. flammeus* Pontopp.).

Barn owl (*Tyto a. alba* Scop.).
Peregrine falcon (*Falco p. peregrinus* Tunst.). B.
Merlin (*Falco columbarius cesalon* Tunst.).
Kestrel (*Falco t. tinnunculus* L.).
Buzzard (*Buteo b. buteo* L.). B.
Montagu's harrier (*Circus pygargus* L.).
Sparrowhawk (*Accipiter n. nisus* L.).
Common heron (*Ardea c. cinerea* L.).
White-fronted goose (*Anser a. albifrons* L.).
Shelduck (*Tadorna tadorna* L.).
Mallard (*Anas p. platyrhyncha* L.). B.
Teal (*Anas c. crecca* L.).
Wigeon (*Anas penehpe* L.).
Shoveler (*Spatula clypeata* L.).
Common scoter (*Melanitta n. nigra* L.).
Cormorant (*Phalacrocorax c. carbo* L.).
Shag (*Phalacrocorax a. aristotelis* L.). B.
Gannet (*Sula bassana* L.).
Storm petrel (*Hydrobates pelagicus* L.). B.
Manx shearwater (*Puffinus p. puffinus* Brunn.). B.
Sooty shearwater (*Puffinus griseus* Gm.).
Fulmar petrel (*Fulmarus g. glacialis* L.).
Little grebe (*Podiceps r. ruficollis* Pall.).
Great northern diver (*Colymbus immer* Brunn.).
Black-throated diver (*Colymbus a. arcticus* L.).
Red-throated diver (*Colymbus stellatus* Pontopp.).
Wood pigeon (*Columba p. palumbus* L.).
Stock dove (*Columba cenas* L.).
Turtle dove (*Streptopelia t. turtur* L.).
Bar-tailed godwit (*Limosa l. lapponica* L.).
Black-tailed godwit (*Limosa l. limosa* L.).
Common curlew (*Numenius a. arquata* L.).
Whimbrel (*Numenius ph. phoeopus* L.).
Woodcock (*Scolopax rusticola* L.).
Common snipe (*Capella g. gallinago* L.).
Jack snipe (*Lymnocryptes minimus* Brunn.).
Turnstone (*Arenaria i. interpres* L.).
Knot (*Calidris c. canutus* L.).
Southern dunlin (*Calidris alpina schinzii* Brehm).
Little stint (*Calidris minuta* Leisl.).

Common sandpiper (*Actitis hypoleucos* L.).
Purple sandpiper (*Calidris m. maritima* Brunn.).
Sanderling (*Crocethia alba* Pall.).
Ruff (*Philomachus pugnax* L.).
Redshank (*Tringa totanus britannica* Math.).
Greenshank (*Tringa nebularia* Gunn.).
Ringed plover (*Charadrius h. hiaticula* L.).
Golden plover (*Pluvialis a. apricaria* L.).
Grey plover (*Squatarola squatarola* L.).
Lapwing (*Vanellus vanellus* L.). B.
British oystercatcher (*Hoematopus ostralegus occidentalis* Neum.).
Stone-curlew (*Burhinus ce. cedicnemus* L.).
Sandwich tern (*Sterna s. sandvicensis* Lath.).
Roseate tern (*Sterna d. dougallii* Mont.).
Common tern (*Sterna h. hirundo* L.).
Arctic tern (*Sterna macrura* Naumann).
Little tern (*Sterna a. albifrons* Pall.).
Black-headed gull (*Larus r. ridibundus* L.).
Common gull (*Larus c. canus* L.).
Herring gull (*Larus a. argentatus* Pont.). B.
Scandinavian lesser black-backed gull (*Larus f. fuscus* L.).
British lesser black-backed gull (*Larus fuscus graellsii* Brehm). B.
Great black-backed gull (*Larus marinus* L.). B.
Kittiwake (*Rissa t. tridactyla* L.).
Arctic skua (*Stercorarius parasiticus* L.).
British razorbill (*Alca torda britannica* Ticehurst). B.
Northern guillemot (*Uria a. aalge* Pont.).
Southern guillemot (*Uria aalge albionis* With.). B.
Black guillemot (*Uria g. grylle* L.).
Little auk (*Alle a. alle* L.).
Southern puffin (*Fratercula arctica grabce* Brehm). B.
Corncrake (*Crex crex* L.). B.
Water-rail (*Rallus a. aquaticus* L.). B.
Moorhen (*Gallinula ch. chloropus* L.). B.
Coot (*Fulica a. atra* L.).
Quail (*Coturnix c. coturnix* L.).

List of flora recorded at Skokholm 1927–1940
(G. = in garden only)

Water crowfoot (*Ranunculus aquatilis* L. agg.).
Lesser spearwort (*Ranunculus flammula* L.).
Lesser celandine (*Ranunculus ficaria* L.).
Creeping buttercup (*Ranunculus repens* L.).
Ivy-leaved crowfoot (*Ranunculus hederaceus* L.).
Field poppy (*Papaver rhozas* L.).
G. Common watercress (*Nasturtium officinale* Br. agg.).
Lady's smock (*Cardamine pratensis* L.).
Hairy bittercress (*Cardamine hirsuta* L.).
Charlock (*Brassica arvense* Kuntze.).
Scurvy grass (*Cochlearia officinalis* L.).
Danish scurvy grass (*Cochlearia danica* L.).
English scurvy grass (*Cochlearia anglica* L.).
Shepherd's-purse (*Capsella bursa-pastoris* Medik.).
Lesser swine-cress (*Coronopus didymus* L., Sm.).
Dog violet (*Viola riviniana* Reichb.).
Heartsease (*Viola tricolor* L. agg.).
Sea-pansy (*Viola curtisii* Forst.).
Milkwort (*Polygala vulgare* L.).
Sea-campion (*Silene maritima* With.).
Red campion (*Lychnis dioica* L.).
Sea pearlwort (*Sagina maritima* Don).
Thyme-leaved sandwort (*Arenaria serpyllifolia* L.).
Mouse-ear chickweed (*Cerostium viscosum* L.).
                                  (*Cerastium tetrandum* Curt.).
                                  (*Cerastium vulgatum* L.).
Chickweed (*Stellaria media* Vill.).
Bog stitch wort (*Stellaria alsine* Grimm).
Lesser stitchwort (*Stellaria graminea* L.).
Sand spurrey (*Spergularia rupicola* Lebel).
Corn spurrey (*Spergula arvensis* L. agg.).
G. Water blinks (*Montia fontana* L.).
Trailing St John's wort (*Hypericum humifusum* L.).

Marsh St John's wort (*Hypericum elodes* L.).
Allseed (*Radiola linoides* Roth).
Tree mallow (*Lavatera arborea* L.).
Sea stork's-bill (*Erodium maritimum* L'Hérit.).
Sycamore (*Acer pseudo-platanus* L.). G.
Furze (*Ulex europceus* L.).
Red clover (*Trifolium pratense* L.).
White clover (*Trifolium repens* L.).
Lesser clover (*Trifolium dubium* Sibth.).
Bird's-foot trefoil (*Lotus corniculatus* L.).
Kidney vetch (*Anthyllis vulneraria* L.).
Common vetch (*Vicia sativa* L.).
Blackthorn (*Prunus spinosa* L.).
Meadow sweet (*Spircea ulmaria* L.).
Bramble (*Rubus fruticosus* L. agg.).
Tormentil (*Potentilla erecta* L., Hampe).
Silverweed (*Potentilla anserina* L.).
Spring potentilla (*Potentilla verna* L.).
Marsh willowherb (*Epilobium palustre* L.).
Water purslane (*Peplis portula* L.).
Pennywort (*Cotyledon umbilicus* L.).
English stonecrop (*Sedum anglicum* Huds.).
Marsh pennywort (*Hydrocotyle vulgaris* L.).
Lesser marshwort (*Apium inundatum* (L.) H.G. Reichb.).
Marshwort (*Apium nodiflorum* (L.) H.G. Reichb.).
Hemlock water-dropwort (*Oenanthe crocata* L.).
Samphire (*Crithmum maritimum* L.).
Cow parsnip (*Heracleum sphondylium* L.).
Sea carrot (*Daucus gummifer* L.).
Hemlock (*Conium maculatum* L.).
Ivy (*Hedera helix* L.).
Common elder (*Sambucus nigra* L.).
Common honeysuckle (*Lonicera periclymenum* L.)
Heath bedstraw (*Galium saxatile* L.).
Lady's bedstraw (*Galium verum* L.).
Marsh bedstraw (*Galium palustre* L.).
Woodruff (*Asperula odorata* L.).
Hemp agrimony (*Eupatorium cannabinum* L.)
Golden rod (*Solidago virgaurea* L.).
Daisy (*Bellis perennis* L.).

Ox-eye daisy (*Chrysanthemum leucanthemum* L).
Corn marigold (*Chrysanthemum segetum* L.).
Sea mayweed (*Matricaria maritima* L.).
Yarrow (*Achillea millefolium* L.).
Groundsel (*Senecio vulgaris* L.).
Sticky groundsel (*Senecio viscosus* L.).
Ragwort (*Senecio jacobaa* L.).
Wood groundsel (*Senecio sylvaticus* L.).
Burdock (*Arctium lappa* L.).
Spear thistle (*Cirsium vulgare* (Savi) Airy-Shaw).
Marsh thistle (C. *palustre* Scop.).
Creeping thistle (C. *arvense* Scop.).
Knapweed (*Centaurea nigra* L. agg.). G.
Great knapweed (*Centaurea scabiosa* L.).
Autumnal hawkbit (*Leontodon autumnalis* L.).
Cat's ear (*Hypochceris radicata* L.).
Corn sowthistle (*Sonchus arvensis* L.).
Dandelion (*Taraxacum officinale* Weber).
Sheep's bit (*Jasione montana* L.).
Bell heather (*Erica cinerea* L.).
Ling (*Calluna vulgaris* (L.) Hull).
Primrose (*Primula vulgaris* Huds.).
Cowslip (*Primula veris* L.).
Pimpernel (*Anagallis arvensis* L.).
Bog pimpernel (*Anagallis tenella* L., Murr.).
Brookweed (*Samolus valerandi* L.).
Ash (*Fraxinus excelsior* L.). G.
Privet (*Ligustrum vulgare* L.).
Centaury (*Centaurium umbellatum* Gilib.).
Water forget-me-not (*Myosotis scorpioides* L. em., Hill).
Field forget-me-not (*Myosotis arvensis* L. Hill). G.
Early forget-me-not (*Myosotis collina* Hoffm.).
Yellow and blue forget-me-not (*Myosotis versicolor* Sm.).
Borage (*Borago officinalis* L.). G.
Bittersweet (*Solanum dulcamara* L.).
Figwort (*Scrophularia nodosa* L.).
Foxglove (*Digitalis purpurea* L.).
Germander speedwell (*Veronica chamcedrys* L.).
Common speedwell (*Veronica officinalis* L.).
Procumbent speedwell (*Veronica agrestis* L.).

Wall speedwell (*Veronica arvensis* L.).
Eyebright (*Euphrasia officinalis* L. agg.).
Red rattle (*Pedicularis palustris* L.).
Lousewort (*Pedicularis sylvatica* L.).
Water mint (*Mentha aquatica* L.).
Wild thyme (*Thymus serpyllum* L.).
Ground Ivy (*Nepeta hederacea* L., Trev.).
Self heal (*Prunella vulgaris* L.).
Lesser skullcap (*Scutellaria minor* Huds.).
Field woundwort (*Stachys arvensis* L.). G.
Common hemp-nettle (*Galeopsis tetrahit* L.).
Henbit (*Lamium amplexicaule* L.).
Red dead-nettle (*Lamium purpureum* L.).
Wood sage (*Teucrium scorodonia* L.).
Common bugle (*Ajuga reptans* L.).
Thrift, sea pink (*Statice maritima* Mill.).
Ribwort (*Plantago lanceolata* L.).
Sea plantain (*Plantago maritima* L.).
Bucks-horn plantain (*Plantago coronopus* L.).
Greater plantain (*Plantago major* L.).
Shoreweed (*Littorella uniflora* L., Aschers.).
Red goosefoot (*Chenopodium rubrum* L.).
White goosefoot (*Chenopodium album* L.).
Wild beet (*Beta maritima* L.).
Orache (*Atriplex hastata* L.).
Sea orache (*Atriplex glabriuscula* Edmonst.).
Curled dock (*Rumex crispus* L.).
Sorrel (*Rumex acetosa* L.).
Sheep's sorrel (*Rumex acetosella* L.).
Knotgrass (*Polygonum aviculare* L.). G.
Amphibious polygonum (*Polygonum amphibium* L.).
Spotted persicaria (*Polygonum persicaria* L.).
Waterpepper (*Polygonum hydropiper* L.).
Sun spurge (*Euphorbia helioscopia* L.).
Petty spurge (*Euphorbia peplus* L.).
Dwarf spurge (*Euphorbia exigua* L.).
Water starwort (*Callitriche aquatica* agg.).
Small nettle (*Urtica urens* L.).
Common nettle (*Urtica dioica* L.).
Creeping willow (*Salix repens* L.).

Cuckoo-pint (*Arum maculatum* L.).
Lesser duckweed (*Lemna minor* L.).
Floating pondweed (*Potamogeton natans* L.).
Lesser water plantain (*Alisma ranunculoides* L.).
Early purple orchid (*Orchis mascula* L.).
Marsh orchid (*Orchis incarnata* L.).
Daffodil (*Narcissus pseudo-narcissus* L.). Planted.
Snowdrop (*Galanthus nivalis* L.). Planted.
Spring squill (*Scilla verna* Huds.).
Bluebell (*Scilla non-scripta* (L.) H. and L.).
Toad rush (*Juncus bufonius* L.).
Common rush (*Juncus communis* agg.).
Heath rush (*Juncus squarrosus* L.).
Field woodrush (*Luzula campestris* L. DC.).
Tufted sedge (*Carex goodenowii* Gay).
Vernal sedge (*Carex caryophyllea* Latour).
Downy oatgrass (*Avena pubescens* Huds.).
Yorkshire fog (*Holcus lanatus* L.).
Couch grass (*Agropyrum repens* L.).
Cock's-foot grass (*Dactylis glomerata* L.).
Crested dog's-tail grass (*Cynosurus cristatits* L.).
Annual meadow grass (*Poa annua* L.).
Smooth meadow grass (*Poa pratensis* L.).
Rough meadow grass (*Poa trivialis* L.).
Silvery hair-grass (*Aira caryophyllea* L.).
Sheep's fescue (*Festuca ovina* L.).
Common reed (*Phragmites vulgaris* Lam. Crép.).
Male fern (*Dryopteris filix-mas* (L. Schott.)
Sea spleenwort (*Asplenium marinum* L.).
Hart's-tongue fern (*Phyllitis scolopendrium* (L. Newm.).
Hard fern (*Blechnum spicant* L. With.).
Bracken (*Pteridium aquilinum* L. Kuhn).

Please contact Little Toller Books
to join our mailing list or for more information
on current and forthcoming titles.

Nature Classics Library

THE JOURNAL OF A DISAPPOINTED MAN *W.N.P. Barbellion*
MEN AND THE FIELDS *Adrian Bell*
A SHEPHERD'S LIFE *W.H. Hudson*
FOUR HEDGES *Clare Leighton*
LETTERS FROM SKOKHOLM *R.M. Lockley*
THE UNOFFICIAL COUNTRYSIDE *Richard Mabey*
RING OF BRIGHT WATER *Gavin Maxwell*
THE SOUTH COUNTRY *Edward Thomas*
SALAR THE SALMON *Henry Williamson*

Also Available

THE LOCAL *Edward Ardizzone & Maurice Gorham*
A long out-of-print celebration of London's pubs
by one of Britain's most-loved illustrators.

LITTLE TOLLER BOOKS
Stanbridge Wimborne Minster Dorset BH21 4JD
Telephone: 01258 840549
ltb@dovecotepress.com
www.dovecotepress.com